READING
FREUD

BOOKS BY PETER GAY

Freud: A Life for Our Time (1988)

A Godless Jew: Freud, Atheism, and the Making of Psychoanalysis (1987)

The Bourgeois Experience: Victoria to Freud, volume II, The Tender Passion (1986)

Freud for Historians (1985)

The Bourgeois Experience: Victoria to Freud, volume I, Education of the Senses (1984)

Freud, Jews and Other Germans: Masters and Victims in Modernist Culture (1978)

Art and Act: On Causes in History—Manet, Gropius, Mondrian (1976)

Style in History (1974)

Modern Europe (1973), with R. K. Webb

The Bridge of Criticism: Dialogues on the Enlightenment (1970)

The Enlightenment: An Interpretation, volume II, The Science of Freedom (1969)

Weimar Culture: The Outsider as Insider (1968)

A Loss of Mastery: Puritan Historians in Colonial America (1966)

The Enlightenment: An Interpretation, volume I, The Rise of Modern Paganism (1966)

The Party of Humanity: Essays in the French Enlightenment (1964)

Voltaire's Politics: The Poet as Realist (1959)

The Dilemma of Democratic Socialism: Eduard Bernstein's Challenge to Marx (1952)

Peter Gay

READING FREUD

Explorations &

Entertainments

Yale University Press *New Haven & London*

Designed by Richard Hendel
Set in Basilia Haas type by
Eastern Typesetting Company,
Hartford, Connecticut
Printed in the United States of America
by Vail-Ballou Press, Binghamton,
New York

The paper in this book meets the
guidelines for permanence and
durability of the Committee on
Production Guidelines for Book
Longevity of the Council on Library
Resources.

10 9 8 7 6 5 4 3 2

Library of Congress Cataloging-
in-Publication Data
Gay, Peter, 1923–
   Reading Freud : explorations and
   entertainments / Peter Gay. p. cm.
   Includes bibliographical references.
   ISBN 0-300-04681-2 (cloth)
   0-300-05127-1 (pbk.)
   1. Psychoanalysis. 2. Freud,
   Sigmund, 1856–1939. I. Title.
   BF173.G3725   1990
   150.19'52—dc20   89-28615
                          CIP

To my friends

John Merriman and Elise Snyder,

the first to call.

In gratitude.

Contents

A Note on Citations

All translations are my own. But since I am
addressing this book to an English-speaking
audience, I have also noted, for convenience,
the places in the English-language versions of
Freud's writings and correspondence where the
reader may find the passages I have quoted
from the original German. When I cite Freud's
published writings, I give first the German title
and page reference and then, in parentheses,
the English page reference.

Abbreviations

Briefe	= Sigmund Freud, *Briefe, 1873–1939,* ed. Ernst and Lucie Freud (1960; 2nd ed., enlarged, 1968). English version, *Letters of Sigmund Freud, 1873–1939,* tr. Tania and James Stern (1961; 2nd ed., 1975).
Freud	= Peter Gay, *Freud: A Life for Our Time* (1988).
Freud-Abraham	= Sigmund Freud and Karl Abraham, *Briefe, 1907–1926,* ed. Hilda Abraham and Ernst L. Freud (1965). English version, *A Psycho-Analytic Dialogue: The Letters of Sigmund Freud and Karl Abraham, 1907–1926,* tr. Bernard Marsh and Hilda Abraham (1965).
Freud-Fliess	= Sigmund Freud, *Briefe an Wilhelm Fliess, 1887–1904,* ed. Jeffrey Moussaieff Masson, assisted by Michael Schröter and Gerhard Fichtner (1986). English version, *The Complete Letters of Sigmund Freud to Wilhelm Fliess, 1887–1904,* ed. and tr. Jeffrey Moussaieff Masson (1985).
Freud-Jung	Sigmund Freud and C. G. Jung, *Briefwechsel,* ed. William McGuire and Wolfgang Sauerländer (1974; 3rd printing, corr., 1979). English version, *The Freud-Jung Letters: The Correspondence Between Sigmund Freud and C. G. Jung,* ed. William McGuire, tr. Ralph Manheim (Freud's letters) and R. F. C. Hull (Jung's letters) (1974).

Freud-Zweig	Sigmund Freud and Arnold Zweig, *Briefwechsel*, ed. Ernst L. Freud (1968; paperback ed., 1984). English version, *The Letters of Sigmund Freud and Arnold Zweig*, tr. Prof. and Mrs. W. D. Robson-Scott (1970).
GW	= Sigmund Freud, *Gesammelte Werke, chronologisch geordnet*, ed. Anna Freud, Edward Bibring, Willi Hoffer, Ernst Kris, and Otto Isakower, in collaboration with Marie Bonaparte, 18 vols. (1940–1968).
Int. J. Psycho-Anal.	= *International Journal of Psycho-Analysis.*
J. Amer. Psychoanal. Assn.	= *Journal of the American Psychoanalytic Association.*
Jones I, II, III	= Ernest Jones, *The Life and Work of Sigmund Freud*, vol. I, *The Formative Years and the Great Discoveries, 1856–1900* (1953); vol. II, *The Years of Maturity, 1901–1919* (1955); vol. III, *The Last Phase, 1919–1939* (1957).
LC	= Library of Congress.
Protokolle	= *Protokolle der Wiener Psychoanalytischen Vereinigung*, ed. Hermann Nunberg and Ernst Federn, 4 vols. (1976–1981). English version, *Minutes of the Vienna Psychoanalytic Society*, tr. M. Nunberg, 4 vols. (1962–1975).
SE	= *Standard Edition of the Complete Psychological Works of Sigmund Freud*, tr. under the general editorship of James Strachey, in collaboration with Anna Freud, assisted by Alix Strachey and Alan Tyson, 24 vols. (1953–1974).

Prefatory Note

Freud—again? One might think that some fifteen years of concentrated attention would last any scholar for a lifetime, especially if they followed upon two decades of growing preoccupation with his thought. The first essay I devoted wholly to him, in 1976, was a lengthy interpretative study introducing a portfolio of photographs of the aged Freud and his famous apartment in Vienna at Berggasse 19. Then, in 1987, after applying psychoanalytic ideas to the history of nineteenth-century middle-class sexuality in two volumes entitled *The Bourgeois Experience,* I publicly asked the question whether psychoanalysis is indeed a Jewish science, in *A Godless Jew: Freud, Atheism, and the Making of Psychoanalysis.* All these investigations and interpretations culminated the following year in a substantial biography, *Freud: A Life for Our Time.* Finally, in 1989, I brought out a comprehensive anthology of Freud's writings as a kind of coda. But, as this volume of essays attests, these earlier publications have not exhausted my interest in Freud. I have collected the eight papers in this volume in the hope that I have not exhausted my readers' interest either.

It remains for me to add that, unlike a fading opera singer repeatedly offering what he labels his final farewell recital, I fully intend in my future publications to leave the person of Freud behind. This is not to say that I am done with his ideas. Not in the least. My conviction that psychoanalytic insights and discoveries are immensely useful—indeed indispensable—to the practicing historian remains unimpaired. But I plan to leave further *biographical* studies of Freud to others.

I wrote two of the papers that follow—"Freud and the Man from Stratford" and "Serious Jests"—after I had completed my biography of Freud, and neither has been published before. Yet both arose from certain pressing questions about Freud's mind and ways of working that I had already addressed at some length in *Freud: A Life for Our Time* but which, I have come to think, deserve further and closer analysis. In contrast, two other papers—"Mind Reading: The Forgotten Freud" and "A Gentile Science?"—are republished here virtually unchanged because they have become, in a rather minor way, "historical" documents, with a life of their own. The four essays that remain have been thoroughly revised and considerably enlarged. They were in their original form progress reports on my search for Freud and left their imprint on the biography which now, in its turn, has moved me to revise and expand them. Together, these eight papers represent yet another series of attempts to approach, and partly resolve, the mystery that is Freud.

Although the book is divided into two sections, "Explorations" and "Entertainments," they overlap and intersect. Certainly my paper on Freud's jokes, "Serious Jests," now included under the rubric of "Entertainments," would have been equally at home under "Explorations." And my paper on Freud's correspondence with his sister-in-law, "The Dog That Did Not Bark in the Night," though scarcely grave in tone and, in its way, an entertaining (at least to me) bit of detective work, is also an exploration of significant moments in Freud's life of which we still know too little. But in the end what matters, I think, in this gathering of essays is that whether serious or jocular, they record my progress on the track of Freud, my attempt at reading him.

I

Explorations

Introduction

"By indirections find directions out." There is in general precious little profit in the advice scattered by that garrulous pedant Polonius, the least favorite character in Freud's favorite play. But at moments his words of wisdom prove downright sensible. In the opening sentence of my piece on the correspondence between Sigmund Freud and his sister-in-law Minna Bernays, I say: "As every biographer of Freud must ruefully acknowledge, Freud left behind some intriguing private mysteries." It was because I hoped to solve some of these mysteries that the stratagem of finding my way to Freud by indirections commended itself to me. I have accordingly adopted that devious method in the following four papers.

Granted, only those as self-assured and naive as Polonius can persuade themselves that they can sound the depths of human nature and claim, without hesitation, "If circumstances lead me, I will find / Where truth is hid, though it were hid indeed / Within the center." Hamlet, upbraiding Guildenstern, comes closer to the heart of the matter: "You would play upon me, you would seem to know my stops, you would pluck out the heart of my mystery, you would sound me from my lowest note to the top of my compass. . . . 'Sblood, do you think I am easier to be played on than a pipe? Call me what instrument you will, though you can fret me, you cannot play upon me." Disregarding Hamlet's energetic protest, I have tried at least to approach the heart of Freud's mystery, within the limits of the available material.

That material is admittedly very rich. It includes thousands of letters published and unpublished. While there are still obstructions preventing access to some of Freud's vast correspondence (like most of his exchange of letters with his fiancée, Martha Bernays, or with Princess Marie Bonaparte), the bulk of it is now open to public scrutiny. We have Freud's letters to Wilhelm Fliess and Eduard Silberstein and his exchanges with Ernest Jones and Max Eitingon, Karl Abraham and Sándor Ferenczi, Oskar Pfister and Carl G. Jung and Arnold Zweig. We have a prize I was lucky enough to be the first outsider to read: Freud's correspondence with his cherished daughter Anna. Equally accessible are such personal documents as his last will and his laconic diary, to say nothing of his immensely revealing, anything but laconic published writings, many of them half-openly autobiographical in nature. Beyond that, there is a treasure house of photographs and home movies, eloquent reminiscences of close followers and distant journalists, intimates and casual visitors, which round out the written and the printed record. As all who have ever occupied themselves with Freud will know, some of this documentation is telling in the extreme: his biographers have seized upon his epoch-making letters to Fliess as they may now seize upon the intimate, extensive reports and recollections of his last physician, Max Schur, and his still fragmentary surviving correspondence with his sister-in-law.

Yet, as Freud has taught us, there is always more to know about people, even fully documented ones. That is why I have tried to read Freud by seeking to understand his desertion of the man from Stratford, his imperious way of naming his children, his characteristic style of scientific determinism, and, most literally, his reading.

1

Freud and the Man from Stratford

I. THE LOONEY CASE

*. . . der grösste
Dichter.
— Freud,
"The
Exceptions"*

Freud, like other cultivated Central Europeans, admired Shakespeare extravagantly though not excessively. He placed *Hamlet, Macbeth,* and other of Shakespeare's dramas in the company of Homer, the tragedies of Sophocles, and Goethe's *Faust,* among the ten most magnificent works in world literature.[1] He quoted Shakespeare frequently, with easy familiarity. He was of course thoroughly conversant with the felicitous German translations that August Wilhelm Schlegel had launched and Ludwig Tieck had completed around the turn of the nineteenth century—translations so authoritative that they encouraged Germans to appropriate the sweet Swan of Avon as *"unser* Shakespeare" and to condescend, only half-jokingly, to the "English version."[2] But

1. See "Contribution to a Questionnaire on Reading" (1907), *SE* IX, 245. For that letter, see below, 96–98.
2. Freud owned the nine-volume version of Shakespeare's *Dramatische Werke* in the Schlegel-Tieck translation, in an edition of 1867, and his writings, both published and

he also had at his fingertips Shakespeare in the original, and quoted
this quite as often as he did the German renderings.[3] In 1878, still
studying medicine at the University of Vienna, he paraphrased Macbeth—in German—in a letter to a close friend.[4] Four years later, a
lover catechizing his fiancée, he quoted a song from *Twelfth Night*—
in English: "Journeys end in lovers meeting, / Every wise man's son
doth know," went on quoting it, and then suggested to Martha Bernays that if she should not understand these "high-spirited lines"
she ought to consult "A. W. Schlegel's German translation."[5]

Plainly, that translation was a crutch that Freud himself did not
need. In the mid-1890s, slaving over a monograph on infantile par-
alyses when he was far keener on developing his "psychology for
neurologists," he reached for a line from Shakespeare to charac-
térize his distracted state of mind: "My heart is in the coffin here
with Caesar."[6] Two decades later, he explored the vicious mind of
Richard III for one of his technical papers on character, and some
twenty years after that, in mid-February 1934, he informed his son
Ernst that he had remained neutral in the bloody civil disorders that
had swept over Vienna a few days earlier because he was critical
of both parties to the conflict. "A plague," he quoted Mercutio in
Romeo and Juliet, "on both your houses."[7]

Shakespeare was on Freud's mind early and late, and Freud called
on him not just casually but also on momentous, emotion-laden oc-
casions. On September 21, 1897, telling his confidant Wilhelm Fliess
in a famous letter that he had felt compelled to abandon his cher-

---

unpublished, offer ample evidence that he had read it to good purpose. See J.
Keith Davies, N. J. Lockley, and S. D. Neufeld, compilers, *Freud's London Library: Preliminary Catalogue* (typescript, 1988), no. 1384.

3. In addition to several individual plays, such as *Macbeth*, Freud owned the
ten-volume edition of Shakespeare edited by A. Dyce (6th ed., 1891). See Davies,
Lockley, and Neufeld, *Freud's London Library*, no. 1386.

4. Freud to Wilhelm Knoepfmacher, August 6, 1878. *Briefe*, 14 (6).

5. Freud to Martha Bernays, July 14, 1882. *Ibid.*, 23–24 (13).

6. Freud to Fliess, April 27, 1895. In English. *Freud-Fliess*, 129 (128). The work
for which Freud's essay was intended was Hermann Nothnagel's vast compen-
dium *Specielle Pathologie und Therapie*, 22 vols. (1894ff.).

7. Freud to Ernst Freud, February 20, 1934. In English. *Briefe*, 434 (420). He
liked the formulation well enough to repeat it five days later in a letter to Arnold
Zweig, February 25, 1934. *Freud-Zweig*, 77 (65).

ished seduction theory of neuroses, and why, he adapted Hamlet's poignant declaration, "The readiness is all," to read, far more buoyantly, "To be cheerful is all."[8] At least once, quoting from memory, he subjected a Shakespearean text to a revealing distortion: musing on the need to face one's death realistically, he transformed the line from *Henry IV, Part Two* which reads, "We owe God a death" into "Thou owest Nature a death"[9]—a creative misquotation, attesting to Freud's impassioned atheism.

Not surprisingly, much though he was taken with *Macbeth*,[10] Freud's most cherished Shakespearean treasure trove was *Hamlet.* In his published writings, he drew on that enigmatic tragedy more than twenty times; in his conversations and his letters, he called on it again and again—in two languages. Thus, trying to dissuade Arnold Zweig from writing his biography, Freud sternly observed that "the truth is not practicable, humans don't deserve it, and besides, isn't our Prince Hamlet right to ask if anyone could 'scape whipping if he were treated according to his merit?"[11]

Freud had a particular stake in *Hamlet.* The play, we know, figured prominently in the train of thought that led him toward the Oedipus complex. Writing to Fliess in the early fall of 1897, he put his discovery tentatively but in confident tones: "It has gone through my head in passing," he wrote, that the oedipal conflict Sophocles' *Oedipus Rex* dramatized might "also be at the bottom of *Hamlet.* I am not thinking of Shakespeare's conscious intention," he added, "but believe, rather, that a real event stimulated the poet to his portrayal, in that the unconscious in him understood the unconscious in the hero. How does the hysteric Hamlet justify his saying, 'Thus conscience does make cowards of us all'? How does he explain his hesitation in avenging his father's death by murdering his uncle—

8. Freud to Fliess, September 21, 1897. *Freud-Fliess,* 285 (265). Actually, Freud misquotes the passage he is "varying": he wrote, "To be in readiness." This was not the only time he would get a passage he was quoting from memory just slightly wrong.

9. Freud to Fliess, February 6, 1899. Ibid., 376 (343).

10. Freud owned the Temple Shakespeare edition of *Macbeth* (3rd. ed., 1897) and a French edition edited and with a long introduction by James Darmesteter (2nd ed., 1887). Davies, Lockley, and Neufeld, *Freud's London Library,* nos. 1387 and 1385. For *Macbeth,* see below, 44–48.

11. Freud to Arnold Zweig, May 31, 1936. *Freud-Zweig,* 137 (127).

Hamlet, the very same who without hesitation sends his courtiers to death, and who is positively hasty in murdering Laertes?" Hamlet, he concluded, must have been tormented by an obscure memory of having harbored murderous wishes against his father.[12] Certainly Freud did; his slip about Laertes is an interesting commentary on the conflict he had stumbled upon in himself and was proposing to generalize: Hamlet, of course, murders the father, Polonius, rather than Laertes, the son. It is as though, caught up in his self-analysis, Freud could not quite face the enormity of the son's homicidal oedipal hostility directed against his father.

Shakespeare, then, spoke to Freud persuasively. Freud was delighted to point out to Fliess that "Shakespeare was right to juxtapose fiction and madness (fine frenzy)."[13] Not that Freud asked Shakespeare to be an expert psychologist and theoretician. In 1930, he wrote to Richard Flatter, who had translated *King Lear* into German and suggested that the aged king might have been a hysteric: "After all, one has no right to demand from an imaginative writer correct, conclusive clinical diagnoses. It is enough if our feelings are not offended in any respect."[14] What Freud asked of a great writer like Shakespeare was psychological penetration without clinical technicalities.

His predilection for Shakespeare was, of course, anything but eccentric. In Freud's intimate circles, an apt quotation from Shakespeare was something of a commonplace. Time after time, Freud's friends and associates, by and large cultivated Viennese, found Shakespearean tags to embellish their thoughts and feelings. Alluding to the diagnostic difficulties presented by that puzzling ailment, hysteria, Josef Breuer, Freud's early mentor, likened them to tragedies with Theseus' disparaging words in *Midsummer Night's Dream:* "The best in this kind are but shadows."[15] Amid the handful of Viennese physicians and laymen who gathered in Freud's apart-

12. Freud to Fliess, October 15, 1897. *Freud-Fliess,* 292–93 (272).

13. Freud to Fliess, draft N, enclosed with letter of May 31, 1897. Ibid., 268 (251). "Fine frenzy" is from *Midsummer Night's Dream.* In English.

14. Freud to Flatter, March 30, 1930. *Briefe,* 414 (395).

15. Breuer and Freud, *Studien über Hysterie* (1895), 221. Breuer is quoting in German, which is rather more apt to his point than the English, for it has the word *Schattenspiel,* which is perhaps best rendered as "shadow play," rather than "shadows."

ment every Wednesday night from 1902 on, speculation about Shakespeare, and resort to Shakespeare as an admirably informed reader of minds, was rife. Hanns Sachs, a member of the committee that Ernest Jones formed in 1912 to protect Freud and the undisputed verities of psychoanalysis, adored Shakespeare, especially the sonnets. He recalled that when he talked with Freud about literature, "Shakespeare was the most frequent topic of our discussions."[16] In 1909, Otto Rank, who had been appointed secretary to the Wednesday Psychological Society three years earlier, called Shakespeare, with unstinting admiration, "the deep psychologist."[17] With this formulation, Rank spoke, as he often did in those years, for Freud.

But, Freud came to ask, who was this admirable psychologist? Who wrote Shakespeare's plays? The man from Stratford or not the man from Stratford? That was the question.

For decades, Freud was perfectly content to accept the common wisdom that Shakespeare had written Shakespeare. It was only after the First World War, when he was in his late sixties, that he began to entertain serious doubts. And he was about seventy when he concluded that Edward de Vere, seventeenth earl of Oxford, was in all probability the true author of Shakespeare's plays. Francis Bacon, the most popular candidate the revisionists had put forward to claim the mantle of Shakespeare, had never impressed Freud very much. As he told Lytton Strachey in December 1928, looking back, he had always laughed at the "Bacon hypothesis."[18] At times, to be sure, he floated some farfetched hypotheses

16. Sachs, *Freud: Master and Friend* (1945), 106. See also ibid., 65.

17. Meeting of December 22, 1909. *Protokolle* II, 338. Rank is referring to Portia's slip of the tongue (act III, sc. 2), "One half of me is yours, the other half yours— / Mine own, I would say."

18. Freud to Lytton Strachey, December 25, 1928. *Briefe,* 400. Many years before, writing to his fiancée on June 22, 1883, Freud argued that Bacon could not have written Shakespeare's plays because "if that were so then Bacon would have been the most powerful brain the world has ever produced, whereas it seems to me that there is more need to share Shakespeare's achievement among several rivals than to burden another important man with it." Unpublished letter quoted in part in *Jones* III, 428. In the same year, on June 19 and 20, in a pair of feuilletons in the *Neue Freie Presse,* the newspaper Freud read, M. Milan made scathing fun of an English woman author, never named, who had dared to claim that Bacon was indeed the author of Shakespeare's plays. (Courtesy of Dr. Al-

of his own. Once, persuaded that Shakespeare's portraits hinted at a "Latin" ancestry, he toyed with the curious notion that Shakespeare's name was a corruption of "Jacques Pierre."[19]

But that was nothing more than transient, lighthearted entertainment. In 1926, Freud came upon J. Thomas Looney's *"Shakespeare" Identified,* published six years earlier, and was largely won over to the Oxford theory.[20] The case for the earl of Oxford imposed itself on Freud as far more plausible than any of its rivals, plausible enough for him to give it public support. In 1930, in an address written as a graceful acknowledgment to the City of Frankfurt for awarding him the Goethe Prize, he broadcast his skepticism, hitherto revealed only to a few, to a wider audience: "It is undeniably embarrassing for us all that we still do not know who authored the comedies,

brecht Hirschmüller.) Jones goes on to say that it was the *methods* of the Baconians which interested Freud and that Freud, "a few years before the First World War," asked Jones to "make a thorough study of them . . . contrasting them with psychoanalytic methods." Freud's reason: "Then the matter would be disproved and his mind would be at rest." (*Jones* III, 428–29.) At this stage in Freud's life, then, when he was in his fifties, he seems to have wanted to rescue the traditional Stratfordian thesis from its critics. Freud owned one of the most determined polemics in behalf of the "Bacon-hypothesis," Sir Edwin Durning-Lawrence's *Bacon Is Shake-speare* (1910). See Davies, Lockley, and Neufeld, *Freud's London Library,* no. 331.

19. *Jones* I, 22.

20. Two years later, he disclosed the agent of his near conversion in letters to Ernest Jones and Lytton Strachey. See Freud to Jones, March 11, 1928, Freud Collection, D2, LC; Freud to Lytton Strachey, December 25, 1928, *Briefe,* 400. Various dates have been given for the time that Freud first came upon Looney's work. In an interesting article, Harry Trosman writes: "Freud did not settle on any one claimant until 1923, when he was sixty-seven years old. At that time he read J. Thomas Looney's book making the case for Edward de Vere." See "Freud and the Controversy over Shakespearean Authorship," *J. Amer. Psychoanal. Assn.* XIII (1965), 476. Trosman offers no documentation for this date. But in his letter to Ernest Jones of March 11, 1928, cited above, Freud says explicitly: "Ich stehe wieder unter dem Eindruck eines Buches, das ich nach einem Jahr zum zweiten Mal gelesen. Ein Buch eines Mannes Looney." Now, literally, this would mean that Freud had first read Looney's *"Shakespeare" Identified* in 1927. But since Jones testifies that Freud had argued in behalf of Oxford in May 1926, and since it was Looney who changed his mind on Shakespeare, we must take Freud's "a book that I read for a second time after a year" not quite literally. In any event, 1923 must be too early.

tragedies, and sonnets of Shakespeare, whether it really was the uneducated son of a Stratford petty bourgeois who attained a modest position as an actor in London, or the nobly born and exquisitely cultivated, passionately dissolute, somewhat déclassé aristocrat Edward de Vere, seventeenth earl of Oxford, hereditary Lord Great Chamberlain of England."[21] In the same year, he reiterated his revisionist doubts in a new footnote to *The Interpretation of Dreams:* "I have lost faith in the assumption that the author of Shakespeare's works was the man from Stratford."[22]

As these carefully drafted formulations show, Freud had some residual reservations about his new conviction. In his 1928 letter to Lytton Strachey, he had privately proffered his recently discovered conjecture with due modesty: "I am naturally all too ignorant to guess what experts on those days can advance against this new Shakespeare candidate. Perhaps it will not be difficult for them to demonstrate that this possibility does not exist. I do not know and should like to know."[23] Using the same tone once again later, in 1935, he recorded his loss of confidence in the "actor William Shakespeare from Stratford," adding that he was *"nearly* convinced" that the name was a pseudonym behind which the earl of Oxford had concealed his authorship.[24] Even at the very end of his life, Freud was not quite sure. As he put it, with becoming caution, in his fragmentary *Outline of Psychoanalysis,* written in English exile: "The name *William Shakespeare* is very probably a pseudonym, behind which a great unknown is concealed."[25] The man who had worked his somewhat grudging conversion, J. Thomas Looney, was held back by no such doubts.

Freud's library offers substantial evidence that after he discovered Looney, his preoccupation with what he called the *Shakespeareproblem* markedly increased. He bought books sup-

21. "Ansprache im Frankfurter Goethe-Haus" (1930), *GW* XIV, 549 / "Address Delivered in the Goethe House at Frankfurt," *SE* XXI, 211.

22. *Traumdeutung, GW* II–III, 273n / *Interpretation of Dreams, SE* IV, 266n.

23. Freud to Lytton Strachey, December 25, 1928. *Briefe,* 400.

24. Footnote added to *Selbstdarstellung* (1925), *GW* XIV, 96n / *Autobiographical Study, SE* XX, 63n. Italics mine.

25. *Abriss der Psychoanalyse, GW* XVII, 119n / *Outline of Psychoanalysis, SE* XXIII, 192n.

porting the Oxford hypothesis,[26] and, after rumors of his adherence spread, like-minded associates and authors plied him, the most eminent of their recruits, with congenial texts. Eva Lee Turner Clark, one of the most fervent and prolific of Oxfordians, who thought Looney's "discovery" nothing less than "brilliant," sent Freud a signed copy of her *Hidden Allusions in Shakespeare's Plays: A Study of the Oxford Theory Based on the Records of Early Court Revels and Personalities of the Times* (1931) and, two years later, of her *The Satirical Comedy: Love's Labour's Lost* (1933).[27] Even more to the point, in 1928, Ruth Mack Brunswick, the young American analyst who had been Freud's analysand and was a member of Freud's intimate circle in Vienna, gave him a copy of Looney's *"Shakespeare" Identified* as a birthday present.[28] Another of his "pupils," Smiley Blanton, an American physician intermittently in analysis with Freud

26. By about 1932, nearly all the works of the prominent pro-Oxford authors were in his possession, including Bernard Mortaunt Ward, *The Seventeenth Earl of Oxford: 1550–1604* (1928); no fewer than five different titles by Percy Allen, including his *The Case for Edward de Vere, Seventeenth Earl of Oxford, as William Shakespeare* (1930) and a polemic he wrote with Ernest Allen, *Lord Oxford and "Shakespeare": A Reply to John Drinkwater* (ca. 1933); Gerald Henry Rendall, *Shakespeare's Sonnets and Edward de Vere* (1930), by which Freud set much store; Gilbert Slater, *Seven Shakespeares: A Discussion of the Evidence for Various Theories with Regard to Shakespeare's Identity* (1931), which, despite its title, comes down on the side of the theory that a committee wrote Shakespeare, with Oxford as principal author; and Hubert Henry Holland, *Shakespeare: Oxford and Elizabethan Times* (1933). See Davies, Lockley, and Neufeld, *Freud's London Library,* nos. 1519, 25–30, 1249, 1400, 646.

27. Clark, *Hidden Allusions,* 162. For the titles, see Davies, Lockley, and Neufeld, *Freud's London Library,* nos. 248 and 251. Another admirer of Looney, Percy Allen, followed suit, sending Freud a signed copy of his *The Life Story of Edward de Vere as William Shakespeare* (1932). See Davies, Lockley, and Neufeld, no. 28.

28. The volume in Freud's library is dated May 6, 1928, and it was given to Freud by "Ruth." Davies, Lockley, and Neufeld, the editors of *Freud's London Library,* suggest (at no. 893) that the donor most probably was Ruth Mack Brunswick. This conjecture strikes me as exceedingly plausible, since as a member of the Shakespeare Fellowship—devoted to preaching, and proving, the Oxford hypothesis—Ruth Mack Brunswick was as persuaded of Looney's arguments as was her mentor, Freud. (See the obituary notice in *Shakespeare Fellowship Quarterly* VII, 4 [October 1946], 54.)

between 1929 and 1938, further enlarged Freud's holdings by sending him current titles on the Shakespeare question.[29]

Blanton did so from shared interests, not shared convictions. In
fact, Freud's commitment to the earl of Oxford almost ruined his
analysis of Blanton. It is a curious story. In December 1929, when
the name of Shakespeare came up during an analytic hour, Freud,
as so often setting his stringent rules of technique aside, asked Blanton whether he believed that the man named Shakespeare had written Shakespeare. Blanton, who was proud of having studied English
literature and drama for a dozen years before going into medicine
and who claimed to know several Shakespeare plays by heart, acknowledged that he "could see no reason to doubt that the Stratford
man had written the plays." Whereupon Freud handed Blanton
Looney's *"Shakespeare" Identified:* "Here's a book I would like you
to read. This man believes someone else wrote the plays." As Blanton
remembered that day, he was "very much upset." If "Freud believes
Bacon or Ben Jonson or anyone else wrote Shakespeare's plays,"
he recalls thinking, "I would not have any confidence in his judgment
and could not go on with my analysis." He was so deeply troubled
that he asked his wife, also in Vienna, in analysis with Ruth Mack
Brunswick, to read the book for him.

Her response reveals, once again, Looney's seductive powers. Margaret Blanton reassured her husband that *"Shakespeare" Identified*
was "a thoroughly sound work, based on solid scholarship, and its
subject was approached with exemplary scientific objectivity."
Whether one agreed with it or not, she told him, "It was obviously
a book to command respectful attention." Her verdict reassured
Blanton; he read the book and "recognized at once" that it was "a
serious work and not just another Baconian exercise in secret ciphers

29. Smiley Blanton (joined on occasion by his wife, Margaret) sent Freud *Hidden
Allusions in Shakespeare's Plays* (1931), which the author, Eva Lee Turner Clark,
had also sent Freud, as well as Clark's *The Man Who Was Shakespeare* (1937).
Toward the end of Freud's life, Blanton sent him Countess Clara Longworth de
Chambrun's *Shakespeare Rediscovered: By Means of Public Records; Secret
Reports and Private Correspondence Newly Set Forth as Evidence on His Life
and Work* (1938); de Chambrun thought that the author of Shakespeare's writings was Shakespeare, but by then it was too late to change Freud's mind once
again. See Davies, Lockley, and Neufeld, *Freud's London Library,* nos. 249,
250, 236.

and codes.''[30] He did not follow Freud into the Oxford heresy but continued his analysis.

Others among Freud's followers were less indulgent toward his eccentricity. In 1935, coming upon an anti-Stratford footnote Freud had added to his *Autobiographical Study,* James Strachey, Freud's principal English translator, was appalled. He pleaded with Freud to omit, or at least modify, the offending passage. In his view, Freud's explicit identification of Looney as the author who had changed his mind only exacerbated the matter: he called Freud's attention to Looney's "unfortunate name," which was bound to have a bad effect on the "average English reader"—a cheap shot that swayed Freud no more than any other argument against Looney. In the end, Strachey got his way, though for the English edition alone. The American edition carried Freud's only slightly hesitant commitment to Oxford in full.[31] The secret was out.

Freud had faced outspoken opposition from the beginning. On May 5, 1926, on the eve of his seventieth birthday, Ernest Jones, Sándor Ferenczi, and Max Eitingon, representing the psychoanalytic establishment in London, Budapest, and Berlin, respectively, visited Freud at Berggasse 19 and listened to him championing Oxford as the author of Shakespeare's plays. Jones later recalled his "admiration at the keenness" that Freud "could devote to such a theme at two a.m.''[32] Hanns Sachs was another target of Freud's old-age enthusiasm ("He lent me the book which presented and defended this new hypothesis"), but Sachs at least remained unconverted.[33] None of this had the slightest impact on Freud.

Indeed, two years later, writing to Ernest Jones in March 1928, Freud reasserted his conviction that Looney's book was an impressive contribution to the Shakespeare question. Until recently, he told Jones, he had been "a convinced Stratfordian, and had especially rejected the Bacon hypothesis as nonsensical." But now he had to

30. Notes by Smiley Blanton as reproduced by his wife and her own comments, in Smiley Blanton, *Diary of My Analysis with Sigmund Freud,* ed. Margaret Gray Blanton (1971), 36–37n.

31. Editorial comment by James Strachey to *Autobiographical Study, SE* XX, 64n.

32. Jones to Freud, April 29, 1928. (Sigmund Freud Copyrights, Wivenhoe.) For a virtually identical account, see *Jones* III, 429.

33. Sachs, *Freud: Master and Friend,* 106–07.

confess that he had been "very much impressed, almost persuaded, by Looney's researches." And he asked Jones to investigate the question whether "one could not construct a reliable analysis of Shakespeare on the basis of the new assumption."[34] Jones would not be drawn in. Having studied Looney's book with care, he told Freud that the second part of *"Shakespeare" Identified* did not fulfill the promises of the first: "The main thesis did not seem to me probable." And he informed Freud that Looney had evidently made little impression in England—or else he, Jones, would surely have heard of it. "The only literary man I spoke to about it was disparaging, largely on the ground of the contemporary evidence about S's identity, which by now is really very considerable."[35] This response, far from deterring Freud, only irritated him.[36]

Freud, then, was impenitent and immovable. Years after these inconclusive, at times slightly intemperate, exchanges, he still held

34. Freud to Jones, March 11, 1928. Freud Collection, D2, LC. The occasion for Freud's letter was condolences to Jones on the death of one of his children. Freud explicitly sought to distract Jones a little from his grief by giving him an intellectual detective's assignment—researching Looney. Whether one interprets this gesture as supreme tact or supreme tactlessness depends on one's own disposition. Jones himself took a middle road. Responding to Freud on April 29, 1928, he expressed his gratitude at "the warmth and thoughtfulness displayed in your letter" but acknowledged that he "missed something in it, some expression of 'tiefe Lebensweisheit'—deep life's wisdom—which no one can utter so well as you. It was as though all my efforts had failed to convey to you our desperate need for some such support." (Sigmund Freud Copyrights, Wivenhoe.)
35. Jones to Freud, April 29, 1928. (Sigmund Freud Copyrights, Wivenhoe.)
36. See Freud to Jones, May 3, 1928 (Sigmund Freud Copyrights, Wivenhoe), and the editorial note by Strachey in *SE* XX, 64n. It is no doubt an unfortunate coincidence that another anti-Stratford author, who gave Shakespeare's writings to Daniel Defoe, was called George M. Battey. (See William F. and Elizabeth S. Friedman, *The Shakespearean Ciphers Examined* [1957], 7.) Looney was aware of the impertinent games that people might play with his name and dealt with the matter with real dignity: "If I were inclined to take exception to anything in your article," he wrote to his admirer Charles Wisner Barrell on June 6, 1937, "it would be your taking any notice of the silly and childish jibes at my patronymic. Publishers and friends foresaw the handle it would provide for the critics, and wished me to adopt a nom-de-plume. I declined very decidedly however, and lost one of the foremost English publishers in consequence." "Discoverer of the True Shakespeare Passes: John Thomas Looney, 1870–1944," *Shakespeare Fellowship Quarterly* V, 2 (April 1944), 19.

to his conviction. In June 1938, shortly after Freud had landed in London as an exile from nazified Austria, Looney wrote him a letter welcoming him to England; Freud promptly replied, hailing Looney as the "author of a remarkable book" and confessing himself Looney's "follower."[37]

What possessed Freud to enlist in so unpromising a cause, to waste time and energy on what must appear to his most well-disposed admirers as little better than a hobby for impassioned cranks? It is true that through the years, intelligent, otherwise rational readers of Shakespeare's plays and poems, men and women demonstrably sane and indeed eminent in other pursuits, have lent themselves to this sport. Some of these—including Lord Palmerston, Henry James, Mark Twain, and Bismarck—had no candidate of their own to propose. But they were disposed to question whether the man from Stratford, to their mind the ill-educated son of illiterate parents, that small-town actor let loose on the London stage, could be the supreme glory of English letters. "I am 'sort of' haunted by the conviction," Henry James wrote to his friend Violet Hunt in 1903, "that the divine William is the biggest and most successful fraud ever practised on a patient world."[38] At least some of the company Freud kept was thoroughly respectable.

Yet the history of the *Shakespeareproblem,* though fairly extensive by the time Freud became one of the players, was anything but respectable. Most of the anti-Stratfordians—Looney and his fellow-champions of Oxford less than the others—emit a distinct odor of crankiness, a single-minded fanaticism and commitment to con-

37. Quoted in A. Bronson Feldman, "The Confessions of William Shakespeare," *American Imago* X (1953), 165. Feldman's article, a fervent, even angry challenge to what he derisively calls "the Stratford cult," is worth reading (pp. 114–66). Referring to Shakespeare's last two sonnets, Feldman comments: "To imagine William Shakespeare of Stratford-on-Avon writing these vacation verses," drawn from the *Greek Anthology* or perhaps a Latin translation, "is a feat equivalent to believing that Nicholas Bottom—the brazen ass of the *Midsummer Night's Dream*—crooned Shakespearean sonnets into the ears of Queen Titania" (pp. 116, 164).

38. Henry James to Violet Hunt, August 26, 1903, in McMichael and Glenn, *Shakespeare and His Rivals: A Casebook on the Authorship Controversy* (1962), 61.

spiracy theories that often barely skirt paranoia. A handful of skeptical pamphleteers in the eighteenth century championed the anti-Stratford cause, and by the late nineteenth century, when the Baconians were riding high, the pace of such publications had risen to a feverish rate. Lawyers insisted that the man who wrote Shakespeare's plays must have been a lawyer, historians that he must have been a historian, diplomats that he must have been a diplomat, travelers that he must have been a traveler. In the late 1880s, the prominent American politician Ignatius Donnelly, a populist with a weakness for outlandish causes, launched—or, rather, popularized—the fashion of reading the works of Shakespeare as a gigantic cryptogram. Once one had solved the cipher the author had concealed in "Shakespeare's" poems and plays, Donnelly argued at interminable length and with impressive ingenuity, Bacon's authorship of these imperishable masterpieces would stand forth dazzlingly clear. Donnelly inspired others to exhaust their mental resources translating Shakespeare's lines into acrostics and anagrams.

But not all anti-Stratfordians manufactured cryptograms. Some detectives, more rational at least on the surface, discovered elaborate schemes on the part of late sixteenth-century playwrights to collaborate in writing the works published under Shakespeare's name. These detectives rarely included Shakespeare himself among the presumed team players, but in any event the notion of a syndicate of dramatists served to explain to their satisfaction the formidable range of "Shakespeare's" allusions to the law, to hunting, to medicine, to Greek and Roman mythology, to ancient and English history, and to exotic places. By the late 1940s, there had appeared more than four thousand books and articles attacking the "Stratford cult."[39] The writers responsible for this massive literature did not merely reject the claim that Shakespeare had written Shakespeare; they also rejected one another's candidates. It has been estimated that some sixty personages have been given the signal accolade of having "really" authored those immortal plays and poems. The catalogue includes Francis Bacon (who long remained a favorite), Christopher Marlowe, Sir Walter Raleigh, the eminent Shakespearean actor Richard Burbage, Queen Elizabeth, the Italian scholar Giovanni Florio and his father, Michele Angelo Florio—and, of course, Edward

39. Ibid., 9.

de Vere, seventeenth earl of Oxford.[40] While the avalanche of these contradictory revelations has slowed, it has by no means ceased. The case against the man from Stratford, to which Freud lent his considerable prestige, remains alive if not well.[41]

The most promising starting point for an inquiry into the reasons Freud dismissed the man from Stratford is the book that impressed Freud enough to make him read it twice. Its author, John Thomas Looney, was an obscure provincial English schoolmaster, for whom his career as a teacher had been, as he put it, "only a makeshift." His passion, he confessed in a rare surviving autobiographical letter, was research, and understanding the world. He was, on his own showing, haunted by problems—as Freud was all his life—and he had come upon the *Shakespeareproblem* after teaching Shakespeare's plays, notably *The Merchant of Venice,* to his pupils year after year.[42] Raised in a pious evangelical household, he began studying for the ministry at sixteen, only to discover, after three years, that he lacked the religious vocation. In its place, after earnest searching, he adopted the philosophy of Auguste Comte, which gave him a firm foundation for his investigations into the world's mysteries. What he learned from Comte was simple but decisive; positivism, he wrote, "taught me to apply the principles, criteria and methods of science to all vital human problems."[43] Here was another link, however tenuous and subterranean, between Looney and Freud, for Freud, too, was a positivist and firmly persuaded that science alone held the key to the enigmas of man and nature.[44]

40. See the list in McMichael and Glenn, *Shakespeare and His Rivals,* 62.
41. On September 25, 1987, a group of Oxfordians staged a well-organized mock trial on Shakespeare's identity in Washington before three justices of the Supreme Court—William Brennan, Harry Blackmun, and John Paul Stevens. After listening to an extensive, earnest debate between Oxfordians and Stratfordians, Brennan decided unequivocally, Blackmun and Stevens somewhat more hesitantly, in favor of the man from Stratford. Some one thousand spectators witnessed the solemn occasion. See Bibliographical Essay, p. 182.
42. See Looney, *"Shakespeare" Identified,* 2; and Charlton Ogburn, *The Mysterious William Shakespeare: The Myth and the Reality* (1984), 145.
43. Looney to Charles Wisner Barrell, June 6, 1937, in "Discoverer of the True Shakespeare Passes," 20–21.
44. It should hardly be necessary to note the famous concluding lines of *The Future of an Illusion:* "No, our science is no illusion. But an illusion it would be

Looney's commitment to science makes him appear the very an-
tithesis of a monomaniac, but it was monomaniacs he seemed destined to inspire. In 1922, a group of his loyal followers founded the
Shakespeare Fellowship in London, designed to "promote study of
the Shakespearean authorship problem along the scientific lines"
that Looney had laid down.[45] An active American branch was formed
some time later, and an American adherent bestowed on Looney an
epithet that could not be surpassed: "the outstanding literary detective of all time."[46] The Looney cult could draw not merely on his
"Shakespeare" Identified but as well on Looney's critical edition of
Oxford's poems, published the following year, in 1921, complete with
a substantial and intense introduction epitomizing his discoveries.
The edition once more shows Looney to be an Oxford enthusiast,
and, by definition, as an enthusiast he was determined to celebrate
what others disparaged.

For others did disparage Oxford's literary ambitions; virtually no
professional student of English poetry was disposed to share
Looney's good opinion of de Vere's verses. Most of them had virtually
nothing to say about his poetry, while C. S. Lewis, in his authoritative
volume in the *Oxford History of English Literature,* devotes one
single scathing sentence to the poet: "Edward de Vere, Earl of Oxford, shows, here and there, a faint talent, but is for the most part
undistinguished and verbose."[47] Looney's desperate search for favorable adjectives about his man's poems yielded only a scanty har-
vest amid the general drought, and he had to be content, in fact
professed to be delighted, with two crumbs from reviewers: "*charming* lyric" and "distinguished for their wit."[48]

Still, overrating Oxford's talents as a versifier is hardly evidence
of mental imbalance on Looney's part. He showed himself, moreover,
keenly alert to the dubious reputation the revisionist enterprise had
acquired and intent on rescuing it from quacks and charlatans. "The

---

to believe that we could get anywhere else what it cannot give us." *GW* XIV,
380 / *SE* XXI, 56. See below, 124.

45. "Discoverer of the True Shakespeare Passes," 19.

46. Ibid. While the article from which I am quoting is unsigned, it was in all
probability written by Louis P. Bénézet, the president of the Shakespeare Fellowship, American Branch, or its secretary-treasurer, Charles Wisner Barrell.

47. C. S. Lewis, *English Literature in the Sixteenth Century Excluding Drama*
(1954), 267.

48. Looney, *"Shakespeare" Identified,* 121–22.

inquiry into the authorship of the Shakespeare plays," he observed defensively, "has . . . long since earned a clear title to be regarded as something more than a crank problem to be classed with such vagaries as the 'flat-earth theory' or surmises respecting the 'inhabitants of Mars.' "[49] He emphatically distanced himself from eccentric investigators like Ignatius Donnelly, whose discovery of a secret Baconian cryptogram in Shakespeare's works he dismissed as "a misleading method," indeed an "inferior form," of investigation. Donnelly's cryptogram was, in Looney's judgment, particularly "unfortunate" because it tended "to bring the enquiry [into who was Shakespeare] into disrepute with minds disposed to serious research."[50] This kind of shooting at his own most exposed troops was calculated to inspire confidence in Looney's methods, and it seems to have won over Freud.

There was more to gratify Freud in *"Shakespeare" Identified* than Looney's self-proclaimed sobriety. Looney regarded himself as a brave discoverer and a righter of wrongs. "The transference of the honour of writing the immortal Shakespeare dramas from one man to another, if definitely effected," he wrote on the opening page, "becomes not merely a national or contemporary event, but a world event of permanent importance, destined to leave a mark as enduring as human literature and the human race itself."[51] This was the sort of heroic self-definition with which Freud could empathize. After all, in the stirring, lonely late 1890s, the founding years of psychoanalysis, Freud had become increasingly aware that, were he to be proved right, he would change the world—nothing less. Looney was presenting himself as the same brand of conquistador as Freud, if on a smaller stage. And he was a conquistador surrounded by dangerous competitors, just as Freud had been in 1884, during his pioneering investigations into the anesthetic properties of cocaine.[52]

Looney made strenuous efforts to appear the most responsible of revisionists. He disdained pandering to self-indulgent pastimes. "At

49. Ibid., 68.
50. Ibid., 78, 11.
51. Ibid., 1.
52. In November 1918, as he candidly revealed in his book, Looney, unable to finish his *"Shakespeare"* as promptly as he had hoped, deposited a summary of his discoveries, in a sealed envelope, with the librarian of the British Museum. Thus, if anyone else should anticipate Looney's book, Looney's priority would be safeguarded.

the beginning it was mainly the fascination of an interesting inquiry that held me, and the matter was pursued in the spirit of simple research," he wrote. "As the case has developed, however, it has tended increasingly to assume the form of a serious purpose, aiming at a long overdue act of justice and reparation to an unappreciated genius who, we believe, ought now to be put in possession of his rightful honours."[53] One of Freud's eighteenth-century German literary models, Gotthold Ephraim Lessing, had performed such acts of rescue—he explicitly called them *Rettungen*—designed to revise undeservedly low reputations. Freud, too, liked to depict himself as a spokesman for unjustly neglected facts of mental life such as childhood sexuality or the dynamic unconscious. What Freud called the "rescue fantasy" was strongly at work in Looney—and scarcely less strongly in Freud.[54]

Looney tightened his grip on Freud with flashes of psychological penetration. "The resort of the faithful few to contemptuous expressions in speaking of opponents"—thus Looney analyzed the Stratfordians confronted with revisionists—"is clearly indicative of uneasiness even amongst the most orthodox littérateurs."[55] In fact, he argued, "orthodox faiths ... are usually intrinsically weakest when most vehemently asserted."[56] Here was Looney, who in 1920 had probably not yet heard of Freud, identifying the stratagems of projection and resistance in action. The defensive maneuvers to which Looney was calling attention were of a sort that Freud could amply and easily document from his clinical experience.

Looney proved an apt psychologist in other ways as well. His chapter on *Hamlet* was bound to confirm Freud's sense of him as an astute reader; like Freud, Looney saw *Hamlet* as Shakespeare's— or, rather, Oxford's—most profound, most instructive confession. *Hamlet,* Looney argues at some length, "is the play which, by its pre-eminence, is entitled to be regarded as 'Shakespeare's' special work of self-delineation."[57] Freud had said much the same thing years before: "Of course," he had asserted flatly in *The Interpretation of*

53. Looney, *"Shakespeare" Identified,* 3.
54. On this point, see esp. Harry Trosman, "Freud and the Controversy over Shakespearean Authorship," *J. Amer. Psychoanal. Assn.* XIII (1965), 492–93.
55. *"Shakespeare" Identified,* 11.
56. Ibid., 15.
57. Ibid., 395.

Dreams, "it can only have been the mental life of the poet that confronts us in *Hamlet.*"[58] For Freud, then, Looney's observations on his opponents and on *Hamlet* must have seemed like so many credentials of moderation and perceptiveness. They disposed Freud to listen.

Looney's case against the man from Stratford is essentially this: there is no evidence that William Shakespeare ever went to school; nor, since his parents were illiterate and Stratford a miserable backwater, could he have acquired at home or in town any of the erudition indispensable to the plays he is supposed to have written.[59] The few authentic signatures we have in Shakespeare's hand only confirm that his grip on literacy was shaky. Moreover, in his long retirement at Stratford, Shakespeare seems not to have engaged in any literary activity whatever and appears to have owned no books. Worse: his last will did not so much as mention any of the masterpieces attributed to him, even though most of them were available only in shockingly corrupt editions. No letters from Shakespeare survive, and virtually complete silence surrounds his activities as a playwright during his London years. In sum, "it is *difficult* to believe that with such a beginning he could have attained to such heights as he is supposed to have done; it is *more difficult* to believe that with such glorious achievements in his middle period he could have fallen to the level of his closing period; and in time it will be fully recognized that it is *impossible* to believe that the same man could have accomplished two such stupendous and mutually nullifying feats. . . . The perfect unity of the two extremes justifies

58. *Traumdeutung, GW* II–III, 272 / *Interpretation of Dreams, SE* IV, 265.
59. "Dirt and ignorance, according to this authority [J. O. Halliwell-Phillips's *Outlines of the Life of Shakespeare,* 2 vols. (1882)]," as Looney firmly puts it, "were outstanding features of the social life of Stratford in those days and had stamped themselves very definitely upon the family life under the influence of which William Shakspere was reared. Father and mother alike were illiterate, placing their marks in lieu of signatures upon important legal documents; and his father's first appearance in the records of the village is upon the occasion of his being fined for having amassed a quantity of filth in front of his house, there being 'little excuse for his negligence.' So much for the formative conditions of his home life. On the other hand, so far as pedagogic education is concerned there is no vestige of evidence that William Shakspere was ever inside of a school for a single day." *"Shakespeare" Identified,* 16.

the conclusion that the middle period is an illusion: in other words William Shakspere did not write the plays attributed to him."[60]

Having wrapped up his negative case, Looney moves on to make the man from Stratford "yield for the adornment of a worthier brow the laurels he has worn so long."[61] By meticulously outlining the methods he had adopted to reach his identification of Shakespeare as Oxford, Looney is bound to have ingratiated himself with Freud. After all, Freud, too, had spelled out the procedures that led him to his results. Looney started from the proposition that the obscurity surrounding the career of Shakespeare the dramatist was "no mere accident" and that, on the contrary, "the very greatness of the work itself is a testimony to the thoroughness of the steps taken to avoid disclosure."[62] The question, then, was, Who could have written those accomplished sonnets, those immortal plays?

In moving toward unveiling his candidate, Looney sternly rejected the most prevalent defense of the Stratfordians, that an obscure and unlettered provincial like Shakespeare could be responsible for highly polished and immensely varied poems and plays because he was, quite simply, a genius: by definition a genius, without schooling, without experience, without a long apprenticeship, who could pour out masterpieces. Looney objected that "masterpieces are the fruits of matured powers." What is more, "if we find that a man knows a thing we must assume that he had it to learn."[63] The convenient epithet "genius" evades the question just how everyone, including the most dazzlingly gifted of creators, must work. Genius or not, the man from Stratford simply could not fill the role the Stratfordians assigned to him.

But who could? To discover the true author of *Hamlet* and *Macbeth,* Looney first studied the writings attributed to Shakespeare with carefully cultivated naiveté in order to sketch a profile of their author's character. He then sought for some outstanding qualities that would give direction to his search. This led him to a tentative identification of a personage who fitted the portrait he had built up. Then he reversed the process: "Having worked from Shakespeare's writings to the man, we should then begin with the man."[64] A diligent

60. Ibid., 36–37.
61. Ibid., 67.
62. Ibid., 73.
63. Ibid., 75.
64. Ibid., 82.

search for corroborative evidence followed, and, finally, Looney tested his conclusion by developing "as far as possible any traces of personal connection between the newly accredited and the formerly reputed authors of the work."[65] It all sounds like the most patient and careful empirical investigation conceivable.

His close reading persuaded Looney that the true author of Shakespeare's writings must have been unconventional, indeed eccentric, a sensitive outsider, "a wasted genius";[66] a gifted lyric poet and literary Englishman with a passion for the theater; a widely traveled, well-informed individual who had been to Italy and knew a great deal about music, sports, and money matters. Perhaps the most telling quality of "Shakespeare" to Looney's mind was that he had enjoyed a classical education. "Place the documents before any mixed jury of educated, semi-educated, and ignorant men, men of practical common sense, and stupid men, and, unless for some prepossession, they would unanimously declare, without hesitation, that the writer was one whose education had been of the very best that the times could offer. And even a moderately educated set of men would assure us that it was not the mere bookish learning of the poor, plodding student who in loneliness had wrested from an adverse fate an education beyond what was enjoyed by his class."[67] Add to these characteristics the inevitable conclusion that the author of Shakespeare's plays was an inveterate conservative, it follows that he must have been an aristocrat: "We feel entitled, therefore," Looney concludes, "to claim for Shakespeare high social rank, and even a close proximity to royalty itself."[68]

Looney is closing in on his prey. Certain other characteristics, such as "Shakespeare's" distrust of women and his preferred verse forms, happily substantiated Looney's conjectures. Comparing "Venus and Adonis" with similar productions by contemporary poets, Looney found his man: Edward de Vere, earl of Oxford. Testing his hypothesis by Oxford's work and life—a procedure that took Looney most of the rest of his book to expound—he felt satisfied. Much remained to be explained, but the more closely Looney examined his evidence the

65. Ibid.
66. Ibid., 85.
67. Ibid., 91.
68. Ibid., 95.

more firmly footed his case appeared to him. In poem after poem, play after play, Oxford alluded to, lampooned, and criticized real persons in his small, tightly knit aristocratic world. This was the principal reason Oxford could not openly acknowledge his literary offspring.

Once Looney had determined that de Vere was Shakespeare, he had no trouble discovering instructive parallels and topical allusions everywhere. Portia's speech on the quality of mercy in *The Merchant of Venice* must be a dramatization of the defense that Mary Queen of Scots, to whom Oxford was sympathetic, delivered before the tribunal that condemned her to death.[69] Again, in the same play, Oxford is barely disguising his own financial difficulties in Bassano's plight.[70] Ulysses' speech in *Troilus and Cressida* celebrating rank and degree expresses Oxford's political ideology to perfection.[71] Othello and Romeo, " 'Shakespeare's' two heroes of tragic love," share Oxford's sensitivity and his "proneness to floods of tears."[72] And Sonnet 125 "seems to be pointing to de Vere's officiating at Queen Elizabeth's funeral."[73]

It is *Hamlet,* though, that inspires Looney's finest flights of identification. The play, as I have already noted, struck Looney—as it struck Freud, though for other reasons—as its author's "special work of self-delineation." He had not a moment's doubt that the protagonist was a self-portrait: Hamlet is precisely as sensitive and singular as Oxford, as resentful of interference in his affairs, as convinced that the times are out of joint, as worshipful of his father, and as grimly disappointed in his mother. Hamlet's speeches on a variety of topics that do nothing to advance the plot of the tragedy—like his hostility to lawyers and politicians and his religious ruminations— mirror Oxford's views. The Danish court looks suspiciously like the Elizabethan court that Oxford knew so intimately. Hamlet's instructions to the players uncannily echo Oxford's way with his own acting troupe. What is more, Polonius, Denmark's chief minister, is a telling caricature of Oxford's powerful father-in-law, Lord Burghley— pompous, sententious, worldly wise, a teacher of opportunistic, en-

69. Ibid., 302–03.
70. Ibid., 309.
71. Ibid., 263.
72. Ibid., 159.
73. Ibid., 335.

lightened self-interest. And Polonius's son, Laertes, is a barely re-
touched portrait of Burghley's son, Thomas Cecil.

Once launched, these conjectures are like the creatures of
Goethe's sorcerer's apprentice: Looney cannot stop this self-
propelling game. Ophelia appears to be directly modeled after Oxford's wife, Lady Oxford. And the honest Horatio? That must be
Oxford's cousin, Sir Horace (or Horatio) de Vere. In fact, Looney
suggests that by introducing his cousin so blatantly into the action
of *Hamlet* Oxford must have been "meditating—just before his
death—coming forward to claim in his own name the honours which
he had won by his work; or, at any rate, that he had decided that
these honours should be claimed on his behalf immediately after his
death, and that Horatio de Vere had been entrusted with the responsibility."[74] Naturally Hamlet himself is Looney's prize exhibit:
the match between Hamlet and Oxford is complete. The case is
proved. "Speaking no longer from behind a mask or from under a
pseudonym, but in his own honoured name," Looney triumphantly
concludes, "Edward de Vere, Seventeenth Earl of Oxford, will ever
call mankind to the worship of truth, reality, the infinite wonder of
human nature and the eternal greatness of Man."[75]

Since Looney was so sure of his case, he could
sweep away objections with a wave of the hand. The most damaging
of these objections was that Oxford died in 1604, while a number
of Shakespeare's late plays, including *Macbeth, King Lear,* and
The Tempest, are usually assigned to later dates. Looney stands
ready to dispose of this argument with fair ease: these so-called late
plays were in fact written earlier. Oxford had ample time—far more
time than the overly busy actor and producer William Shakespeare—to turn out all the plays that supposedly originated after
1604.[76] In a substantial appendix, Looney confronts the objection in
more detail by analyzing *The Tempest.* His conclusion: this play is
too mediocre to be Shakespeare's, which is to say Oxford's, work
at all. And so, a modern Prospero, Looney breaks his staff—over
Shakespeare's head.

74. Ibid., 407. For all the parallels, see ibid., 390–414.
75. Ibid., 427.
76. See ibid., 317–22.

These, then, were the arguments that Freud found persuasive. Others found them far less so. Generations of modern scholars have pretty well demolished the claims for Oxford or Bacon or Queen Elizabeth and the whole tribe of ghostwriters presumed to be hiding behind the man from Stratford. We now know that John Shakespeare was not some illiterate rustic but was trusted enough in Stratford to be appointed burgess, alderman, and bailiff; if he signed documents with a cross or an emblem, this was a fairly widespread habit among contemporaries who could demonstrably read and write. As for his son William, while we do not have his report card, there is no reason to assume that he did not attend the local school. And if he did, he was bound to have acquired a fair amount of learning, even if he did come away with little Latin and less Greek. It is true that his poems and dramas display a generous sampling of metaphors drawn from many pursuits, are set in a variety of locations, and suggest a certain familiarity with the law or with history. But his plays yield as abundant a crop of errors as they do accurate allusions. The famous seacoast of Bohemia in *The Winter's Tale* testifies not to the playwright's esoteric knowledge that briefly in the late thirteenth century the Bohemian realm extended to the Adriatic but, quite simply, to his ignorance.[77] What is more, as Ernest Jones told Freud in 1928, we know far more about Shakespeare's life as a member of a prominent acting company than the anti-Stratford party have been willing to concede. All in all, though it would plainly be desirable to know more, we know enough to affirm with a certain confidence that Shakespeare was Shakespeare. The case for any other claimant calls for so much ingenuity, so much imagination, as to dull Occam's razor.

77. Jan Kott economically summarizes the case against the learned and traveled Shakespeare: "He did not know geography. He gives Bohemia a seashore. Proteus boards a ship to go from Verona to Milan, waiting moreover for the tide. Florence, too, is for Shakespeare a port. Shakespeare did not know history either. In his plays Ulysses quotes Aristotle, and Timon of Athens makes references to Seneca and Galenus. Shakespeare did not know philosophy, had no knowledge of warfare, confused customs of different periods. In *Julius Caesar* a clock strikes the hour. A serving maid takes off Cleopatra's corset. In King John's time gunpowder is used in cannons." *Shakespeare Our Contemporary* (1964; tr. and ed. Boleslaw Taborski, 1974), 26.

Looney's plea for Oxford is not without a certain charm.[78] He makes his argument more economically than other Oxfordians: Dorothy and Charlton Ogburn's *This Star of England* (1952), heavily and respectfully indebted to Looney, takes up more than 1,250 pages, while their son Charlton's defense of Oxford, loyally tracing his parents' footsteps, requires merely 892 pages. But it must be admitted that Looney liberally quotes his proof texts out of context[79] and that his solemn search for literary parallels between Oxford's poetry and Shakespeare's writings yields improbable, farfetched likenesses, visible only to someone intensely wishing to see them. Most treacherous of all, Looney's case depends heavily on identifications—Hamlet is Oxford, Polonius is Burghley, Ophelia is Lady Oxford—far too loose to be persuasive.

But precisely these identifications attracted Freud to Looney. As a psychoanalyst, he was predisposed to see the creator in his creation. Before Shakespeare the man had become problematic to him, he had already derived Leonardo da Vinci's depiction of Saint Anne as a young woman, as youthful as her daughter, the Virgin Mary, from Leonardo's dim memories of the two young women who had mothered him. In the same vein, he had interpreted Michelangelo's statue of Moses in Rome as an autobiographical revelation.[80] In his paper of 1908, "Creative Writers and Daydreaming," he had already laid it down bluntly that poets or playwrights or novelists in essence translate their most private fantasies—which is to say, by and large their discontents—into literature. In short, psychoanalytic aesthetics

78. William T. Hastings's slashing verdict on *"Shakespeare" Identified*—"a masterpiece of errors of fact and false logic, as well as amazingly childish naiveté"—is rather harsh. "Shakspere was Shakespeare," *American Scholar* XXVIII (1959), 483. The essay is conveniently excerpted in McMichael and Glenn, *Shakespeare and His Rivals,* 232–46; the quotation is at p. 239.

79. Hastings offers one telling instance: Looney quotes a "trivial and pretentious commonplace book about the literature of the past and the present" by one Francis Meres, published in 1598, as extolling Oxford for being "the best in Comedy" but suppresses two vital facts: (1) that Meres listed no fewer than seventeen writers as being "the best for Comedy," so that Oxford's place is considerably diminished, and (2) that all three of Meres's catalogues, listing the outstanding contemporary writers of tragedy, comedy, and works bemoaning the perplexities of love, contain Shakespeare's name. Ibid.

80. See below, 49–50.

invites biographical criticism. Hence Looney's parallel-hunting was in itself, for Freud, neither eccentric nor vulgar.

Unlike such aesthetically sophisticated and academically trained psychoanalysts as Ernst Kris, Freud had little confidence in the independent productivity of the creative imagination. In sharp contrast, he trusted the ability of the psychoanalyst-biographer-critic to find the man in the work and explain the work by the man. Goethe had said in a famous sentence that all his writings were but fragments of a great confession. Freud had found a way of making authors confess more fully than they had before. His much-quoted remark in his case history of "Dora" definitely applied, in his judgment, to imaginative writers: "He who has eyes to see and ears to hear, becomes convinced that mortals can keep no secret. If their lips are silent, they gossip with their finger tips; betrayal forces its way through every pore."[81] It will emerge that this claim applies to Freud as well.

II. BEYOND THE FAMILY ROMANCE

One did not have to be a psychoanalyst to welcome the kind of literary sleuthing in which both Looney and Freud were engaged as they hunted for the true author of *Hamlet* and *Midsummer Night's Dream.* From the mid-nineteenth century on, while Freud was growing up and reaching his maturity, biographical literary criticism was increasingly in the air. It had its detractors, but the most conspicuous students of literature were part-time biographers, some virtual professionals. The most influential, erudite, and prolific—for many decades, the most persuasive—critic of the age, Charles Augustin Sainte-Beuve, was principally a student of writers' lives, nothing less than a self-proclaimed psychologist. His gigantic output stands as an expansive exemplification of the saying "tel arbre, tel fruit—as the tree, so is the fruit," which he quotes with approval.[1]

From a rather different perspective, in his widely read *History of English Literature,* the little less influential French critic and histo-

81. "Bruchstück einer Hysterie-Analyse" (1905), *GW* V, 240 / "Fragment of an Analysis of a Case of Hysteria," *SE* VII, 77–78.
1. See René Wellek, *A History of Modern Criticism, 1750–1950,* vol. III, *The Age of Transition* (1965), 35, 282.

rian Hippolyte Taine linked life and work without apology. He did
not discount the impact that cultural forces, especially politics, exercise on authors. But he was persuaded that an author's ruling
passion will struggle for, and necessarily find, graphic expression in
his work. This, he argued, held particularly true for William Shakespeare, that "extraordinary species of mind," that "all-powerful,
excessive master of the sublime as well as of the base." With Shakespeare "all came from within—I mean from his soul and his genius;
circumstances and the externals contributed but slightly to his development." To be sure, Taine adds, "he was intimately bound up
with his age; that is, he knew by experience the manners of country,
court, and town; he had visited the heights, depths, the middle ranks
of mankind; nothing more. In all other respects, his life was commonplace."[2] His poetry supplied the supreme clue to the poet: "If
we would become acquainted more closely with the man, we must
seek him in his works."[3] One must "reconstruct" Shakespeare's
world, "so as to find in it the imprint of its creator."[4] The greatest
rewards of this reconstructive procedure, Taine suggests, are generated by a reading of *Hamlet.* Thus in the crucial scene with his
mother, "Hamlet, it will be said, is half-mad; this explains the vehe-
mence of his expressions." The inescapable conclusion follows: "The
truth is that Hamlet, here, is Shakespeare."[5]

The brilliant English essayist, editor, economist, political scientist,
and literary critic Walter Bagehot held much the same position. In
a leisurely essay of 1853, "Shakespeare—The Man," he argues that
for all the paucity of information about him, Shakespeare had left
telltale traces of himself in his writings. "Some extreme skeptics,
we know, doubt whether it is possible to deduce anything as to an
author's character from his works." Bagehot demurs: "Surely people
do not keep a tame steam-engine to write their books; and if those
books were really written by a man, he must have been a man who
could write them; he must have had the thoughts which they express,
have acquired the knowledge they contain, have possessed the style
in which we read them."[6] Licensed by this tautology, Bagehot con-

2. Taine, *History of English Literature,* tr. H. van Laun (1873), 204–05.
3. Ibid., 211.
4. Ibid., 214.
5. Ibid., 212.
6. Bagehot, "Shakespeare—The Man," in *Literary Studies* (*Miscellaneous Essays*), 3 vols., ed. Richard Holt Hutton (1879; ed. 1910), I, 37.

structs a Shakespeare endowed with "a first-rate imagination working on a first-rate experience," a writer blessed with a "fine
sensibility," who took a "keen interest" in the general outlines and,
better, the "minutest particulars and gentlest gradations" of objects.
Quoting at length from Shakespeare's depiction of the hunt in
"Venus and Adonis," Bagehot observes with characteristic panache,
"It is absurd, by the way, to say we know *nothing* about the man
who wrote that; we know that he had been after a hare. It is idle to
allege that mere imagination would tell him that a hare is apt to run
among a flock of sheep, or that its so doing disconcerts the scent of
hounds." Plainly, Shakespeare was "a judge of dogs, was an outdoor
sporting man, full of natural sensibility." Besides, "he was not merely
with men, but of men"; he had "in his own nature the germs and
tendencies of the very elements that he described." He knew the
common people; he enjoyed, as his invention of Falstaff leaves no
doubt, "a capacity for laughter"; he was certainly "a natural reader."
Bagehot draws much more out of the poems and the plays than this:
Shakespeare's politics and religion, his class attitudes and genial
good humor. He was, Bagehot tells us, "beloved and even respected,
with a hope for every one and a smile for all."[7] From this position
to Freud's reading Shakespeare's Oedipus complex by reading
Shakespeare's *Hamlet* is only one step—if a large one.

The Germans rather lagged behind in the biographical exploration
of poets and their work. It is no accident that the first major biography of Goethe should be by an Englishman, George Henry Lewes.
Published in 1855, some twenty-three years after Goethe's death, it
was promptly translated into German and for decades remained the
unrivaled life. In a paper on the riddle of *Macbeth,* the psychoanalyst
Ludwig Jekels cites Georg Gottfried Gervinus, the mid-nineteenth-
century German publicist, historian, democrat, and student of
Shakespeare, as urging critics to throw a bridge between Shakespeare's inner life and his published work: "With Shakespeare, as
with every rich poetic nature," he quotes Gervinus writing in 1849,
"no outer routine and poetic propriety, but inner experiences and
emotions of the mind were the deep springs of his poetry."[8] But

7. Ibid., 38, 40, 42, 48, 55, 61, 81, 86.
8. From Gervinus, *Shakespeare,* 2 vols. (1849–1850; tr. F. E. Bunnett, 1875), I,
22. In Jekels, "The Riddle of Shakespeare's Macbeth," (1917; tr. 1943), which
is in Jekels, *Selected Papers* (1952), 105. Jekels gave that paper first to the
Vienna Psychoanalytic Society, on March 7, 1917. See *Protokolle* IV, 298.

even a glance at Gervinus's bulky two-volume commentary on Shakespeare's plays discloses that he failed to carry out his own largely implicit program. And in any event, he had no followers. It was not until late in the nineteenth century, when responsible literary biographies were becoming more common, that German literary historians and critics joined the rest of Europe in seeking the man in the work.

Probably the epochal figure in the serious game of literary detection, certainly for Freud, was the fertile, adventurous Danish critic Georg Brandes, who more than anyone else shaped late nineteenth-century European literary and philosophical tastes.[9] It was, significantly, Brandes's two-volume *William Shakespeare,* first published in Danish in 1895 and 1896 and immediately translated into German, that made this kind of criticism directly available to Freud. He had the book in his library, and we know that he read it to good purpose, for he quotes it on a crucial page in *The Interpretation of Dreams,* in the passage about *Hamlet* and the Oedipus complex.[10] Later, in a discussion at the Vienna Psychoanalytic Society dealing with "the relation between the creation and the life of the imaginative writer," Freud praised Brandes without reserve. If Shakespeare was "a favorable object of the psychological method," Freud thought, this was true all the more because Brandes had "done very good exploratory work."[11]

What Freud found particularly relevant in Brandes's biography was the information that Shakespeare had apparently written *Hamlet* shortly after his father's death. Indeed, Brandes melodramatically juxtaposes these two salient events in Shakespeare's life: "He lost his father, his earliest friend and protector, whose honor and repute were so close to his heart. In the same year," Brandes continues

9. When in March 1900 Brandes came to Vienna to lecture, Freud and his wife went to hear him. See Freud to Fliess, March 23, 1900. *Freud-Fliess,* 446 (406). That Brandes viewed America with contempt could have done him no harm in Freud's eyes. (For Brandes's anti-Americanism, see his gratuitous attribution to Americans of "lack of spiritual finesse—*Mangel an geistiger Feinheit.*" Brandes, *William Shakespeare* [1895–1896; German tr. 1896], 120. The first German edition of that biography is in Freud's library. See Davies, Lockley, and Neufeld, *Freud's London Library,* no. 152.)

10. See the editor's note in *SE* XXI, 91n. The passage in *The Interpretation of Dreams* is at *SE* IV, 265.

11. Meeting of December 11, 1907. *Protokolle* I, 250–51.

breathlessly in a one-sentence paragraph, *"Hamlet* began to form in Shakespeare's imagination."[12] Freud must have found this formulation extremely seductive. What he added was the important diagnostic detail that the death of Shakespeare's father evidently revived in the mourning playwright long-repressed oedipal feelings.

Given his biographical bent, it was only natural that Brandes should be an unabashed parallel-hunter. To be sure, he denigrated as "half-educated" those obsessed revisionists who insisted on giving Shakespeare's plays to someone else, and spurned Ignatius Donnelly's *The Great Cryptogram: Francis Bacon's Cipher in the So-Called Shakespeare Plays* as an "insane book."[13] Yet Brandes was not averse to speculating about the experiences that must have formed the lines Shakespeare put down on paper. To take one instance, Shakespeare wrote *The Merchant of Venice* at a time of considerable personal prosperity, "his mental life dominated by ideas all turning on acquisition, property, riches, and wealth." The harmonious, sunny conclusion of this play is "as it were an emblem of a feeling of inner wealth and of the equilibrium he had now achieved."[14] Brandes did not propose to be naive: to discover, say, King James I in Hamlet was to confuse the possibilities available to a writer with the "impulses of which he himself was unconscious"[15]—a formulation that must have endeared Brandes to Freud even more.

Still, Brandes sought the writer in his writings and was disappointed when he did not find him. Thus he confessed that to his taste, *Macbeth* was "one of the less interesting works of Shakespeare's, considered not from the artistic but from the purely human point of view. It is a rich, highly moral melodrama; but I felt Shakespeare's heart beating in it only in a few places."[16] Again, he disputed the claims of those who professed to recognize in Iago the historical King Richard III: "No, surely Shakespeare encountered Iago in his own life."[17] Since, expectedly, *Hamlet* furnishes a particularly well stocked hunting preserve for irresponsible reductionist readings,

12. Brandes, *William Shakespeare,* 481.

13. Ibid., 123n.

14. Ibid., 210, 239.

15. Ibid., 491. Brandes uses the term "unconscious" more than once in his biography.

16. Ibid., 598.

17. Ibid., 610.

Brandes took care to caution against them: "No imaginative work of immortal value is generated this way"[18]—a warning that only served to legitimize Brandes's own ventures into biographical conjecture. Like Looney after him, Brandes took credit for prudence to allow himself to be audacious. "Shakespeare," he insisted, "needed no poetic efforts to transform himself into Hamlet." Quite the contrary, "he could allow this figure to drink his innermost heart's blood; he could communicate to it the beating pulse of his own veins."[19]

Shakespeare's relatively tranquil external fate, Brandes mused, might seem to fall far short of his inventiveness; still, he had undergone enough trials, including the death of a father, the infidelity of a beloved woman, and the treachery of a trusted friend, to become Hamlet-like. "He experienced everything like Hamlet—everything."[20] Shakespeare had managed to endow his imagined hero with independent life, and yet "he blended with Hamlet; he felt as Hamlet did, he drew him to himself and into himself."[21] Brandes realized—and acknowledged on an early page[22]—that it had become commonplace to say, We know nothing about Shakespeare. But his bulky biographical study implies, and at times proclaims, that, handed so abundant an outpouring of deeply felt writings, the critic must not resign and treat Shakespeare as a mysterious stranger. When James Joyce's Stephen Dedalus, in *Ulysses,* entertains his listeners with his imaginative theories about the author of *Hamlet*—"Rutlandbaconsouthamptonshakespeare or another poet of the same name in the comedy of errors"—he was, if a little extravagant, in the critical mainstream of his time. In short, biographical criticism pervaded, largely dominated, the atmosphere in which cultivated men like Freud read their Shakespeare. All that psychoanalysis did was furnish sharper scalpels or, to vary the metaphor, more finely ground lenses, to assist the critic in detecting the hidden personal agenda in a writer's work.

Freud, then, was disposed both as a psychoanalyst and as an educated Central European to be receptive to Looney's

18. Ibid., 510.
19. Ibid., 512.
20. Ibid.
21. Ibid., 514, and see 517.
22. Ibid., 4.

ideas. But his belated enthusiasm for the earl of Oxford had more tangled roots than this. It would be begging the question to blame his allegiance, however hesitant, on an old man's right to indulge his crotchets. No doubt, with advancing age, Freud's willful, stubborn confidence in his judgment against the evidence also increased. He came to adopt a hardening posture that could only work against that admirable attitude of systematic doubt and hesitant conclusions which Freud himself had repeatedly—and sincerely—proclaimed to be the mark of the scientific mind. Just as he defied all the most authoritative available opinions in his conjectures about the identity of the author of Shakespeare's plays, he later offended not only the pious but also rationalist scholars by insisting that Moses must have been an Egyptian. Quite as defiantly, in the teeth of unanimous rejection on the part of responsible biologists, he persisted in arguing for the Lamarckian theory that acquired characteristics can be inherited. And in 1936, when he was eighty, he speculated in a letter to Thomas Mann, after reading one of the volumes in Mann's Joseph tetralogy, that Napoleon Bonaparte must have lived out his life in obedience to fantasies about Joseph.

It is not that the old Freud grew imperious about his views. His theories about Shakespeare (as we have seen) or Moses (as we shall see) show him in a tentative, even a troubled mood. In his letter to Thomas Mann about Napoleon, Freud confessed that he did not take his own notions too seriously but found them charming. Moreover, whatever we may think of his conclusions, Freud's newly awakened interest in the mysteries of female sexuality and his radical reevaluation of his theory of anxiety, both of which date from his late sixties, show him capable of changing his mind drastically about some cherished ideas of his own. And even if we were to convict Freud of some perverse desire to be different, the question would remain: what are the grounds of this perversity?

Not surprisingly, when students of Freud the Oxfordian have asked this sort of question, they have chosen to proceed psychoanalytically. This is only fair: since Freud has shown that psychoanalyzing writers can often yield astonishing rewards, others have felt justified in visiting Freudian exploratory techniques on Freud himself. And it is true that Freud's joining the anti-Stratford forces seems to call for an investigation reaching more deeply into the recesses of his unconscious than an appeal to cultural and literary causes ever could.

Ernest Jones, who had done battle with Freud over the Oxford hypothesis from the beginning and who could never quite understand Freud's caprice, associated it with Freud's views about two other figures that loomed large in his fantasy life, Leonardo da Vinci and Moses. "It can hardly be chance that with each of these questions of identity arose in one form or other, evidently disguised variants of the theme to which Freud gave the name 'Family Romance.'" Jones suggests that "something in Freud's mentality led him to take a special interest in people not being what they seemed to be." For Freud, then, embracing the notion that Shakespeare was not Shakespeare was, Jones thought, "some derivative of the Family Romance phantasy," part of his childhood wish that he might have been the son of his prosperous half brother Emanuel rather than of his impecunious father. At the heart of his stubborn Oxford fantasy, Jones concludes, "seems to be a wish that a certain part of reality could be changed."[23]

It is an ingenious thesis, and not without some merit.[24] But neither Jones nor those who later echoed him have considered the curious fact that Freud did not dismiss the man from Stratford until late in

23. *Jones* III, 430. In his paper on this matter ("Freud and the Controversy over Shakespearean Authorship," *J. Amer. Psychoanal. Assn.* XIII [1965], 475–98), Harry Trosman takes essentially the same position: "Freud had the type of mind that could never accept the obvious or the popular. His great achievement was to see mystery and concealment where others accepted the manifest unquestioningly. . . . Freud suggested the specific variant of the family romance to which the Shakespearean authorship controversy has reference. . . . The issue of the Shakespearean authorship controversy appears to be a long-standing unresolved preoccupation with doubts concerning rightful paternity." Trosman, 493, 495.

24. In 1965, Norman Holland added an interesting twist to Ernest Jones's psychoanalytic explanation of Freud's "Oxfordism." Borrowing from the theory of the Oedipus complex, Holland added to Jones's thesis that Freud's fantasy enshrined a wish to change reality: "Freud's doubts about authorship are part of a general pattern of ambivalence in his personality, of which he himself was well aware." His "feelings toward Shakespeare were not devoid of such filial ambivalence." The artist, in Freud's view, does change reality—or, better, "wishes a changed reality into being"—by means of "poetic license." (Holland, *Psychoanalysis and Shakespeare,* 58.) Paul Roazen's view of the Shakespeare question, which also draws on oedipal theory, is far more extravagant. Freud, Roazen conjectures, "felt guilt toward his father," in part because he felt compelled "to obliterate his parents." Again and again, as Freud's treatment of Leonardo da Vinci, Oedipus, and Moses show, he returned "to the fantasy of

life—not the time for a family romance to blossom. True, Freud had a considerable investment in the conventional identification of Shakespeare. For Freud, as I have said, the unsettling emotional event in Shakespeare's life that propelled him to write *Hamlet* was the death of his father in 1601. Freud first hinted at this notion in 1897; he had almost certainly read Brandes's life of Shakespeare by then.[25] Ten years later, he made it explicit at a meeting of his Wednesday Psychological Society: the relationship of "*Hamlet* to the personal circumstances in the writer's life are particularly evident. The work is a reaction to the death of his father."[26] It was, after all, the compelling evidence these bereavements supplied for an intimate link between life and art that made *Hamlet* supremely the psychoanalyst's play, the modern *Oedipus Rex.*

Now, if the man from Stratford was not Shakespeare the playwright, the date of his father's death would become irrelevant. It might well be, as Freud told Lytton Strachey, that the seventeenth earl of Oxford "shows himself, in Hamlet, as the first modern neurotic."[27] Besides, it was a matter of record that Oxford had lost his father when he was twelve, and it was possible that his mother had remarried all too promptly.[28] Still, these facts of Oxford's life, partly shrouded in

being raised fatherless." And this fantasy sees to it "that the true father always turns out to be a man of high rank." Oedipus, of course, was a king; Moses, an aristocrat. "He even speculated that Shakespeare was not the man of humble origins at all, but instead the Earl of Oxford. These were the ego models that Freud needed to sustain him in his work." In this "special version of the oedipal complex," Freud "unconsciously thought of himself as his own father." (Roazen, *Freud: Political and Social Thought* [1968], 176–77.) Thus, in Roazen's version, Freud's family romance stands as a bit of nasty, largely unconscious snobbery.

25. See Freud to Fliess, October 15, 1897. *Freud-Fliess,* 293 (272).

26. Meeting of December 11, 1907. *Protokolle* I, 251.

27. Freud to Lytton Strachey, December 25, 1928. *Briefe,* 401.

28. "His mother, we also learn," Looney writes, once again quite unconscious of raising matters of psychoanalytic concern, "remarried. We have tried in vain to discover the exact dates at which he was brought to court, and when his mother remarried, not as matters of mere curiosity, but because we believe these points may have their bearing both on our problem and upon questions of Shakespearean interpretation." Unfortunately, the dates must remain a matter of speculation. (*"Shakespeare" Identified,* 193–94.) In 1934, Freud tried to connect Oxford—father of three daughters—to King Lear. See Freud to James S. H. Bransom, author of *The Tragedy of King Lear,* March 25, 1934. *Jones* III, 457.

uncertainty, somehow lacked the powerful emotional resonance similar facts had held for the man from Stratford. Freud was only too well aware of the difficulty; as he alerted Ernest Jones in 1928, if the earl of Oxford was "really Shakesp., we shall have to alter a good deal in our analytic constructions." There might be, he added in an access of optimism, a real gain if the new thesis proved correct.[29]

But while the gain was speculative, the loss was palpable enough. "I read your last contribution to the *Psychoanalytische Bewegung*," dealing with *Hamlet* and death, "with some uneasiness," Freud wrote Theodor Reik in March 1930. "I have been troubled by a change in me which was brought about under the influence of Looney's book, *"Shakespeare" Identified.* I no longer believe in the man from Stratford."[30] It will emerge that the word "troubled" carries a good deal of weight. Not that Freud was generally disposed to evade doubts when they assailed him. He always showed himself ready, in far more fundamental psychoanalytic issues, to shake up the psychoanalytic establishment and himself with new ideas, with radical departures. In itself, then, Freud's desertion of the man from Stratford was hardly out of character. But the nagging question remains: why shift when he did and not before? If Freud needed to appease the craving for a more illustrious parentage for himself— and for his presumable stand-in, Shakespeare—he would not have had to wait for Looney. More prestigious pedigrees for the author of Shakespeare's works than undistinguished provincial parents could provide had been available while Freud was a younger man. In the decisive late 1890s, after the death of his father and while he was in the midst of his self-analysis, the case for Bacon was an undisputed favorite, and Freud was sufficiently acquainted with it.

What is more, the family romance, that widespread psychological phenomenon Freud first described in the late 1890s, is the privilege, virtually the monopoly, of adolescent and adult neurotics. Certainly Freud's first sustained treatment of what he called the *Familienroman,* a two-page psychoanalysis of Conrad Ferdinand Meyer's nov-

29. Freud to Jones, March 11, 1928. Freud Collection, D2, LC. I might note that Ernest Jones, too, had a stake in the conventional view: basing himself on Freud's comment in *The Interpretation of Dreams,* he had written a paper on Hamlet's Oedipus complex in 1910, a paper he republished in revised and expanded form through the years. It did not become a book (*Hamlet and Oedipus*) until 1949.
30. Freud to Reik, March 23, 1930, in Reik, *The Search Within* (1956), 649.

ella *Die Richterin,* clearly aimed at a clinical understanding of neurotics.[31] And the title of Freud's short paper on the subject, supplied after the paper was first printed, was "Der Familienroman der Neurotiker." Beethoven, to name just one striking exemplar of a neurotic plagued with the urgent need to invent less appalling parents than reality had provided, demonstrated in his life that the family romance need not wholly fade away after puberty.[32] Still, unlike Beethoven, who was, after all, never analyzed, Freud should have been able to shed such fantastic constructions after his self-analysis. One might argue that it was precisely the psychoanalysts' professional stake in the man from Stratford that kept Freud from yielding to his own family romance earlier.

But the evidence for Freud's being in any way prey to this self-induced neurotic legend is skimpy in the extreme. It seems that he indulged in imagining a different, a better parentage just once—at least to the best of my knowledge, it was just once. And that was not in the late 1890s, when his oedipal demons, revived and refreshed, visited him most energetically, but much earlier, after his first visit to England, in 1875, when he was a young medical student. Nor was his a highly visible dream of paternal glory: Freud had to tease it out with an ingenious interpretation of one of the famous slips he allowed himself in *The Interpretation of Dreams.*[33] Freud is recounting his painful disillusionment with his father when Jacob calmly told him of the time he had knuckled under to an anti-Semitic bully who had knocked his new fur cap into the gutter. Freud recalled that he had contrasted his father's unheroic behavior (he picked up the cap from the muck) with the vow that another Semite, Hannibal's father, Hasdrubal, had exacted from his son to take revenge on the

31. For a brief discussion of Freud's psychoanalysis of Meyer's *Die Richterin,* see below, 112–14. Freud's paper first appeared in Otto Rank's *Der Mythus von der Geburt des Helden* (1909; 2nd ed., 1922) and was then printed as a separate essay in a collection of Freud's papers, *Neurosenlehre und Technik* (1931), where it was given the title "Der Familienroman der Neurotiker." For some reason, the editors of the Standard Edition docked the second half of the title, and it is as "Family Romances" that the paper has become known to English-speaking psychoanalysts. (See *SE* IX, 236.)

32. For the role of the family romance in Beethoven's life, see the impressive psychoanalytic biographical study by Maynard Solomon, *Beethoven* (1977).

33. For the slip, see *Interpretation of Dreams, SE* IV, 197, 197n; for its interpretation, *Psychopathology of Everyday Life, SE* VI, 219–20. See *Jones III,* 430.

Romans. But, of course, as Freud well knew, Hasdrubal was Hannibal's brother, not his father, and in *The Psychopathology of Everyday Life,* he explained how he had managed to mistake a brother for a father: on his visit to England, he had become better acquainted with his half brother Emanuel, who had emigrated to Manchester and prospered there, and Emanuel's son, John, roughly Freud's age. This conjunction stimulated him, Freud reports, to weave fantasies about just how different his life would have been if he had been born the son of Emanuel rather than of Jacob Freud. Then Freud would have been, one may fill out his daydream, member of a comfortable rather than a pinched household, and an Englishman to boot—a pleasant but scarcely exalted wish. In short, the family romance cannot solve the conundrum of why Freud gave the author of Shakespeare's plays and poems an exalted family tree.

Repeatedly throughout his life, in almost oppressive reiteration, Freud would confess that certain riddles, technical and literary, bothered him exceedingly.[34] They troubled him as an unresolved chord troubles a musician. Conundrums did not just fascinate him; they tortured him. He spoke of them in the vocabulary of authentic suffering, like a man pursued by demons, who cannot rest until he has found a way of appeasing them. He found the sheer abundance of ideas flooding him a mixed blessing.[35]

In June 1912, with his longed-for summer holiday at last in the offing, he wrote to Karl Abraham: "At present, my intellectual activity would be confined to the corrections for the fourth edition of my [*Psychopathology of*] *Everyday Life* if it had not suddenly occurred to me that the opening scene in Lear, the judgment of Paris, and the choice of caskets in the Merchant of Venice are really based on the same motif which I *must* now track down."[36] The language

34. In the following five or six pages, I have drawn on evidence already gathered in my *Freud,* esp. pp. 313 and 608, as well as on some new material.

35. One of his adherents, unfortunately unidentified, once exclaimed about Freud, in considerable agitation: "You see, the man has absolutely original ideas of his own, thoughts no man else ever had before. They come in such a flood, they fill his head to an extent he himself cannot master—a ceaseless fount!" Reported by M. Wulff, a psychoanalyst in Tel Aviv, in Israel Psycho-Analytical Society, *Max Eitingon in Memoriam* (1950), 141–42.

36. Freud to Karl Abraham, June 14, 1912. Karl Abraham papers, LC. Italics mine.

is unvarnished: Freud confesses to a sense of urgency about the need for resolving the puzzle that has somehow occurred to him. It is as though he were feeling compelled to pass a stringent test—a test, moreover, which he had set for himself. One might think that Freud would take pleasure in musing on two favorite plays and an agreeable Greek myth. But he exhibited, rather, a mixture of pleasure and pain, of playfulness and compulsion, as he dug for the roots of the motif he *must* track down.

This is how he sounded, early and late. Patients were enigmas to be solved: "E.," a five-year analysand, "has at last concluded his career as a patient with an evening invitation to my house," Freud wrote triumphantly to Fliess in April 1900. "His riddle is *almost* completely solved."[37] Then, in late 1909, Freud reported to Jung: "Yesterday, before the Society, I launched the Leonardo lecture, which I didn't like myself, so that I can count on a little peace from my obsession."[38] "Obsession" is a strong word, and Freud did not use it casually. Again, in May 1911, he told Sándor Ferenczi, "I am tormented today by the secret of the tragic school, which will surely not withstand PsA."[39] He advised his patient, the English psychoanalyst Joan Riviere, after she had told him of some analytic explanation that had occurred to her, " "Write it, write it, put it down in black and white; that's the way to deal with it; you get it out of your system.' " While the advice meant little for Riviere's way of working, she came to see it as "true for him," necessary for his own creative work. It was in the same spirit that he had previously told her, " 'Get it out, produce it, make something of it—*outside you,* that is; give it an existence independently of you.' "[40] Perceptive as she was, Riviere did not catch the tormented tone of this bit of confessional advice, this strain of pregnancy and of being compelled to relieve it by giving birth. The same obsessive note informs Freud's response when his American patient Joseph Wortis asked him whether he found writing difficult: " 'No,' he answered, 'because I have usually

37. Freud to Fliess, April 16, 1900. *Freud-Fliess,* 448 (409).

38. Freud to Jung, December 2, 1909. *Freud-Jung,* 298 (271).

39. Freud to Sándor Ferenczi, May 21, 1911. Freud-Ferenczi Correspondence, Freud Collection, LC.

40. Riviere, "A Character Trait of Freud's" (1956), in *Psychoanalysis and Contemporary Thought,* ed. John Sutherland (1958), 145–49, quotations at 146. For an example of Freud's total absorption in his work, see him writing *Totem and Taboo. Freud,* 324–25.

not written until a thing was ripe and I felt a real compulsion to express myself.' "[41] The metaphor of the author as the father or mother of his work, commonplace by Freud's time, was often under his pen, and he never anticipated an easy pregnancy.[42]

Probably the most persuasive testimony to Freud's torment of creativity stems from his work, begun some time after the advent of Hitler, on the speculative essays that would together become *Moses and Monotheism.* Throughout he was ridden by imperious spectres. Who was Moses? How could one reconcile his stern monotheism with the primitive volcano-god Yahweh that the ancient Hebrews had long worshiped? When late in 1934 Freud ceased work on the essays for some time, he stopped not just because he feared the censorious and bigoted Catholic authorities but also because he was beleaguered by "inner misgivings." His "historical novel," as he provisionally titled his venture in a blend of self-deprecating humor and serious skepticism, would not stand up to the criticism he was expending on his unconventional notions. But he was unwilling—indeed, quite unable—to give up his enterprise, and once again he spoke as though he were being driven by obscure forces he could not control: "Leave me alone with Moses," he instructed Arnold Zweig, who had asked after the book, with a show of irritation rare in their correspondence. "That this probably final attempt to create something has run aground depresses me enough. Not that I have got away from it. The man, and what I wanted to make of him, pursues me incessantly."[43] In the spring of the following year, he confessed, again to Arnold Zweig, "Moses will not let my imagination go."[44] Writing to Max Eitingon just a few days later, he used more

41. Wortis, *Fragments of an Analysis with Freud* (1954), 152.

42. The topic calls for further exploration. Here are a few tantalizing instances: "I want to keep holding back on the theory of sexuality," Freud told Fliess on November 19, 1899. "An unborn piece is still attached to what has already been born." *Freud-Fliess,* 426 (387). Again to Fliess, on October 23, 1900, he sent a handshake on his birthday, unlike the previous year, when he "could salute you with the firstborn of the dream book." Ibid., 469 (428). Once again, quite baldly, Freud wrote Jung on February 12, 1911: "For some weeks I have been pregnant with the germ of a larger synthesis and expect my confinement this summer." *Freud-Jung,* 432 (391). There are other instances.

43. Freud to Arnold Zweig, December 16, 1934. *Freud-Zweig,* 108 (97–98).

44. Freud to Arnold Zweig, May 2, 1935. Ibid., 117 (106).

emphatic, more clinical language: the book on Moses "has become a fixation for me."[45]

The long-delayed publication of *Moses and Monotheism,* possible only after he had reached England, liberated him from his self-generated pursuers. But he could not forget the pressures that had been goading him for years: candidly he reminded his readers of the compulsive quality the project had had for him from the outset. It was splendid to be a free man at last. Now "I may speak and write— I have almost said, think—as I wish or must."[46] There was in those words far less feeling of joyous closure, of inner freedom, than one might have expected: he had for years thought and written about Moses because he had been somehow forced to do so. The problem of Moses, he wrote, had "tormented me like an unlaid ghost."[47] And he concluded, "Unfortunately, an author's creative power does not always follow his will; the work turns out as it can, and often confronts its author as it were independently, indeed, like a stranger."[48] These are revealing phrases.

When he was younger, Freud could afford to wait until the solutions to haunting problems came to him. He felt that he might allow the observations he was accumulating and the theoretical ideas which he hoped would bind those observations into a coherent whole to mature in his unconscious. But, as his letters to Fliess show over and over, even during the heroic years of discovery, Freud felt the torment of the incomplete. Later in life, as the time available to him grew shorter, his patience grew shorter as well, particularly as he repeatedly set dates for his probable demise. This, too, is why when he was getting old he entered into the two most eccentric commitments of his life, both revisionist in the extreme—the identification of Moses as an Egyptian and of Shakespeare as the earl of Oxford. As he once confessed to Max Eitingon, one of the two matters in his life that had "always perplexed him to distraction" concerned the

45. Freud to Max Eitingon, May 12, 1935. (Sigmund Freud Copyrights, Wivenhoe.)

46. "Vorbemerkung II," *Der Mann Moses, GW* XVI, 159 / "Prefatory Note II," *SE* XXIII, 57.

47. "Zusammenfassung und Wiederholung," *Der Mann Moses, GW* XVI, 210 / "Summary and Recapitulation," *SE* XXIII, 103.

48. Ibid., 211 / 104.

identity of the author of *Hamlet* and *Macbeth*.[49] (The other was telepathy.) By now Freud's choice of language is familiar, but it remains striking. It is no accident, then, that when Freud informed Reik of his desertion of the man from Stratford, he chose the rather grim term "troubled." He meant it.

If the riddles that Shakespeare set Freud—or, rather, that Freud insisted on discovering in Shakespeare—were more prominent and more haunting than others that troubled him, they are tributes to Shakespeare's persistent hold on his imagination. Curiously enough, Shakespeare's probably most baffling and problematic play, *Hamlet,* was for Freud among the least challenging of these riddles. He came upon his historic solution for the central psychological question the tragedy raises—why does Hamlet hesitate to kill the king, his stepfather?—with apparent ease: Hamlet's unresolved oedipal conflicts paralyzed him. Freud's response after reaching that explanation was not his usual one of a man breathing free after intense, tormenting preoccupations but, rather, the satisfaction of having discovered an important but really quite simple truth— simple for a psychoanalyst. He took pride in having been the first to pierce the obscurity of a drama that, more than any other, had engrossed so much attention and generated so many debates for more than two centuries.[50] Had he not succeeded where even his admired Goethe had failed? "When I wrote down what seemed to me the solution of the mystery," he congratulated himself in a letter to Ernest Jones in 1909, "I had not undertaken special research into the Hamlet literature but I knew what the conclusions of our German writers were and saw that even Goethe had missed the mark."[51]

In sharp contrast, another Shakespearean tragedy, *Macbeth,* harassed him with far more protracted questions. "I have begun to study *Macbeth,* which has long been tormenting me," he wrote to Sándor Ferenczi in 1914, "without having found the solution so far."[52] He

49. Freud to Eitingon, November 13, 1922. Quoted in *Jones* III, 430.

50. For that claim, see "The Moses of Michelangelo" (1914), *SE XIII,* 212. L. C. Knights reports the consensus of scholars in 1960: "*Hamlet* is, I suppose, that play of Shakespeare's about which there is most disagreement." *An Approach to "Hamlet"* (1960), 1.

51. Freud to Jones, June 1, 1909. In English. Freud Collection, D2, LC.

52. Freud to Ferenczi, July 17, 1914. Freud-Ferenczi Correspondence, Freud Collection, LC.

knew the play inside and out. When during one analytic session Smiley Blanton, that scholarly physician, attributed the line "untimely ripped from his mother's womb" to *Julius Caesar*, Freud instantly corrected him: "No," he told Blanton, "it was said of Macduff in *Macbeth.*"[53] The tragedy was a long-standing preoccupation for Freud. A decade and a half before he devoted some fascinating pages to it, he had suggested succinctly that *Macbeth* is about childlessness.[54] Then, in 1915, in a paper on analytic patients wrecked by success, he restated this interpretation in greater detail though with less conviction. Lady Macbeth "collapses after having reached success, after she has striven for it with unwavering energy." Early in the tragedy, she shows "no vacillation and no sign of any inner battle, no other endeavor than to conquer the scruples of her ambitious and yet tender-minded husband. She is willing to sacrifice her very womanliness to murderous intentions." After the murder of Duncan, though, she shows a measure of disappointment, and, after bravely covering over her husband's collapse during the terrible banquet scene, she more or less leaves the action to him. Sleepwalking, in unmitigated terror of her blood-soaked visions, she seeks to undo the deed that cannot be undone. "Remorse," Freud observes, "seems to have prostrated her," the very woman "who had seemed so remorseless." And then she dies. "Now we ask ourselves, what has shattered this character, which seemed forged from the hardest of metals?"[55] This is the riddle of *Macbeth* that had, as he told Ferenczi, so long tormented him, and for which he had found no solution.

He never really discovered one, as he frankly confessed. "I find it impossible to reach a decision here."[56] The play, Freud bravely continued to speculate, does scatter strong hints that it is essentially concerned with the sad theme of childlessness. But they were only hints. And unfortunately, it was not Lady Macbeth alone who remained elusive. Macbeth, too, was unfathomable. "What can these motives be, which could turn in so short a time the hesitant ambitious man into an uninhibited hothead, and the steel-hard instigator into a contrite sick woman, filled with remorse? This is in my view insoluble." He

53. Blanton, *Diary of My Analysis with Freud,* 56.
54. See *Interpretation of Dreams, SE* IV, 266.
55. "Die am Erfolge scheitern," in "Einige Charaktertypen aus der psychoanalytischen Arbeit," *GW* X, 373–74 / "Those Wrecked by Success," *SE* XIV, 318.
56. Ibid., 375 / 320.

offered in mitigation the "triply layered obscurity" that obstructed an understanding of the play: the poor state of the text, the unknown intentions of the poet, and the secret meaning of the legend.[57]

Yet Freud pressed on. Almost pathetically, he grasped at the straw that the psychoanalyst Ludwig Jekels had offered in an unpublished paper, suggesting that Shakespeare had split a single protagonist into two, so that Macbeth and Lady Macbeth were simply two sides of one character.[58] This was a possible explanation dictated, for Freud, more by despair than by conviction. "It is so hard," he acknowledged, "to leave a problem like that of *Macbeth* as insoluble,"[59] and he toyed with Jekels's suggestion only because he found it so painful to abandon a riddle that continued to haunt him.

Freud left one muted but eloquent document testifying to his passion for puzzle solving and to his interest in *Macbeth* as a mystery far more than as a poem. He owned a French edition of the tragedy with a lengthy introduction by the editor, James Darmesteter, a virtuoso of languages who specialized in Near Eastern texts and also wrote extensively on English literature. Darmesteter's commitment to biographical criticism was complete: "For too long," he wrote in an essay on Shakespeare, "we have studied Shakespeare as though we were studying a revealed book, without dreaming of applying to him the ordinary laws of historical criticism." He complained that Shakespeare's innumerable living and diverse characters—Romeo, Macbeth, Lear, Hamlet, and many others—have been treated as "the almost artless and unconscious productions of a remote genius, who contained in himself all the contrasts and all the harmonies." Only recently, Darmesteter thought, have people discovered that not even Shakespeare can escape the general laws of the human spirit, that he changed as all other humans do. This was a view with which

57. Ibid., 378–79 / 323.

58. Ibid. Interestingly enough, A. C. Bradley, though of course without resorting to psychoanalytic terminology (or for that matter to psychoanalytic ideas), comes to much the same conclusion: "Not that they are egoists, like Iago; or, if they are egoists, theirs is an *égoisme à deux.* They have no separate ambitions. They support and love one another. They suffer together." *Shakespearean Tragedy* (1904; 2nd ed., 1905), 350.

59. "Die am Erfolge scheitern," *GW* X, 379 / "Those Wrecked by Success," *SE* XIV, 323. On this unpublished paper of Jekels's, different from the published paper of 1917 on the riddle of *Macbeth,* see the editors' note in *SE* XIV, 323n.

Freud powerfully sympathized. Would he not write about Leonardo da Vinci, "There is no one so great that it would be a disgrace for him to be subject to the laws that govern normal and pathological activity with equal severity"?[60] The mind that had devised a Romeo, as Darmesteter put it, was not the same mind that had devised a Hamlet. Hence, "the real interest in Shakespeare's history is the history of his genius." One needs to date his productions, grasp the progress of his experiences: "The cold genius can create only a statue of marble; life comes only from life."[61]

Freud, as his copy attests, read Darmesteter's edition of *Macbeth* carefully, even taking the trouble to correct some typographical errors.[62] To judge from the lines he penciled against the margins (and once, just once, into the text) as tokens of particular attention, his interest was aroused mainly by the psychological mysteries, the hidden conflicts, of the principal characters as well as by textual conundrums. "She thinks," runs one passage of Darmesteter on Lady Macbeth that Freud noted, "he must be king. But she fears his weakness: he desires and does not dare; his wishes are criminal and he recoils before the crime."[63] Again, in a tantalizing hint at what Freud would come to call oedipal conflicts: "She would have given the blow herself, if the sleeping Duncan had not resembled her father."[64] Lady Macbeth, Darmesteter observes (using terminology that Freud must have found supremely congenial), "marches ahead blindly, like an unconscious and fatal force."[65] What particularly interested Freud were the obscure workings of the mind; he noted Darmesteter's comment on "the admirable sleep-walking scene": That scene has been anticipated in the second act "in germ," in Macbeth's

60. *Leonardo da Vinci, GW* VIII, 128 / "Leonardo da Vinci and a Memory of His Childhood," *SE* XI, 63.
61. Darmesteter, "Shakespeare" (1881), in *Essais de littérature anglaise* (2nd ed., 1883), 17–19, 45. This essay was also included as an "Introduction" in the critical edition of *Macbeth* that Freud owned. In his paper of 1917, Jekels still used Darmesteter's essay on *Macbeth* (the first edition of 1881). See Jekels, "The Riddle of *Macbeth*," 112–13.
62. Thus Freud corrects two wrong dates, "1811" and "1812," to "1611" and "1612." See "Introduction," Shakespeare, *Macbeth*, "Edition classique," edited by James Darmesteter (2nd ed., 1887), lxiv.
63. Ibid., lxviii.
64. Ibid., xxxix.
65. Ibid., lvii.

. . . .

words, "Will all great Neptune's Ocean wash this blood / Clean from
my hand?" Those words, "dropped on Lady Macbeth at the moment
of her firmest hardness of heart, have insinuated themselves unperceived and worked in silence."[66] Freud noted, too, Darmesteter's
closing comment: "Macbeth is not the villain who calculates; nothing
in him of Iago. He is Hamlet in crime; hence the strange sympathy
that stays with him to the end."[67]

The text of *Macbeth* presents cruxes that Freud found only marginally less absorbing. He paid particular attention to the editor's
comparisons between Shakespeare's tragedy and its source, Holinshed's *Chronicles of Scotlande:* "Shakespeare," Darmesteter writes,
"omits, or pushes back into the shadows, those motives that are too
general or which would offer attenuating circumstances; he puts into
high relief the two particular traits he finds in the chronicle, though
one of them is barely hinted at: the actions of the witches, and the
action of Lady Macbeth."[68] There are other puzzles that Darmesteter
finds noteworthy—as does Freud: from which source or sources did
Shakespeare derive those parts of the play, "the most original ones,"
not to be found in Holinshed, such as the appearance of Banquo's
ghost and the sleepwalking scene?[69] Again, Darmesteter has a footnote on the Gaelic origins of Macbeth's name that Freud evidently
found of interest.[70] These are precisely the sorts of questions that
could kindle Freud's impatient compulsion to tackle enigmas.

Yet in the end it is the psychological secrets of *Macbeth* to which
Freud responded wholeheartedly. The one passage he underlined
in Darmesteter's introduction concerns Lady Macbeth's *"inexplicable contradictions."*[71] Inexplicable contradictions which Freud
could not leave alone, or—to come closer to the heart of his creative
mechanisms—which would not leave Freud alone.

Why not? What did Freud need to accomplish
with his obsessive problem solving? What are the sources of these
pressures that pursued him all his life, right into old age? I am

66. Ibid., lxxi.
67. Ibid., lxxix.
68. Ibid., lv.
69. Ibid., lx.
70. See ibid., lxvii n.
71. Ibid., lvi.

reluctant to make heavy weather of what I, following Freud, have called his tormented way of working. There was, after all, a sound dash of playfulness in his researches.

But these researches also attest to something else. Freud once observed that scientific inquisitiveness is a derivative of the child's sexual curiosity, the sublimation of the vital, anxiety-laden questions: where do I come from? what did my parents do to produce me? what is the difference between boys and girls, and what does it mean to me? As biographers of Freud have not failed to observe, these questions exercised a particular fascination for him because of his intricate family constellation: a mother half his father's age, two half brothers as old as his mother, a nephew older than he. Freud, we may note, gave a hint of this fascination in his autobiographical study: he recalled that he had been driven on, when he chose to study medicine, not by the desire to heal but by what he called *"eine Art von Wissbegierde"*—literally, "a sort of greed for knowledge." The translators of the Standard Edition of his writings chose the most pallid possible equivalent, "a sort of curiosity," which does little to convey the intensity of Freud's secret needs.[72]

In a sportive exercise of 1914, "The Moses of Michelangelo," Freud hinted at the shape these needs took in his maturity and exhibited once more the driven nature of his working habits. Since 1901, when Freud had glimpsed Michelangelo's larger-than-lifesize statue for the first time, it had dazzled and baffled him. On each of his return visits to Rome, he would make pilgrimages to the *Moses*, at times daily, studying it, measuring it, drawing it. By 1912 he told his wife that he thought he might write a few lines about it.[73] Silent and awesome, the statue virtually defied Freud to penetrate its unsettling enigmas. Late in life, as I have reported, Freud would confess that the Moses of the Old Testament haunted him like an unlaid ghost. Michelangelo's *Moses* had been tribulation enough.

What, Freud asked himself, does the statue represent? Had Michelangelo depicted Moses as an enduring representative of a religious founder? Or had he captured Moses in a moment of action? If so, action of what sort? Is Moses rising to smash the tablets he

72. See *Selbstdarstellung, GW* XIV, 34 / *Autobiographical Study, SE* XX, 8. It must be said that even the more ordinary word for "curiosity" or "inquisitiveness," namely, *Neugier,* includes the word for "greed," *Gier.*
73. See his letter to Martha Freud, September 25, 1912. *Briefe,* 308.

had brought from Mount Sinai, as the Book of Exodus so eloquently describes him doing? Or is he manfully controlling his rage at the spectacle of the children of Israel worshiping the golden calf? In 1914, after years of pondering and hesitating, reading and consulting other pieces of sculpture, Freud was at last ready to commit his answer to paper. As we would expect, he chose to side with a minority of Michelangelo scholars; as we would expect, too, he found his answer in the character and personal experience of the sculptor. The divine Michelangelo, that temperamental, wrathful Renaissance titan among artists, had portrayed in Moses his own desperate effort to control his rage in the face of powerful and capricious patrons. For Freud, Michelangelo's Moses was, precisely like Shakespeare's Hamlet, an aesthetic creation to be explained through the mind of its creator.[74]

Freud's paper on Michelangelo's *Moses,* then, is a small monument to his characteristic way of understanding art and literature alike— through biographical criticism. But, as I have noted, the paper also helps map the path to sublimation that his childhood sexual inquisitiveness had taken. Speaking anonymously, Freud described himself as a layman rather than a connoisseur, one who found himself "more strongly attracted by the subject matter of a work of art than by its formal and technical properties." Hence music was almost inaccessible to him, for, he confessed, he derived pleasure from a work of art only if, after contemplating it for a long time, he could "grasp it in my own way, that is, make comprehensible to me by just what means it makes an impression." And he attributed his inability to enjoy what he could not comprehend to a "rationalistic, or perhaps analytic, turn of mind."[75]

Freud did not mean to say that the knowledge he sought was purely intellectual; he wanted to respond perceptively to the artist's inten-

74. And more: Michelangelo's effort at disciplining his passions was comprehensible to Freud, and congenial, partly because Freud was in these years involved in combat with Adler and Jung, laboring to stay cool and keep the good of the psychoanalytic movement in the forefront of his mind.

75. "Der Moses des Michelangelo," *GW* X, 173 / "The Moses of Michelangelo," *SE* XIII, 211. While the authorship of the anonymous paper, published in *Imago,* was transparent—Karl Abraham rightly asked Freud in a letter of April 2, 1914, "Don't you think that one will recognize the lion's claw?" (Abraham papers, LC)—Freud did not lift the "secret" until 1924.

tions and emotional states. But he insisted that the road to this kind of understanding—at least his road—lay through a rational process. He could decipher artistic intentions and emotions only if he could "discover the meaning and the contents of what is represented in the work of art, that is to say, *interpret* it." Such an act of analytic comprehension, he added, should not diminish aesthetic pleasure; he offered in proof the clarity he had brought to the deciphering of *Hamlet* and of its astonishing, enduring power over its audiences. The source of that power could not be the splendid language of the tragedy alone; it must be something more, and it was psychoanalysis that had unriddled that added element.[76]

But useful as it was, Freud's greed for knowledge was by its nature insatiable. Success brought satisfaction, but only for a limited time. Then the urge to know was renewed, much as Gertrude's appetite for her first husband, the elder Hamlet, "had grown / By what it fed on." Only Freud had sublimated that appetite into psychoanalytic research. Thoroughly disguised and elevated as it was, the erotic element in Freud's greed for knowledge is unmistakable.

It was an early acquired but indelible element. Freud deeply desired but could never be certain of his mother's love. She cherished him, her first-born, and said so often and emphatically. At the same time, she presented her Golden Sigi with rivals for her attention again and again—five sisters and two brothers in the space of ten years. That one of these brothers, little Julius, died as an infant, far from lightening Freud's burden, only increased it, for that death generated in Freud vivid and persistent feelings of guilt for having wished his brother gone.

This was a burden that must have been particularly hard to bear as Freud was wrestling with and gradually overcoming his oedipal phase. In his *Interpretation of Dreams,* he recalled a disagreeable and revealing childhood episode: at the age of seven or eight, he had invaded his parents' bedroom and urinated in their presence. Freud's father, generally so indulgent, had been annoyed and predicted, in his anger, that "the boy will come to nothing." Evidently the incident made a deep impression on Freud since, as he remembered many years later, he frequently returned to it in his dreams

76. "Der Moses des Michelangelo," *GW* X, 172–74 / "The Moses of Michelangelo," *SE* XIII, 211–13.

and would couple it with enumerations of his many successes, as though to say to his father, "You see, I *have* amounted to something after all."[77]

I suggest that Freud needed to persuade his mother of the same thing, just as desperately if not more so. He had to convince her all his life that he was lovable, capable of amounting to something after all, in a sense potent. Seeking to guarantee, if possible to monopolize, his mother's attention, he had to perform great feats again and again. And for him, it was in the domain of knowledge alone that he could excel, not in art or poetry, business or war. Being a fine student at Gymnasium was one way. Solving the riddles of the world was another.

These riddles took many forms, grave and amusing, literary and historical and psychoanalytic, but they were always solidly anchored in the very ground of Freud's inner experience. Baffling himself over the theme of the three caskets, the nature of tragedy, the posture of a statue, the identity of Moses—and of Shakespeare—these were necessary exercises through which he could reiterate his claim to paternal and, even more, maternal love. To move from the indistinct figure of the man from Stratford to the presumed solidity of the earl of Oxford was part of a lifelong quest.

I said earlier that I did not want to make heavy weather of Freud's problem solving. But to judge from his own conduct, my psychoanalytic conclusion seems appropriate enough. On September 7, 1938, a few months after Freud had reached safety in England from nazified Austria, the Blantons came to visit him for the last time. Margaret Blanton went in alone and stayed for about ten minutes. She had a pleasant chat with Freud, but when she told him that she and Smiley planned to make a pilgrimage to Stratford-on-Avon, Freud asked her—"with sudden and uncharacteristic sharpness," she recalled—whether her husband really still believed "that those plays were written by that fellow at Stratford." For a moment, Margaret Blanton was sorely tempted to tell Freud of that tense day some eight years earlier when her husband had almost abandoned his analysis for fear that Freud was a faddist. But she chose not to. "I suddenly realized," she writes, "that if the professor had a sense of humor, I had never seen it manifest itself." She was wrong about Freud's sense of humor, as more intimate associates could have told

77. See *Interpretation of Dreams, SE* IV, 216.

her. But her intuition that the question of the real Shakespeare was not a trivial matter for Freud was sound enough. "I think," she recalled, "he would not have been amused."[78] She was right. To know the answers to profound secrets was as necessary as it was dangerous. And Freud wanted to know, or, rather, had to know, as Faust had had to know, and Hamlet—and Oedipus.

78. Blanton, *Diary of My Analysis with Freud,* 114n.

2

. . . .

Six Names in
Search of an
Interpretation

*He who knows a
word for a thing,
masters the thing.
This is the core
of the "magic of
names," which
plays such an
important part in
magic in general.
—Otto Fenichel,*
The Psychoan-
alytic Theory
of Neurosis

The six names which together add up to my text
are Mathilde, Jean Martin, Oliver, Ernst, Sophie,
and Anna. To speak of them as being in search of
an interpretation is more than lighthearted literary license. Names, as Freud insisted in *Totem and
Taboo,* carry a heavy unconscious freight of meaning. "For primitive peoples—as for savages today
and even for our children—names are by no
means something indifferent and conventional, as
they seem to us, but something significant and essential. A human being's name is a principal com-
ponent in his person, perhaps a piece of his soul."[1]
Here Freud, usually so brilliant in tracing remnants of childish and "savage" traits in civilized
adults, unexpectedly failed to make the connections that were his specialty. The act of naming
retained substantial residues of archaic and ar-
cane magical beliefs even in rationalist modern
cultures—even for Freud himself.

It is as though the giver of names acquires power

1. *Totem und Tabu: Einige Übereinstimmungen im Seelen-
leben der Wilden und der Neurotiker* (1913), *GW* IX, 136 /
*Totem and Taboo: Some Points of Agreement Between the
Mental Life of Savages and Neurotics, SE* XIII, 112.

over what he has named, or, at the least, by the act asserts his sovereignty over his domain. Certainly naming embodies a gratifying reversal of roles: it means doing to others what others had once done to oneself. Even when convention, piety, or legislation—in short, cultural pressures—constrict the range of the namer's choice and dictate, or at least strongly commend, preferences to him, there remain, within the available pool of propriety, alternatives for the work of selection. Both what that work must exclude and what it may include offer clues to culture and, more interesting still, to the character and mental history of the namer himself. That is why they invite interpretation.

Freud's history as a nomenclator particularly courts scrutiny because at critical moments he showed a far more than ordinary interest in names, including his own. His given first name was Sigismund, but in Gymnasium and during his first years at the university he experimented with Sigmund, and in the mid-1870s he definitively adopted the name under which he was to become famous.[2] There has been some conjecture that Freud shortened his name from Sigismund to Sigmund because the former, widespread among Jews, served as a favorite butt in anti-Semitic jokes. But since Freud never commented on his reasons, this must remain speculation.[3] Whatever the reason, the change was his idea, an assertion of symbolic control over the shape of his identity. And there is a family tradition, reported by Freud's sister Anna, that when his last sibling was born in 1866—Freud was then ten years old—it was his suggestion for a name, Alexander, that carried the day. Freud, his sister reports, had been taken with Alexander the Great's prowess as a general and his statesmanlike magnanimity.[4]

2. It is curious to follow his vacillations: in 1872, not long before graduating from Gymnasium, he signed one of his letters "Sigmund," but three years later, as a student at the University of Vienna, he inscribed "Sigismund Freud, stud. med. 1875" in his copy of Darwin's *Die Abstammung des Menschen.* (See *Freud,* 5n.)
3. For that speculation, see Ronald W. Clark, *Freud: The Man and the Cause* (1980), 36.
4. See *Jones* I, 18. Unfortunately, the source from which Jones draws his report of the incident, Anna Freud Bernays's reminiscences of Freud, who had died just the year before ("My Brother, Sigmund Freud," *American Mercury* LI [1940], 335–42), is not wholly untainted, being demonstrably inaccurate in some details. Considering how well and how long Ernest Jones knew Freud, I thought it safe to follow Jones's authority on this episode.

Whatever the significance of this episode—and I shall return to it
below—it, too, testifies that the bestowal of a name is an exercise
of power. Later, speaking of the act of naming as a paterfamilias
and a psychoanalyst, Freud observed that the "suppressed megalo-
mania of the father" is transferred in thought to the child.[5] Mathilde,
Jean Martin, Oliver, Ernst, Sophie, and Anna, then, may light up
some obscure corners in (as well as confirm some accepted conjectures about) Sigmund Freud.

What these names reveal, with considerable force, is the extent
of Freud's domestic sovereignty. He was at once the typical late
nineteenth-century middle-class family man and the cosseted genius;
a liberal, genial father whose children were as well behaved as if
he had been strict with them. Without raising his voice or brusquely
asserting himself, he found the family routine that fitted his tastes
and kept his daily occupations free of distractions. He detested the
sound of someone practicing the piano, and so the Freud children,
unlike the children of other respectable bourgeois in those years,
went without piano lessons. He detested the spartan accommoda-
tions of third-class travel, and so, even if the rest of the family during
lean years had to make do with wooden benches, his wife would
arrange for him to ride alone, grandly, in first-class comfort.[6]

True, important household decisions were indisputably in Martha
Freud's domain. When in her twenties Anna Freud wanted to exchange one of her rooms for another at Berggasse 19, where she
was living with her parents, and appealed to her father, Freud gently
but flatly placed the authority for such a move on her mother's
shoulders: "I cannot force her, I have always let her have her way
in the house."[7] Martin Freud, whose informal and intimate reminiscences convey the flavor of his family's daily life, categorically
asserts that "my mother ruled her household with great kindness
and an equally great firmness."[8] But when it came to naming their
six children, Freud was wholly in charge. It was *his* friends, *his*
teachers, *his* heroes, *his* ego ideals, who prevailed—each time.

He made this point explicitly in *The Interpretation of Dreams*.
Speaking of his children, he said: "I set store on their names being

5. See *Die Traumdeutung* (1900), *GW* II–III, 450 / *The Interpretation of Dreams*,
SE V, 448.

6. Martin Freud, *Sigmund Freud: Man and Father* (1958), 44.

7. See *Freud,* 428n.

8. Martin Freud, *Sigmund Freud,* 32.

determined, not according to the fashion of the day, but in memory of valued persons."[9] This is a striking declaration underscoring Freud's freedom from convention, but beyond that his domestic dominance. There was, after all, nothing in Jewish tradition that automatically entitled the father to impose his will in so consequential a domestic matter. In the biblical epoch, it was generally, though not always, the mother who conferred a name on a child.[10] And the fragmentary evidence we have from later centuries of Jewish life, and from Freud's own time, leaves the ultimate authority for choosing a name open.[11] It was for the most part a family decision, a matter for negotiation or of accident. Since it was a generally observed custom among the Ashkenazim, the Central European Jews who were Freud's tribe, to name the child after a deceased relative or to borrow the initial of such a relative, much obviously depended on just whose father or mother had recently died.

But in the Freud household the act was the father's monopoly. Certainly it was Sigmund, not Martha, who named their first child, born on October 16, 1887, Mathilde, and named her "as a matter of course" after Frau Dr. Breuer.[12] "Natürlich": she was the wife of the highly regarded Viennese internist Josef Breuer, in whose house the poverty-stricken young Freud had long been a frequent and welcome guest, and to whose emotional and financial magnanimity he owed more than he liked. The Freuds' second child, Jean Martin, was born two years later and given a half-French name most unusual for an Austrian child; this, too, documents one of Freud's extensive debts, this time an intellectual one. This first son was named after the great French neuropathologist and Parisian social lion Jean-Martin Charcot, with whom Freud had worked closely for some immensely profitable months in the winter of 1885. Significantly, Charcot, too, was a giver of names: in the affectionate and admiring obituary that Freud wrote of his master in 1893, he recalled the myth

9. *Traumdeutung, GW* II–III, 491 / *Interpretation of Dreams, SE* V, 487.
10. See J. (Joseph Jacobs), "Names (Personal)," *The Jewish Encyclopedia,* ed. Isidore Singer et al., 12 vols. (1901–1905), IX, 152.
11. While most Jewish authorities agree that it was the father who made the ultimate decision, "in practice, however," writes Jacob Z. Lauterbach, "these questions were first settled between the parents." *Studies in Jewish Law, Custom and Folklore,* selected by Bernard J. Bamberger (1970), 65.
12. See Freud to Emmeline and Minna Bernays, October 16, 1887. *Briefe,* 231 (223).

of Adam naming the animals as he reported how Charcot had dis-
criminated among and assigned names to mental ailments that his
predecessors had failed to recognize and distinguish.[13]

With his second son, Oliver, born fourteen months later, Freud
went further afield. The name records Freud's devotion to the figure
of Oliver Cromwell, "a great historical personage," Freud reports,
"who had powerfully attracted me in my boyhood years, especially
since my stay in England." Speaking of Oliver in his *Interpretation
of Dreams,* he substantiates, in passing, his domestic hegemony in
the sphere of naming and hints at the high drama he associated with
that performance: "Throughout the year of waiting" for Oliver's
birth, "I had resolved to use this very name if it should be a son,
and I greeted the new-born with it, highly *satisfied.*"[14] The ceremony
of greeting his son with Cromwell's name was anything but casual.
It meant a great deal to Freud.

His next boy, Ernst, in no way deviated from the pattern Freud
had established: he was named after Ernst Brücke, in whose physiological laboratory Freud had spent six happy, productive years,
and who had died just three months before the Freuds' fourth child
was born. And their last two children once more throw light on their
father's rather than their mother's life experience: Freud named
Sophie after a niece of Samuel Hammerschlag, who had been his
religion teacher and remained a supportive and selfless friend, and
Anna after one of Hammerschlag's daughters. Had their sixth child
been a boy rather than a girl, its name would, of course, have been
different, but Freud's right to name it would have remained unimpaired. "Had it been a son," Freud told his "Liebster Wilhelm" on
December 3, 1895, addressing Fliess as he had for years in the
familiar form, "I should have given you telegraphic news, for he
would have borne your—*deinen*—name."[15] The contribution of Martha Freud to this sixfold act of naming seems negligible. It was enough
for her to superintend a crowded household, protect her husband
from tedious intrusions, and bear six children in eight years.

If, in surrendering the right to a share in choosing
her children's names, Martha Freud yielded to her husband's over-

13. See "Charcot" (1893), *SE* III, 11–23, esp. 13.
14. *Traumdeutung, GW* II–III, 450 / *Interpretation of Dreams, SE* V, 448.
15. Freud to Fliess, December 3, 1895. *Freud-Fliess,* 159 (153).

riding authority, this was not her only concession to his strongly held convictions. Her orthodox upbringing could not withstand her husband's imperious atheism. Freud seems to have been, by and large, humorous and gentle in his domestic relations, just as he enforced discipline on his children with a light hand. But he refused to compromise his irreligious principles even in the face of his young wife's visible distress. Born into a strictly observant family, Martha Bernays had at first interposed some mild objections to her fiancé's freethinking ways and to his articulate detestation of all religious ritual. But she was won over to his bellicose unbelief—or, rather, chose to make no difficulties about it—and, once again, the names of their children attest to his complete ascendancy.

As I have observed, Central European Jews habitually remembered, with their children's names, grandparents or other cherished deceased relatives. All sorts of superstitious beliefs, woven around attempts to ward off demons intent on harming the newborn, accompanied this practice. Even when, in the enlightened nineteenth century, such magical precautions were despised or forgotten, the custom survived. Yet it was not invariable. Josef Breuer, largely emancipated from time-honored Jewish rituals and customs, named his firstborn, Leopold, after his father—who was very much alive— and his second child, Bertha, after his mother, who had died during his infancy.[16] For centuries other Jews had paid tribute to the culture in which they lived by naming children after local places or local worthies. In Freud's age, there were Austrian Jews who advertised their loyalty to the House of Habsburg by calling their boys Franz Josef.

But Freud was little more of a patriot than he was a traditionalist. In my writings on Freud, I have made much of his determined and articulate unbelief. I could scarcely have done anything else: his irreligiosity was fundamental to his scientific stance, essential to his psychoanalytic theory.[17] He was a good Jew in the sense that he

16. G. H. Pollock, "The Possible Significance of Childhood Object Loss in the Josef Breuer–Bertha Pappenheim (Anna O.)–Sigmund Freud Relationship. I. Josef Breuer," *J. Amer. Psychoanal. Assn.* XVI (1968), 718–19. "Custom," in short, does not mean "law." Thus the prominent German-Jewish family the Ephraim, court jewelers and businessmen in Berlin, would give the father's name to each son as a middle name—in the father's lifetime.

17. See, for a detailed discussion, Peter Gay, *A Godless Jew: Freud, Atheism, and the Making of Psychoanalysis* (1987).

never denied his "racial" ancestry, took pride in the achievement of Jews across the centuries, and regarded the quality of his Jewishness as a mysterious bond with fellow Jews, a bond still resistant to psychoanalytic explanation. Indeed, the names of Mathilde, Sophie, and Anna—his girls—support the view that Jewishness indeed meant something to him; these names speak of the domestic side of his temperament and of his preference for social companionship, which was largely Jewish. So, in its own way, does "Oliver," for among Cromwell's merits, in Freud's eyes, was that he had permitted Jews to settle in England after centuries of exclusion.

But the names of his Martin and his Ernst demonstrate that Freud's Jewish identity subsisted in a larger mental world: that of the European scientific, most specifically the materialist, positivist mind. With his relentless introspection and symmetrical dualistic theory of the drives, Freud has often been misdescribed as a child of romanticism. But Ernst Brücke, whom Freud fondly remembered as "old Brücke," belonged to what has been called, in historians' shorthand, the "school of Helmholtz," a small but extraordinarily influential group of natural and medical scientists who derided the hazy, quasi-mystical "scientific" speculations of German romantic philosophers, insisting rather on the supremacy of matter and of observation and experimentation in the making of scientific discoveries.[18]

The world of these medical scientists, clustered in the University of Vienna, became Freud's world. It was a world for which he was, as an adolescent atheist, thoroughly prepared and into which he plunged with a will. Unlike many other talented young Viennese Jews of his time, Freud did not mingle much in the lively society of the salons. He did not go to poetry recitals or to concerts. His Vienna was medical Vienna. And that Vienna was, in Freud's student days, dominated by professorial physicians imported from Germany. Carl Claus, who headed the Institute of Comparative Anatomy and who supported the young Freud's first independent researches on the gonads in eels, had come to Vienna from Göttingen. Hermann Nothnagel, in whose Division of Internal Medicine Freud worked from October 1882 to April 1883, had been, like Brücke, born in northern

18. *Freud*, 34–35; Siegfried Bernfeld, "Freud's Scientific Beginnings," *American Imago* VI (1949), 165.

Germany and trained in Berlin. And, precisely like Brücke, in his lectures to students and to a wider public, Nothnagel championed the antiromantic view of nature and of the human body that he had brought to Vienna from "the north." With other luminaries, including the celebrated surgeon and talented amateur musician Theodor Billroth, this group, with Brücke the most impressive of them all, helped make medical Vienna a German city. It was in that city, and that city alone, that Freud developed and felt most at home.

He could feel at home, despite frigid blasts of anti-Semitism, largely because these German scientists, Nothnagel in the vanguard, made it possible for Jews like Freud to see themselves as other than pariahs. For Brücke was, for all his severity in the laboratory, a political liberal, an anticlerical (which in Austria meant, of course, anti-Catholic) known to have Jewish friends. And Nothnagel, who kept in touch with Freud after he had completed his studies at the university, sending him patients and sponsoring his academic advancement, was even more actively hostile to the anti-Semitic camp that was making such worrisome inroads on Vienna from the 1870s on. In 1891, when Freud, the fledgling nerve specialist, was beginning to experiment with radically innovative approaches to mental distress, Nothnagel became one of the founders of the Society for Combating Anti-Semitism and gave outspoken lectures in its behalf.

Then, in the summer of 1894, Nothnagel faced down anti-Semitic students demonstrating in his university and obstructing the conduct of classes. In view of what was to happen in Austria and Germany toward the end of Freud's long lifetime, it is worth resurrecting an item from the *Lancet* of July 7, 1894: "We learn with feelings of pain and indignation, that . . . the medical students of Vienna University have made a hostile demonstration against Professor Nothnagel, who happens to have protected the race which has furnished Germany with some of its most distinguished scientific men. The deplorable anti-Semitic agitation would seem to have penetrated that seat of learning; and because Professor Nothnagel has taken an active part in shielding Jewish students of medicine from the persecution to which they are subjected, he himself is attacked and prevented from carrying on his clinical work. We trust that the leaders in this outrage will be promptly dealt with by the authorities, for it reflects shame and discredit upon the university when one whose reputation is world-wide should be subjected to such insults."[19] Freud's reaction to the incident is not on record; his letters to Fliess of the early summer of 1894 are taken up with his heart problems, his suffering under the abstinence from cigars that his authoritative friend had imposed—and his shamefaced confessions of lapses from that abstinence.[20]

Freud never called a son "Hermann" after Nothnagel, but it is obvious from the name of his second son how much the Brücke-Nothnagel ambience meant to him. "Ernst" provides eloquent testimony also to the solidity of Freud's positivism, a philosophy of science he had learned in large measure from Germans—which meant, in those days, from all of Western Europe, since these Germans were, at least as scientists, good Europeans. "Martin" offers further supporting evidence of this positivism, for Jean-Martin Charcot, unexcelled clinician, unsurpassed observer, enacted in his famous public demonstration lectures at the Salpêtrière the rules of scientific conduct that the positivist mind demands. He was the servant of what he saw, or, better, he allowed what he saw to lead him to what he could not see. Their reputation to the contrary, nineteenth-century positivists were by no means invariably shallow empiricists; it was only that they refused to load nature with entities or meanings that metaphysicians alone could detect—or invent. Once challenged by the independent-minded Freud for contradicting a theory established among contemporary scientists, Charcot replied with an aphorism that Freud never tired of recalling, and thus preserved for posterity: theory is all very well, but it does not prevent phenomena from existing—"La théorie, c'est bon, mais ça n'empêche pas d'exister."[21] By the 1890s, when Freud was on the track of phenomena that were strange, indeed incredible, this open-minded and adventurous scientific attitude would stand him in good stead. The names of two of Freud's sons, then, remind us that, however loyal Freud proclaimed himself to be to the essence of Judaism, however helpful he thought being a marginal Jew in a Catholic society had been in freeing him from accepted prejudices, the intel-

19. Quoted in Max Neuburger, *Hermann Nothnagel. Leben und Wirken eines deutschen Klinikers* (1922), 443–44.
20. See esp. Freud to Fliess, June 22, July 14, July 27, 1894. *Freud-Fliess*, 76–83 (83–88).
21. "Charcot," *SE* III, 13, 13n.

lectual instrument that led him to his psychoanalytic theories was not Jewish or Austrian. "Martin" and "Ernst" show Freud in the antimetaphysical, determinist tradition and celebrate it.

Freud's own name bears witness how tenacious a rival tradition, the Jewish tradition, could be. His father, Jacob, though increasingly liberating himself from his family heritage, yet gave Freud a Jewish middle name, Schlomo, choosing this name to commemorate his own father, who had died less than three months before his son Sigismund Schlomo was born.[22] It was a name that Freud would, significantly, never use. Indeed, when it came time for Freud to name his own children, he deliberately set even this faded remnant of tradition aside: it was a sign of his total assimilation that he gave none of his boys and girls a Jewish name. Rather, as we have come to see, their names represent a radical departure from, even defiance of, Jewish usage: three of his children celebrated gentiles, three Jews, none celebrated a member of his family. Or didn't they?

If the names of Freud's six children generate rich associations to his social habits, religious stance, and scientific commitments, they also supply important evidence for his unconscious life. I submit that ultimately all his children's names lead back to one figure, and to Freud's long-standing struggle with it: his father, Jacob. Freud became emotionally enmeshed with names as a son as well as a father. Jacob Freud would proudly show off his obedient son: "My Sigmund's little toe is cleverer than my head, but he would never dare to contradict me."[23] And it was true: if Freud did contradict his father or found him wanting, he did so in the privacy of his mind, waiting until Jacob Freud's death before recording his deep disappointment in him. But this disappointment had been at work in Sigmund Freud long before. After all, as we know, Jacob Freud had, as he once calmly confessed to his dismayed son, picked up from the gutter the cap that an anti-Semitic bully had knocked off his head.[24] The episode seems to have preoccupied Freud for years, and found it haunting his dreams.[25]

22. *Jones* I, 2.
23. Fritz Wittels, *Sigmund Freud: His Personality, His Teaching and His School* (1924; tr. Eden and Cedar Paul, 1924), 60.
24. See above, 39.
25. *Interpretation of Dreams, SE* IV, 197.

Similar powerful feelings of ambivalence troubled his relations to other potent father figures in his life. Whatever Josef Breuer was later to become for him, in 1887, when Mathilde Freud was born, he was a fatherly friend. Fourteen years Freud's senior, settled, experienced, successful, presiding over a flourishing household, Breuer unstintingly gave the young Freud companionship, encouragement, and money. He "lent" Freud considerable sums, provided him with patients, and supported his ambitions with the delicacy of an affectionate parent. And for years Freud, at home in Breuer's house, spending evenings there, taking baths after a hot day, talking for hours about patients—especially Anna O.—responded warmly.

Freud responded perhaps even more enthusiastically to "old Brücke." He always remained for Freud "my teacher," with the full weight of that paternal title; Brücke, Freud insisted, was the "greatest authority" he had encountered in all his life.[26] If Breuer spoiled Freud like a favorite child, Brücke kept him in line like an obedient son so that, with him, Freud's sterner, more disciplined identifications with admirable models emerged. Brücke's dramatic, if disguised, appearance in Freud's famous "non vixit" dream, which Freud analyzed at length in *The Interpretation of Dreams*, points unmistakably to Brücke's dominant role in Freud's development. A leading character in that dream was Freud's friend, competitor, and colleague Josef Paneth, who had died young, in 1890, and whom Freud identifies in his interpretation with the laconic initial "P." Freud, so he dreamed, gave P. a "piercing" look under which he turned pale and indistinct and melted away. The interpretation shows that the dream figure Freud had been a stand-in for Brücke, and P. a stand-in for Freud himself. It had come to Brücke's attention that Freud, then a demonstrator in his Physiological Institute, was sometimes late. One morning, accordingly, Brücke showed up promptly at the opening time of the laboratory and waited for Freud. "What he said to me," Freud recalled, "was terse and pointed. But it was not the words that mattered. The overwhelming thing was the terrible blue eyes with which he looked at me and before which

26. For Brücke as Freud's "greatest authority," see "Nachwort" to *Die Frage der Laienanalyse* (1927), *GW* XIV, 290 / "Postscript" to *The Question of Lay Analysis, SE* XX, 253.

I faded." Everyone, Freud concludes, "who can remember the great master's eyes, stunningly beautiful until his old age, and who ever saw him in anger, will easily empathize with the feelings of the youthful sinner."[27]

These are the anxious feelings of a loving and remorseful son— loving, remorseful, but in the end striking for independence. For the materialist Brücke, mental operations were principally rooted in physiological states and somatic insults. Freud, though of course always conspicuously loyal to Brücke's commitment to positivistic science, would in the 1890s develop psychoanalytic propositions which hold that psychological events often evolve from psychological causes—and more, that even physiological symptoms may be rooted in mental conflicts, as in hysterical conversion symptoms. But the luster of Freud's affection and admiration for this unmatched instructor, inventive deviser of medical instruments, adventurous student of chemistry, professional aesthetician, and indefatigable propagandist for the natural sciences shines undimmed through Freud's reminiscences for years after.[28]

Charcot, too, was a father to Freud. In that exhilarating fall and winter in Paris, when Freud had the privilege of coming to know Charcot well—Charcot must have sensed that his Viennese visitor was a man of no common gifts—Freud's fantasies moved beyond admiration for a distant authority to affection for a figure infinitely

27. *Traumdeutung, GW* II–III, 425 / *Interpretation of Dreams, SE* V, 421–22.
28. In my biography, I have made my case in somewhat different language. Noting that Freud's feelings for Brücke were "filial, nothing less," I also noted that "much of Brücke's irresistible appeal to Freud was precisely that he was *not* Freud's father. His authority over Freud was earned rather than bestowed by the accident of birth; and at this critical juncture [during his years at medical school], when Freud was training himself to become a professional investigator into human mysteries, such authority was necessary to him. Jacob Freud was genial and good-humored, soft, yielding; he virtually invited rebellion. Brücke, in contrast, was reserved, precise to the point of pedantry, an intimidating examiner and exacting chief. Jacob Freud liked to read and had a measure of Hebrew erudition; Brücke was nothing if not versatile" (*Freud,* 33). Yet the highly visible differences between Jacob Freud and Ernst Brücke did not keep Brücke from functioning emotionally as Freud's father. It was as though Freud used his second father to gain some distance from the first. This was a pattern he would repeat in later relationships.

worth imitating, yet impossible, it then seemed, to equal. Charcot's lectures, Freud told his fiancée, gripped him like a religious experience: "I walk away as from Notre Dame, with a new perception of perfection." This was not the way Freud usually sounded about anyone. Then, in a telling metaphor of generation, Freud wondered to Martha Bernays: "Whether the seed will one day bring forth fruit, I do not know." Before attending a formal party at Charcot's house and fortifying himself with a bit of cocaine for the ordeal of speaking French all evening, Freud encouraged his fiancée to spread the word in Hamburg and Vienna, "even with exaggerations, such as that he kissed me on the forehead (à la Liszt and so on)"—recalling a striking vignette about a great father, Liszt, doing homage to a greater son, Chopin. In a complicated image that it would take a Freud to unravel, he teased Martha Bernays from Paris: he might well fall in love with Mademoiselle Charcot, who was about twenty, natural and friendly, and looked exactly like her father. "Nothing is more dangerous than when a young girl bears the features of a man one admires."[29] These complexities of Freud's unconscious wishes rival those of Dora.

Samuel Hammerschlag's paternal attitude confirms my diagnosis of Freud the son wrestling with his fathers. Freud himself acknowledged that their relationship, their "secret sympathy," was as intimate as could be: "He always regards me as his son."[30] The obituary he wrote for his paternal teacher must be read in conjunction with an informal essay that Freud contributed some ten years later to a celebratory volume on the fiftieth anniversary of the Gymnasium where he had first met Hammerschlag. For all students, Freud wrote, the personality of the teacher is more important than the subject he professes; indeed, "for many, the road to the sciences led through the persons of the teachers alone." These men became, in short, "our substitute fathers."[31] Freud seems to have had some fleeting moments of impatience with his religion teacher, but in public Freud remained as good a son to Samuel Hammerschlag as he had been

29. Freud to Martha Bernays, November 24, 1885; January 18 and 20, 1886. *Briefe*, 189, 199, 202–03 (185, 193, 196–97).
30. Undated remark, *Jones* I, 163.
31. "Zur Psychologie des Gymnasiasten" (1914), *GW* X, 205–07 / "Some Reflections on Schoolboy Psychology," *SE* XIII, 241–44. See also "Obituary of Professor S. Hammerschlag" (1904), *SE* IX, 255–56.

to Jacob Freud.[32] While Freud notes the ambivalent attitudes pupils transfer to their teachers from their mixed feelings about their fathers, with Hammerschlag the negative side of his feelings emerged only rarely.

This side did emerge, subtly, with his idealization of Cromwell. For Freud's choice of "Oliver" for his second son hints once again at his protracted efforts to resolve his conflicting emotions about his biological father. Biographers have freely—often too freely—commented on Freud's identifications with giants of the past: Hannibal, Leonardo da Vinci, Michelangelo, Goethe. Certainly, as I have already observed, Freud ranked Oliver Cromwell among these admirable world historical personages, in part because of his hospitable attitude toward the Jews. Cromwell's decision to readmit Jews to England was logical enough for him; it followed from the Puritans' preoccupation with the Old Testament and the Chosen People. But in view of the age-old, at times bloodthirsty anti-Jewish sentiment disfiguring the history of Christian nations in Europe, Cromwell's was a daring act, if somewhat attenuated in practice.[33] Yet, even if compromised, such conduct was in striking contrast to Jacob Freud's humble, anything but heroic behavior. Writing to his fiancée in the summer of 1882, in one of his rare explicit references to Cromwell, Freud dilates on his own "aching for independence," a besetting wish that conjures up England in his imagination, "with

32. For hints at irritation, see Freud to Martha Bernays, November 24–26, 1885: "Hammerschlag is extraordinarily sensitive; Breuer's father once called him an egg without a shell." (Sigmund Freud Copyrights, Wivenhoe.)

33. "In November, 1655, Manasseh Ben Israel, a learned Portuguese Jew, settled in Amsterdam as a physician, petitioned the Protector to allow the Jews to reside and trade in England, and to grant them the free exercise of their religion. Cromwell, who was personally in favour of this petition, called together a committee of divines, merchants, and lawyers to confer with the Council on the question. The Protector himself took part in the conferences. 'I never heard a man speak so well,' said one of his hearers, but the divines feared for their religion and the merchants for their trade, so the legal toleration the Jews asked for was not granted. Cromwell, however, granted them leave to meet in private houses for devotion, and showed them such encouragement and favour that their resettlement in England really dates from the Protectorate." Charles Firth, *Oliver Cromwell and the Rule of the Puritans in England* (1900; World's Classics ed., 1953), 355–56.

its sober industriousness, its generous devotion to the public weal, the stubbornness and sensitive feeling for justice of its inhabitants." All this, graphically reviving the "ineffaceable impressions" of his visit to England seven years earlier, which had "had a decisive influence" on his life, now moved him to take up once again "the history of the island, the works of the men who were my real teachers—all of them English or Scotch." He told Martha Bernays that the "most interesting historical period" of the English past for him was "the reign of the Puritans and Oliver Cromwell with its lofty monument of that time—*Paradise Lost*."[34] And Milton's masterpiece, we know, remained a great favorite with him.[35]

To be sure, Cromwell did not embody all, or even most, of the lessons England had to impart to Freud. Certainly it was Darwin and his fellow nineteenth-century investigators, and their impressive predecessors, the philosophers of the Scottish Enlightenment and Isaac Newton, who furnished him with his intellectual ancestry. But Cromwell's sobriety, courage, and devotion to public duty, all worthy qualities, could only remind Freud of the rather pitiful figure his father had cut on more than one occasion. Moreover, Cromwell, I must note, had been a symbolic parricide, a most reluctant parricide but one who, once persuaded that the good cause demanded the execution of Charles I, pressed for it with unbending consistency. And, of course, that "lofty monument" of Cromwell's time, *Paradise Lost,* was the story of a great rebellion, the very prototype of all rebellions: the revolt of children, both angels and humans, against their father. After disobeying, Adam and Eve had been expelled from the dreamy paradise of unlimited infantile gratification and thrust into the real world; their unfilial act of self-assertion compelled them to grow into and act as full human beings. Was it an accident that as he interpreted his "non vixit" dream, Freud found that he had been playing the part of Brutus? After all, like Cromwell, though even more notorious, Brutus had been a symbolic parricide. "Strangely enough," Freud remembered, "I really did once play Brutus," at fourteen, and, it seems, with conviction.[36] "Strangely

34. Freud to Martha Bernays, August 16, 1882. Quoted in *Jones* I, 179.
35. See below, 97.
36. See *Traumdeutung, GW* II–III, 427 / *Interpretation of Dreams, SE* V, 424.

enough," Freud tells us. But was it so strange, any more than it was an accident that he should have dreamed about it? There are, as we know, no uncaused accidents in the mental universe that Freud uncovered and, therefore, no such accidents in his own. Overdetermined as Freud's choice of "Oliver" may have been, it is charged with covert criticism of his beloved, his ineffectual father, concealing repressed aggression against him.[37]

Freud's conflicting feelings about his father preoccupied him most strongly during the years when he was fashioning his hard-won insights into the systematic theory of mind he would call psychoanalysis. He was, almost self-consciously, a Joseph, brooding much on his father; his life was filled with friends named Joseph, and in *The Interpretation of Dreams* he commented that he identified himself with the Joseph of the Old Testament.[38] Like that Joseph, Freud was a child of his father's last wife and a great favorite; he had proud visions and suffered for them; most important, he gained first notoriety and then fame for acting as an interpreter of dreams. And his father's name was Jacob.

Much was at stake in names, then, and Freud came to know it. After all, one of the names he had purloined for his science was that of Oedipus, the unriddler of fatal riddles and killer of his father. Freud recognized that winning the oedipal struggle might be as costly as losing it, and he was self-aware enough to apply this recognition to himself. Reminiscing late in life about his visit to Athens, in 1904, he recalled that, standing on the Acropolis, he had been haunted by a mysterious feeling of unreality about the whole experience. Analyzing it, Freud discovered in himself a largely unconscious feeling of guilt deriving from his uncomfortable awareness that he had surpassed his father. An access of what he called *Pietät,* filial piety, interfered with his pleasure in seeing that supreme monument to

37. At this point I should emphatically insist that what Freud called overdetermination must be treated with the seriousness it deserves and does not always get. Freud may never have said, "Sometimes a cigar is just a cigar." (I certainly have never found the aphorism in any of his writings or recorded conversations.) But "overdetermination" constitutes a sound caution against overprivileging single motivations among a complex network of causal agents.
38. See esp. *Interpretation of Dreams, SE* V, 484n.

the glory that was Greece.[39] Doubtless, the oedipal struggle was risky no matter how it came out.

Freud's biographers have been right to fasten on the late 1890s as the years of decision for the maker of psychoanalysis. But the preceding decade had its own importance for Freud's life. Those were the years in which he established a tranquil and eventually a substantial household complete with six children, a bourgeois accomplishment that Freud, for all his exalted fantasies, by no means despised. In that decade, he also set up his private medical practice, published his first book, on aphasia, as well as interesting papers on a wide range of subjects, and was collaborating with the eminent Josef Breuer on another book which, he had high hopes, would prove of seminal importance. He was introducing radical innovations in his therapeutic techniques and growing aware that epoch-making discoveries were slowly moving to the forefront of his mind. By 1895, he had begun a kind of self-analysis, though he did not yet call it that. And in July 1895, while his wife was pregnant with their last child, Freud dreamed the complex and revealing dream about Irma's injection, the first he fully analyzed; it was to become famous, a paradigm for dream interpretation.

Meanwhile, some of his masters, his favorite surrogate fathers, were dying—Brücke in 1892, Charcot in 1893. Around the same time Breuer was dying to him in another way, becoming increasingly unavailable as a source of emotional support and scientific companionship. Freud found these deaths—two physical, one spiritual—hard to absorb. He mourned the first by naming a son after Ernst Brücke and the second, as he had already bestowed Charcot's name on a son, with a lucid and loving obituary. The cooling of his long-standing friendship with Josef Breuer is another matter and throws a glaring, far from pleasant light on Freud's belated, but for that all the more intense, efforts to gain his independence from paternal figures. In 1887, it is important to remember, the year that Freud named his first child Mathilde after Breuer's wife, Freud was an impecunious young physician with a small practice. In the early

39. See "Brief an Romain Rolland (Eine Erinnerungsstörung auf der Akropolis)" (1936), *GW* XVI, 250–57, esp. 256–57 / "A Disturbance of Memory on the Acropolis. An Open Letter to Romain Rolland on the Occasion of His Seventieth Birthday," *SE* XXII, 239–48, esp. 247–48.

1890s, when the two men were working together on what was to become, in 1893, their joint paper, "Preliminary Communication," and, two years later, their book *Studies on Hysteria,* the two scientists of the mind were increasingly estranged, largely over Freud's confident, scandalous hypothesis that the etiology of all hysterias must be sexual in nature. While Breuer, with his intelligent and amorous patient Anna O., had unwittingly laid the groundwork for psychoanalysis, it was Freud who drew the consequences from Breuer's case—Freud rushed in where Breuer feared to tread. And now, in the mid-1890s, as their views were being presented to the Viennese medical community, Breuer refused to follow where Freud was leading. This was enough reason for intimacy to cool. But beyond that, as Ernest Jones has rightly conjectured, Freud's irritable, often quite unjust faultfinding with his hitherto exemplary friend Breuer must have sprung from deeper, almost wholly unconscious sources.

These were the years when Freud was trying to come to terms with his ambivalence about his father. That ambivalence was, as I have shown, of long standing, and it had led him when he was only ten into another act of naming—that of his youngest brother, Alexander. This choice of name marries circumspection to self-assertion. Alexander was a commander superior to his father, Philip, and the historical conquistador Alexander the Great was a figure with whom the growing Freud might readily identify. But then, Philip of Macedonia had been a potent and aggressive monarch in his own right. Thus Freud could in fantasy best his father without humiliating him, gratifying two wishes at once or, perhaps, diplomatically disguising a most ambitious wish behind the recognition of his father's eminence.

But in the mid-1890s Freud needed sterner stuff. "It is plain," Jones remarks, "that Freud now resented the burden of the old debt of gratitude he owed Breuer, one that could in part be estimated in the concrete terms of money," and money—need I add?—stands for many profound matters in our minds. Early in 1898, it seems, after years of mounting irritation, Freud "made the attempt to repay an installment" on his debt to Breuer. But Breuer, "probably loath to accept what he must have long regarded as a gift, wanted to set off against it an amount he considered Freud should be paid for medical attention on a relative of his. Freud seems to have interpreted this as an endeavor to retain the old tutelage, and bitterly resented

Breuer's response."[40] There is surely no filial bondage harder to undo, and none more harshly felt, than that imposed by a generous father. No doubt, from the mid-1890s on, writing to his confidant Wilhelm Fliess, Freud was being unjust to Breuer. As Tacitus said long ago, we never forgive the people we have injured.

But, as always with Freud—as with other humans—his feelings about Breuer were far from clear-cut. It is true, in the mid-1890s, at the edge of greatness, Freud was alone, just as he later remembered it. His intense emotional dependence on Fliess was as much a symptom of his isolation as its cure. Indeed, Freud was finding his subterranean struggle with his father a crucial and wrenching experience. How much that father was on his mind, and continued to be, even (perhaps especially) in the decade in which he was working out the principles of psychoanalysis, emerges from some of the dreams he was willing to publish in *The Interpretation of Dreams.* In two important papers, George Mahl has shown that these dreams disclose conflicting affects over and over: admiration and rebelliousness, compassion, guilt, and murderous rage, wishes to console his father and to kill him.[41] None of Freud's words are more familiar, and more moving, than his declaration that *The Interpretation of Dreams* was part of his self-analysis, "my reaction to my father's death, that is, the most significant event, the most decisive loss, of a man's life."[42] But it was not his death that first gave Jacob Freud a share in the history of psychoanalysis. He acquired that earlier, in the years when Freud was becoming his own man. As I have pointed out, the naming of one's children is a reversal of roles. Freud's six children document with their names that Freud played his role as paterfamilias, as he himself said, with satisfaction. And some students of his life have suggested that as he was making his way in the world, he was dissolving his identification with his biological father to adopt, in turn, spiritual and scientific fathers. On this plausible view, he was continuing his dependency, only shifting his rulers.

But there is a less dismaying way of reading his children's names. As his sense of self increased, he was no longer simply a son but a

40. *Jones* I, 252–56. For a detailed analysis of this troubled relationship, with some new materials, see *Freud,* 67–69, 140.

41. See Bibliographical Essay, p. 184.

42. "Vorwort zur zweiten Auflage," *Traumdeutung* (1908), *GW* II–III, x / "Preface to the Second Edition," *Interpretation of Dreams, SE* IV, xxvi.

son-as-father. It would be just, I think, to see Freud's succession of emotional allegiances—to Brücke or Breuer or others—as a progression, an increasingly self-confident loosening of old ties and forging of new ones. The enrichment that internalization "as a completed process" may provide implies, as Hans Loewald has put it, "an emancipation from the object."[43] Looking back from the distance of maturity, in 1914, Freud could articulate what that progression meant. "Everything hopeful, but also everything objectionable, that characterizes the new generation, is determined by this detachment from the father."[44] It was a detachment from identifications and object choices imposed on him by his fate of being born Jacob Freud's son, and a substitution of identifications and objects freely chosen: of loved friends, admired teachers, estimable colleagues, ideal figures from the past. From this perspective, the names Freud gave his six children record his heroic and historic bid for inner freedom, a freedom that was the essential condition for his discoveries.

43. Hans W. Loewald, "On Internalization" (1973), in *Papers on Psychoanalysis* (1980), 83.
44. "Psychologie des Gymnasiasten," *GW* X, 207 / "Reflections on Schoolboy Psychology," *SE* XIII, 244.

3

. . . .

Freud and
Freedom

*We all still show
too little respect
for nature which
is (in Leonardo's
obscure words
that recall Ham-
let's speech) "full
of countless
causes which
never enter
experience."*
—*Freud,*
Leonardo
da Vinci and
a Memory of
His Childhood

*Indeed, analysis
does not set out
to prevent morbid
reactions, but
should give the
patient's ego* free-
dom *to decide
one way or another.*
—*Freud,* The Ego
and the Id

Freud was a determinist, yet his psychology is a
psychology of freedom. This sounds like an authentic paradox, but, as a number of modern philosophers going all the way back to Hobbes have
argued, the paradox is merely apparent.[1] In A. J.
Ayer's words, "from the fact that my action is
causally determined" it "does not follow that I am
not free."[2] To be sure, it may turn out that Freud's
coupling of determinism with freedom proves
hopelessly incoherent or contradictory. After all,
it is notorious that he repeatedly expressed contempt for most philosophy and most philosophers.
He thought formal philosophy to be largely nonsensical or self-evident. But philosophically sophisticated or naive, Freud's ideas on these issues
can be examined with profit, not merely as an
exercise in the history of ideas but also as an exploration of his fundamental ways of thinking.

1. As Donald Davidson has put it emphatically: "Hobbes,
Locke, Hume, Moore, Schlick, Ayer, Stevenson, and a host
of others have done what can be done, or ought ever to
have been needed, to remove the confusions that can make
determinism seem to frustrate freedom." "Freedom to
Act," in *Essays on Actions and Events* (1980), 63.
2. Ayer, "Freedom and Necessity," in *Philosophical Essays*
(1954), 278.

It should be plain from the outset that on clinical and theoretical grounds, Freud needed both determinism and freedom. Determinism spelled the very essence of science to him, and psychoanalysis was, by his accounts, a science. That is why he insisted, in an important paper of 1932, "The Question of a Weltanschauung," that psychoanalysis needs no world view of its own.[3] But psychoanalytic therapy, though proceeding on the fundamental assumption that there are no uncaused accidents in mental life, aims at the removal of obstructions to free action and at the establishment of mental balances in which freedom is more than a cheap slogan.

That capacious and suitably vague philosophical term *determinism* has long been used in several distinct senses and remains controversial; after centuries of heated objections by Roman Catholic theologians, in recent decades it has been French existentialists and Anglo-American philosophers of action who have sought to vindicate free will and questioned the whole doctrine of determinism, however defined. It cannot be my purpose to rehearse, let alone my ambition to solve, the debate here. Surely Isaiah Berlin has been right to remind us that "the problem of free will," which is only the problem of determinism in another guise, "is at least as old as the Stoics," has "tormented ordinary men as well as professional philosophers," and remains far from "a definite solution."[4] But Freud thought and wrote as though these controversies were largely irrelevant, typical philosophers' games. He followed his deterministic course of thinking without uneasiness, with no sense of its obscurities or of its highly problematic nature. He understood it to mean, quite straightforwardly, that just as there is no event in the physical universe without its cause (or, better, its causes), so there is no mental event or mental state without *its* causes. And Freud treated this conviction, first imbibed at the medical school of the University of Vienna, as more than a necessary ground for his psychology; it served him as an immensely instructive clue to the mysteries of mind. It was for him an instrument of discovery.

Freud demonstrated the heuristic value of psychic determinism through all his work, but nowhere more accessibly than in *The Psychopathology of Everyday Life* of 1901, the popular book on which he worked concurrently with his masterpiece, *The Interpretation of*

3. See *SE* XXII, 158–82.
4. Berlin, "Introduction," *Four Essays on Liberty* (1969), xi.

Dreams. The *Psychopathology* is among Freud's most deftly persuasive, widely translated, frequently reprinted books, even though—or, rather, just because—its theoretical yield is modest. I cannot overstate its strategic value for the acceptance of Freud's strange and shocking theories; in this sprawling, overstocked treasure house of mental mistakes and odd compulsions, he leaped from ordinary incidents—from slips of the tongue, the misreading of texts, the forgetting of names—to a comprehensive theory of the mind. Here were mental aberrations that readers could recognize and, finding them unthreatening, often downright comical, freely acknowledge.

It was with a shrewd appreciation of the explanatory range and compelling force of such aberrations that Freud more than a decade later opened his only marginally less successful *Introductory Lectures on Psychoanalysis* with an expansive section on *Fehlleistungen,* on the mind's making—which is to say, actively generating—mistakes. Each homespun illustration was just one more argument in favor of the universal determination that, Freud insisted, governs mental life. And Freud's demonstration that all events have their causes was accompanied by his demonstration that these events also have their meanings—and the causes reveal their meanings. To take one much-quoted incident from the *Psychopathology* that Freud clipped from a Vienna newspaper: The president of the lower house of the Austrian Parliament is on the podium ceremonially opening a new session which he fears will be unruly and difficult. Solemnly, he declares the sitting "closed" when, of course, he meant to proclaim it "opened." This "mistake" was not a bit of spontaneous verbal sport but a meaningful revelation generated by the speaker's unconscious anxiety about the session he was about to inaugurate.[5]

5. See *The Psychopathology of Everyday Life* (1901), *SE* VI, 59. It would be useful not to confound meaning with cause, though Freud, almost deliberately it would seem, did not keep them apart. After all, a piece of mental behavior—a neurotic symptom or a dream—may be meaningless, virtually nonsensical, and still have a cause. Many nineteenth-century psychologists, anxious to discover somatic or constitutional roots for the baffling actions of madmen and the equally baffling reports of dreamers, interpreted these actions, and these reports, in just this way. For Freud, in contrast, meaning was indissolubly linked to cause; it was precisely because each instance of mental life, whether a slip or a symptom, could be traced to antecedent causes that the psychologist could count on finding meaning for it. And conversely, it was because each such instance had a meaning

Such instances are only too familiar, and their very familiarity guaranteed them a hearing. They testified to the ubiquity of cause and the pervasiveness of meaning in the life of the mind, even when they appear to be wholly absent.

If Freud is right about the ubiquity of cause, why had his predecessors overlooked it across the centuries? Freud could account for that by postulating a dynamic unconscious, a domain inaccessible to direct inspection but in which the most influential mental causes—passions, anxieties, conflicts—reside and from which they seek outlets. The unconscious is a rich repository of causes. Yet, being unconscious, it has a way of concealing its contribution to mental work or of letting out its dangerous inhabitants only after they have been thoroughly masked. Causal relationships are like a string of small islands whose deep connections are hidden by the sea. Much mental determinism is so hard to recognize, in short, because it is either disguised or concealed.

A dramatic instance of disguised causal relations is the case of Freud's gifted lawyer-patient, the obsessive neurotic who has entered history under the nickname of the Rat Man. The Rat Man indulged in all sorts of bizarre behavior which he knew to be determined—knew it only too well, for he could not help engaging in it. He entered treatment with Freud because he felt compelled to think certain thoughts and do certain things. He was obsessed by fears that a revolting and terrible punishment would be visited on his father and on the woman he loved—rats boring their way into their anuses. He was no less obsessed by sadistic thoughts that he vigorously repudiated as wholly uncharacteristic of him, by self-destructive impulses that he could not shake off, and by pedantic, absurd prohibitions that kept him caged within his closed universe of suffering. A trivial debt he owed to a fellow officer preempted much valuable time and forced him to devise elaborate schemes he was painfully sure he must carry through lest that punishment be loosed on those he loved most in the world. What his psychoanalytic treatment managed to uncover were the true causes of these com-

that it must be sure to have a cause—or causes. Reviewing, in 1924, the fundamentals of the psychology he had founded, Freud included among these "the thorough-going meaningfulness and determination of even the apparently most obscure and arbitrary mental phenomena." See on this point the discussion in *Jones* I, 366.

pulsions, causes—notably a profound ambivalence toward his father—that were not legibly reflected in his symptoms. Deeply loving his father, the Rat Man could not consciously face his feelings of hatred for him, and in consequence that hatred fought its way to the surface by indirections. What psychoanalytic therapy did for him was to substitute a true for a false determinism. The causal connection the Rat Man saw between his compulsive needs and the punishment that so worried him proved to be inauthentic, the creation of his neurosis. In actuality, both the needs and the punishment were symptoms, effects of that basic cause—his ambivalence. Many puzzling events have this quality: one knows that they have their causes, but one is likely to find the wrong ones. This is what scholars before Freud had done with Hamlet's notorious hesitation over killing his uncle; its true cause, Freud believed, was not the one that others thought they had discovered.[6]

Still more difficult to clarify is the situation in which the causal nexus is concealed. One of Freud's most conspicuous failures, his aborted analysis of Dora, serves as a striking illustration. The eighteen-year-old who came to Freud in October 1900 crippled by hysteric symptoms terminated her treatment eleven weeks later with much of the work still to be done, and her abrupt departure moved Freud to a critical self-examination. At first he interpreted her "desertion" as a neurotic, self-destructive act of revenge, but as he explored the failure further, he graduated to a fuller and more just explanation. Dora's leaving him was not a sheer accident or, for that matter, wholly her doing: he had overlooked the potent clinical phenomenon of transference—the patient investing in her analyst passionate feelings of love and hate that properly belong to other persons truly important to her. He might have added, to complete the causal analysis of Dora's deserting him just before New Year's Day 1901, that he had also failed to take account of his countertransference—his own unconscious involvement with this pert, attractive, and irritating analysand. He had somehow refused to complete the process that defines psychoanalysis: the unremitting search for causes.

Another eloquent testament to Freud's commitment to scientific determinism is the so-called fundamental rule of psychoanalysis: the

6. See above, 44.

analysand is told—it is one of the few things he *is* told—to hold back nothing that comes into his mind, no matter how absurd, trivial, inconsistent, or obscene. This is the procedure known as "free association," a procedure the patient rarely carries out, indeed persistently tries to evade. But the rule obeyed or defied, its name is misleading in an instructive way. It generates a picture of the mind playing freely over the materials that present themselves in informal, often startling sequences and of the patient reporting them without neatening up or censoring the outpouring of his associations. But, as the psychoanalyst Roy Schafer has pointed out, there is really nothing free about the analysand's "free association"; on the contrary, the fundamental rule works, to the extent that it works at all, precisely because the conscious mind is compelled to review a mass of thoughts, feelings, and memories over which it has no control and which are determined by unconscious impulses. "From this perspective," Schafer writes, "the point of the free-association method is to make it plain just how unfree the analysand is." Freud did not intend to deceive his readers into thinking that his system was a voluntaristic one; the method of free association actually liberates the patient, but only to recognize what his deepest desires and anxieties are. "The designation 'free,' " to quote Schafer again, "makes sense only as referring to one's freeing oneself from the usual self-imposed constraints of verbal reasonableness, coherence, and verbal decorum."[7] The psychoanalytic process demonstrates, as do dreams, slips of the tongue, and symptoms, that man's mind cannot escape the laws that govern it.

Deterministic systems are by and large closed systems. In the defender of free will they induce claustrophobia. He sees them as turning humans into the helpless victims of uncontrollable and normally unknown forces, as reducing them to mere puppets slavishly obeying an invisible and omnipotent puppeteer. The movements man is allowed to perform in such a system, the advocate of free will is bound to say, are never autonomous, let alone spontaneous. They are (he will say if he is tired of this metaphor) steps in a ballet rigidly choreographed in advance by an inaccessible

7. Schafer, *Language and Insight* (1978), 40. See also Anton O. Kris, *Free Association: Method and Process* (1982).

and implacable choreographer. Choices, alternatives, the whole panoply of mental freedoms are discredited as childish, or mere self-
serving fictions; the determinist—better, the fatalist—treats them
with disdain as the last survivals of naiveté. Isaiah Berlin has spoken
of flowers that deck men's chains. The advocate of free will, I might
add, is bound to see them as artificial flowers at that. No sense of
responsibility can flourish or even survive in such a prison.

The charge is extreme, but whatever its justice, Freud's determinism is different. His structure is open to the world, hospitable
to change and to possibilities; it makes room for the exercise of
rational mental and moral effort. In the 1920s, in some reflections
on his theory of dreams, Freud comments, "of course one must hold
oneself responsible for one's wicked dream impulses. What else is
one to do with them?"[8] His confident tone makes this observation
only the more telling. Men are responsible for what they do, even
for what they dream—"of course." But how can they assume responsibility for their thoughts and their dreams if these are merely
the last links in a chain of causes? Freud's commitment to chance
or "accident" is the first step to a resolution of this difficulty.

It is, however, only a first step. Central as Freud's ideas about
chance or accident were to his way of thinking, we must tease them
out from casual asides, no less weighty for being embedded in texts
dealing with other matters. In short, he believed that in important
ways nothing is chance and that in other no less important ways
everything is chance.

I have expounded on the first of these alternatives at some length.
We have seen that, according to Freud, what often seems spontaneous or uncaused is actually symptomatic—a result, not mere hap-
penstance. Instancing "many apparently accidental injuries"
happening to his patients, Freud found himself persuaded that they
were "really self-injuries" caused by "a tendency toward self-
punishment."[9] If this view, appropriately outlined in *The Psychopathology of Everyday Life,* is not a surprising posture for a scientific
determinist like Freud to adopt, it *is* surprising, at least at first glance,
that Freud could also argue, in his essay on Leonardo da Vinci, "I

8. "Einige Nachträge zum Ganzen der Traumdeutung" (1925), *GW* I, 567 / "Some
Additional Notes on Dream-Interpretation as a Whole," *SE* XIX, 133.
9. *Zur Psychopathologie des Alltagslebens,* (1901) *GW* IV, 198 / *Psychopathology
of Everyday Life, SE* VI, 178–79.

believe that one has no right . . . to consider chance unworthy of deciding our fate." To do so is simply to "relapse into the pious world view that Leonardo himself helped to overcome." Indeed, "we like to forget that in fact everything in our life is chance, beginning with our origin out of the encounter of spermatozoon and ovum; chance," he scarcely clarifies the matter by adding, "which nevertheless has its share in the lawfulness and necessity of nature."[10]

The formulation is less than helpful, but plainly by "accident" or "chance" Freud does not mean consequences without causes. He seems to visualize a mental event or state as resembling a frequently flooded pond that is fed by many streams and canals, each with its own source, its own tributaries, and its own geological past. These suppliers of water intersect; some of them run dry at times, others can be dammed up at their mouths, so that it is not wholly predictable which of them will contribute waters to the pond and cause it to overflow. Not predictable but, for the patient and the resourceful investigator, traceable after the event. Since there are always more accesses of water than are necessary to flood the pond, there are always more possibilities than the actuality needs. "Everything in our life is chance," but not in the sense, once again, that a person's mental history is wholly or even partially random. A human being comes into the world, after all, with a certain constitutional physical and mental endowment, in a certain place, at a certain time, into a certain family. There are all too many oppressive unchangeable necessities in life, necessities that the most energetic activity cannot alter. "It doesn't follow," Donald Davidson has written, "from the fact that at noon today I became exactly 55 years, 72 days, 11 hours, and 59 minutes old, that I was free to become this age (rather than another) on this date."[11] A patient of Freud initiated into sexual activity by a lubricious governess might not have had that particular adult to seduce him if, say, the boy's mother, who engaged this governess, had failed to attend a certain woman's club meeting at which she had first heard this woman highly recommended. But from this switching of causal tracks it does not follow that her son, grown up, *might* not have ended up on Freud's couch anyway. One can

10. "Eine Kindheitserinnerung des Leonardo da Vinci," *GW* VIII, 210 / "Leonardo da Vinci," (1910), *SE* XI, 137.
11. Davidson, "Freedom to Act," *Essays on Actions and Events,* 74.

paint the possible, though by no means inevitable, scenario: he might
have been sexually enlightened by another governess (it is almost
certain that there would have been such an employee in his household) or have picked up the sexual stimuli that overwhelmed him in
other ways. And even if he had never been seduced, some other
events might have produced a similar erotic history for him, if perhaps with somewhat differing symptoms.

Not all chances are equally remote or equally obtrusive. The network of experiences in which personal life is enmeshed makes room
alike for improbable contingencies and (though, of course, far more
often) for highly probable occurrences. To return to Dora for a moment, one of her symptoms, a difficulty in walking, almost a limp,
had emerged after a high fever. Her puzzled physician had attributed
that fever to a mild appendicitis but failed to diagnose the foot-
dragging. Freud took the physical syndrome to be a "real hysterical
symptom," born from the way Dora's neurosis had seized on an
attack of influenza. This physical ailment was the "chance event"
which her hysteria had then utilized for "one of its utterances."[12]
Dora's bout of influenza was one of those bits of reality that, although
it impinged on her life, might well have passed her by. Had it not
invaded her troubled existence, her neurosis would have differed,
however subtly, from the neurotic-having-used-her-influenza-for-
psychological-ends whom Freud tried to cure in the fall of 1900.

There is, then, room for play in Freud's world, and it is the task of
chance to provide that play. As Freud put it in one of his last papers,
it is difficult to distinguish "what is rigidly laid down by biological
laws and what is mobile and changeable under the influence of
accidental experience." It may be difficult to distinguish, but Freud
saw irresistible invasions of the fortuitous in everyone's early life:
the fact and character of infantile seduction, "the time when siblings
are born, the time when the difference between the sexes is discovered, the direct observation of sexual intercourse, the solicitous
or rejecting conduct of the parents"—any of these things can speed
up the sexual maturation of a child.[13] How decisively or how casually
such events, none of them inescapable, will shape the child's future

12. "Bruchstück einer Hysterie-Analyse" (1905), *GW* V, 265 / "Fragment of an
Analysis of a Case of Hysteria," *SE* VII, 102.
13. "Über die weibliche Sexualität" (1931), *GW* XIV, 536 / "Female Sexuality,"
SE XXI, 242.

depends on the events, on their location—and on the child. In any event, the power of accident over individual lives is no accident.

For Freud, this conception of chance had more than explanatory import. It was part of psychoanalytic polemics. In a brief preface to the third edition of his *Three Essays on Sexuality,* he notes that he has throughout the book given preference to the "accidental factors" determining sexual life, leaving "the dispositional ones in the background." After all, he adds, "the accidental plays the principal role in analysis."[14] What Freud is doing here is privileging the power of nurture, at least in psychoanalysis. This is rather ironic, for Freud has often been accused of biological determinism. Actually, psychologists of his day thought him not biological enough. What his teachers and his professional colleagues, the psychologists and psychiatrists, had for decades regarded as ultimately decisive in mental malfunctioning was "bad" heredity or some physical trauma.[15] To them, Freud was little better than a single-minded environmentalist. Indeed, in 1912, Freud found it necessary to defend himself, a little irritably, against the charge that he had "denied the significance of inborn (constitutional) factors because I have stressed that of infantile impressions. Such a reproach stems from the narrowness of the causal need—*Kausalbedürfnis*—of mankind," which likes to posit a single cause if at all possible. Rather, he argued, there are "two sets of etiological factors," namely, "*Daimon* and *Tyche*," endowment and chance, which together regularly "determine a person's fate."[16] While his contemporaries placed heavy emphasis on unchanging characteristics, popularized by such unscientific clichés as "national character" and "blood," Freud, with his somewhat idiosyncratic use

14. "Vorwort zur dritten Auflage" (1914), in *Drei Abhandlungen zur Sexualtheorie* (1905), *GW* V, 29 / "Preface to the Third Edition," *Three Essays on the Theory of Sexuality, SE* VII, 131.

15. I have discussed this issue at some length in *Freud,* 119–24. See also two pioneering essays, making for Britain the point which I have generalized here, William F. Bynum, Jr., "Rationales for Therapy in British Psychiatry," and Michael J. Clark, "The Rejection of Psychological Approaches to Mental Disorder in Late Nineteenth-Century British Psychiatry," in Andrew Scull, ed., *Madhouses, Mad-Doctors, and Madmen: The Social History of Psychiatry in the Victorian Era* (1981), 35–57, 271–312.

16. "Zur Dynamik der Übertragung" (1912), *GW* VIII, 364–65n / "The Dynamics of Transference," *SE* XII, 99n.

of the words *chance* or *accident,* instead stressed the pervasive play of experience, especially early experience, in the shaping of mind.

That experience, Freud was persuaded, is very rich indeed. The stark simplicity of Freud's dualistic theory of drives, his conviction that the Oedipus complex is universal, and those massive granite blocks from which the structure of psychoanalysis is built—conflict, defense, repression—have invited many of his readers to see in Freud a theoretician who knows one big thing, a propounder of essentially simple generalizations, in short, a hedgehog.[17] Nothing could be further from the real Freud. Rather, he was a fox, a fox who at times affected hedgehog's clothing. He had an uncanny gift for detecting parallels and discovering relationships and found fertile use for that talent in exploring the resemblance of dreams to jokes and psychoses, of children to neurotics and "savages." This was Freud, the discoverer of the laws governing mind, the maker of strong, if hitherto unperceived designs.

But there is another Freud, equally characteristic though somewhat less conspicuous: the celebrant of variety. Freud was not a psychological reductionist any more than he was a pan-sexualist— an epithet against which he protested vigorously, justly, and in vain. To call his view of human nature monotonous is equivalent to calling the game of chess monotonous because it has few pieces and rests on few rules. Just as in chess, in human life a handful of ingredients produces never-ending, ever-surprising variations. Uniformity and variety cooperate and alternate in Freud's view of man, to point both to recurrent patterns and to individuality.

Freud's great case histories are tributes to his perception and cheerful acceptance of this immense, inexhaustible variety of human types and human experience. They offer a diverse menu of mental suffering: obsessions, phobias, delusions, fetishism, anxiety attacks, hysterical aches—each characteristic of a group of syndromes, yet each unique. And Freud (as is often forgotten) drew his observations and developed his theories from a widely assorted cast of characters: precocious small boys, spoiled Russian aristocrats, nubile Austrian adolescents, dissatisfied French nobility, troubled poets and com-

17. I have in mind, of course, Isaiah Berlin's famous pamphlet *The Hedgehog and the Fox: An Essay on Tolstoy's View of History* (1953), in which he distinguishes between two types of mind: the hedgehog, which knows one big thing, and the fox, which knows many things.

posers, English and American physicians in search of psychoanalytic training, classic paranoiacs whom he knew only from books, and writers he came to value as friends. He was puzzled all his life by how these analysands had come to "choose" the particular neurosis that brought them to his couch, but he was sure of two things: that while each patient could teach him something about other patients, each was irreplaceably himself or herself; and that while the process of neurotic choice remained obscure, it must be traced back to the unconscious, to early desires and fears, and to traumatic but eventually repressed irruptions. Even if the act of choosing had been thoroughly forgotten, had for many never been conscious at all, it had occurred. As crippled, hedged in, and driven by unknown forces as humans might be, they were for Freud choosing animals.[18]

The problematic nature of choice, then, must occupy a prominent place in Freud's psychology of freedom. An obvious, somewhat overworked example of psychological constraints calling out for psychoanalytic understanding is the young man who falls in love over and over again, convinced that he is choosing freely from a sizable pool of eligible partners. Yet it turns out on analysis that his presumably untrammeled serial infatuations are mere reenactments of unresolved oedipal conflicts, for his women strikingly resemble one another—and his mother.

But the analysis of choice is particularly difficult because the very persons most intimately involved in the process of choosing often submit contradictory testimony. They *feel* free, yet are unfree; they feel under compulsion, but for reasons different from those they quite sincerely advance. The Rat Man, whom I have briefly discussed, is a splendid instance of such misreading of one's situation. A good part of the resulting confusion stems from what Freud once called

18. On firmly narrowing the range of choice, modern philosophers have agreed with Freud, though of course in their own vocabulary. Thus Alasdair MacIntyre writes: "One can hardly doubt that more and more of behaviour will be included in accounts which show such behaviour to be causally dependent on antecedent conditions." "Determinism," *Mind* LXVI (1957), 29. See also Isaiah Berlin: "It is plainly a good thing that we should be reminded by social scientists that the scope of human choice is a good deal more limited than we used to suppose. . . . And this certainly alters our ideas about the limits of freedom and responsibility." "Historical Inevitability" (1954), *Four Essays on Liberty,* 73.

"the astonishing behavior of patients," behavior in which they combine "a conscious knowing with not-knowing."[19] A patient may "know" that he is performing compulsive ceremonies, another one that her limp derives from no physical disability. Both may even "know" that their ailments are neurotic symptoms. Still, this "knowledge" may not enable these patients to stop their neurotic behavior, disagreeable though it may be for them. The promise of the Gospel of John has not been fulfilled: these peculiar ways of knowing the truth have not made them free.

A poignant exemplar of such ineffectual knowledge, such open-eyed slavery, is the victim of anorexia nervosa, who may literally starve herself to death, knowing that she must eat to live but unable to persuade herself to take the steps that will ensure her survival. One such sufferer, a bright college student quoted in the *New York Times* in the spring of 1978, perceptively and pathetically remarked: "It's like there are two of me. There's the intelligent Rochelle, who knows all about nutrition and what the proper things to eat are. But then there's the emotional Rochelle, who's dominating and won't let me take the upper hand and do the proper things." She went on, facing her dismal, virtually inescapable future in fear and impotence: "Of course, the possibility of death terrifies me. I'm not suicidal! I'm terrified of catching a cold because the doctors have said that I'd get pneumonia and it would kill me. But that doesn't make me eat more. It just doesn't seep in."[20] *It just doesn't seep in.* Rochelle seems to command all the requisite instruments of freedom: she knows her condition, charts her loss of weight with mounting anxiety, predicts the consequences of her crazy eating habits with terrible lucidity. She knows and she does not know. It would seem that she is choosing her starvation, yet this is not the right way to put it, for she is not free to choose otherwise.

Not all illusions of free choice are the monopoly of some profound psychopathology. They may be rooted less in the inaccessible unconscious, which preserves infantile wishes and anxieties intact, than in the preconscious, which stores cultural ideals or prohibitions of which individuals have only intermittent inklings since they make up an almost automatic element in their structure of thought and

19. "Zur Einleitung der Behandlung" (1913), *GW* VIII, / "On Beginning the Treatment," *SE* XII, 142.
20. *New York Times,* May 11, 1978, B9.

behavior. One good instance of this is fashion, which for centuries cultural critics have liked to call a tyrant. Fashion, a pendant to private pathology, can become a kind of social pathology. Consider a conventional young couple moving into their first house and preparing to buy their first set of furniture. They think they have rationally defined the extent and the boundaries of their freedom: the size of their house is one limit for them, the amount of disposable funds is another. Within these limits, they will assert with complete sincerity, they are free to choose from among a vast variety of offerings: as long as the pieces are not too large or too expensive, they will buy what they like. After they have completed their purchases, they will continue to maintain that they were guided by their taste alone. Did they not visit showroom after showroom until they found lamps and tables and chairs that "spoke to them"?

Nothing is easier than to demolish this feeble if well-meant claim to personal autonomy and to demonstrate that this couple's taste was molded firmly, perhaps exclusively, by outside agencies. They bought what went for good taste among their friends. To be sure, psychological forces better hidden than the implicit imperatives of their social environment may have influenced the couple and hence fenced them in even more narrowly than the bounds of fashion. I am thinking of the survival of identifications with parents' tastes or longings, or the struggle for dominance between husband and wife. Just as the child develops its superego, in Freud's words, not on the model of its parents but on that of its parents' superegos, so the wishes of the young couple may reflect not so much what actually stood in their elders' houses as the pieces of furniture these elders had dearly *wanted* to possess. Whatever the forces at work, we seem entitled to amend the old adage that beggars can't be choosers to say that choosers, only too often, can't be choosers either.

I want to illustrate the issues involved in Freud's version of determinism with another fiction, an invented but plausible tale in which an individual finds himself placed before incompatible alternatives but in which abstention is, by the nature of the demands on him, ultimately impossible. Consider a professor of acoustical engineering, popular with his colleagues, relatively well paid, and with sufficient time for his passion, private researches into loudspeakers. This engineer, who lives and teaches in the Midwest, receives an offer from a firm in southern California noted for its innovative sound

systems, which seductively promises him not only life in the sun but
a still higher salary and even more time for his "own" work than
his university has been willing to allow him. He is tempted indeed.
His wife, with whom in good American fashion he discusses his
situation, declares herself neutral: she is happy in the native part of
her country but professes that she can be just as happy in Los
Angeles. It is up to him, she tells him, to make the decision. He has
a month to decide.

Thrown on his own resources, the engineer is, by all the evidence,
torn one way and the other. He wants to go and he wants to stay.
As day follows day, in his ruminations and his fantasies, he makes
up his mind more than once. At times he sees himself moving, at
other times he sees himself staying put. In his perplexity, he has
dictated two letters, one accepting the offer and the other rejecting
it, which his secretary keeps locked away in her desk. There they
both are, signed but not mailed. His friends, with whom he canvasses
his dilemma freely, are so puzzled by his indecision that they hesitate
to make even small bets on the outcome—so balanced does he seem
on the knife-edge of choice. The clues point, with equal plausibility,
in either direction. The engineer feels troubled, but he also feels
free, and may really *be* free. Then, on the twenty-ninth day, he makes
his decision. He will stay. His secretary tears up the letter of acceptance, his friends give him a party, and the chief of his department
informs him privately that he may expect a sizable raise next academic year.

As we anatomize this agonizing process of choosing, we need not
concentrate on the engineer's unconscious alone. The drama of decision played itself out across his mind, including his conscious ego.
He had made sure to inform his chairman of the tempting offer and
of his state of mind and had shrewdly negotiated for better conditions. Still, his unconscious must have played a far from negligible
part in visualizing his future. His indecisiveness had been real enough
and had run deep; all through his happy ordeal, he had reasons,
including unconscious ones, that he could use to support either
course of action. His father, a practical man of business, had long
disdained his academic post as unworthy of his talents, a fact of his
life that had not entered into the engineer's conscious calculations
at all. As he had constructed his parallel lists, "staying" on the left
and "moving" on the right—a well-tested resource of academics

debating their future with themselves—he had not entered his father's firmly voiced preferences on either side, though they might legitimately have fitted on either list, or on both. Two aspects of his unresolved oedipal problems, powerful if repressed ambivalent feelings toward his father, struggled for supremacy in him without his being aware of that conflict at all. And there were other, equally submerged struggles at work, pushing and pulling on him as it were from behind the scene. Among these were his overprotective impulses toward his wife (who, he correctly sensed, for all her strenuous neutrality, was sending him subtly pleading messages to remain in the region in which she had grown up), impulses competing with resentment against her soft dictatorship. And there were other conflicting impulses as well which it would take a psychoanalyst to detect and unravel.

How free, then, was the engineer at that crucial moment when he told his secretary, "Mail the letter to L.A. that says 'No,' and tear up the one that says 'Yes' "? The engineer himself, as I have said, felt in control of his destiny, yet wholly, frankly undecided for almost a month. "I swear," he told a friend later, "that half an hour before I directed my secretary which letter to send, I had no idea which way I would jump." Is freedom, then, essentially a state of inner confusion, nothing better? Or is that confusion merely a symptom of concealed determinism?

As it now stands, this vignette is not as useful a test of Freud's deterministic psychology of freedom as it might be. It becomes far more instructive in this variant: suppose that the managers in California, knowing their man better than he knows himself, shrewdly anticipating an impending rejection and aware that any hard pressure would prove counterproductive, invite the acoustical engineer to take a whole year or even two to decide. They suavely tell him that they can wait. And the engineer, appalled by his indecisiveness and his bouts of anxiety, resolves to enter psychoanalysis. In the course of his treatment he begins to confront some of the conflicts that had long bedeviled him outside the sphere of awareness: his haunting oedipal mixed feelings—an unconscious identification with his father battling an equally unconscious rebelliousness against him—as well as his complex attitudes toward his wife. As he grows more introspective, more self-aware, these irrational survivals recede. They become less pressing, even less relevant to his process of decision making. A year or so later he can reflect about the offer from California with most if not all of the elements entering choice on the table rather than behind his back. He can weigh practical matters far more rationally than earlier and pay attention to his feelings without being flooded by them. He can now, as the analysts would say, test reality with a fair measure of success.[21] Is he free now to move or to stay, or at least freer than before? Freud would say that he is.

As this revised anecdote suggests, even though psychoanalysis acts to circumscribe the area of freedom in which humans fancy they live, it also acts in the opposite way. After all, as a therapy, its precise intention is to *enlarge* the area of freedom. There have been many philosophers who have argued that freedom is the recognition of necessity or (a good deal more subtly) obedience to a law that one has made for oneself.[22] But however valuable, even bracing, recognition of the hold that necessity has on us may turn out to be, freedom is not defined by necessity, even self-imposed necessity. One may reasonably argue, and a psychoanalyst is bound to argue, that it is better to know realities than not to know them, and those realities certainly include the boundaries to one's freedom. This was Freud's view, as exemplified by his insistence on being told the truth, however unpalatable, even about his painful and ultimately fatal cancer. He dismissed Felix Deutsch as his personal physician because he had protectively failed to tell him the true diagnosis of the lesion in his mouth. And late in April 1939, when he was very old and—the cancer having recurred and now incurable—close to death, he told his former analysand and now close friend Princess Marie Bonaparte that his family and friends were attempting to soothe him with a well-meaning but mendacious atmosphere of remaining hope: "The cancer is in shrinkage, the reaction manifestations are tem-

21. See on this point Robert Waelder, "Das Freiheitsproblem in der Psychoanalyse und das Problem der Realitätsprüfung," *Imago* XX (1934), 89–108; its English version, "The Problem of Freedom in Psychoanalysis and the Problem of Reality Testing," can be found in the *Int. J. Psycho-Anal.* XVII (1936),
22. See for just one instance among thoughtful psychoanalysts the paper by Robert P. Knight, "Determinism, 'Freedom,' and Psychotherapy" (1946), which quotes (with approval) Kant, Hegel, and Engels to this effect, and an unattributed but Kantian epigram: "That man is free who is conscious of being the author of the law that he obeys." *Clinician and Therapist: Selected Papers of Robert P. Knight,* ed. Stuart C. Miller (1972), 140–41.

porary. I do not believe it, and," he added stoically, "do not like being deceived."[23] He resented such bedside chatter as an insult to his dignity—and an assault on his freedom.

The recognition of necessity, then, though not an element in freedom, can become a precondition for it, and in two ways: it may point, however obliquely, to regions of autonomy that had been invisible or indistinct as long as the boundaries of compulsion's kingdom had not been firmly mapped. Moreover, such recognition may relieve the sort of anxiety that uncertainty is bound to induce and thus may enhance one's capacity for making choices. But Freudian therapy is only in part aimed at the calm and candid acceptance of one's powerlessness. In two celebrated summaries of therapeutic action, Freud suggests clearly enough that psychoanalysis aims to reduce, as much as to acknowledge, constraints. Freud said again and again that the purpose of psychoanalytic treatment is to make the unconscious conscious—as in my earlier formulation, to put on the table what had been behind the patient's back; and he said once, in a much quoted epigram and lovely metaphor on the same subject: "Where id was, there ego shall be. It is a work of culture rather like the draining of the Zuider Zee."[24]

One short text, buried in a footnote in *The Ego and the Id*—I have already quoted it as one of my two epigraphs to this essay—clarifies what Freud thought to be at stake: "Analysis does not set out to prevent morbid reactions, but should give the patient's ego *freedom* to decide one way or another."[25] The psychoanalyst is not another Rousseau, trying to force his patients to be free; he cannot guarantee

23. Freud to Marie Bonaparte, April 28, 1939. *Briefe*, 474–75.

24. "Die Zerlegung der psychischen Persönlichkeit," *Neue Folge der Vorlesungen zur Einführung der Psychoanalyse* (1933), *GW* XV, 86 / "The Dissection of the Psychical Personality," *New Introductory Lectures on Psycho-Analysis, SE* XXII, 80.

25. *Das Ich und das Es* (1923), *GW* XIII, 280n / *The Ego and the Id, SE* XIX, 50n. Italics in original. I first called attention to this text in an early article, the first in which I expressed an interest in Freud, some thirty-five years ago: "The Enlightenment in the History of Political Theory," *Political Science Quarterly* LXIX (1954), 374–89; my quotation is at p. 379n. This article is reprinted in a slightly revised version in my *The Party of Humanity: Essays in the French Enlightenment* (1964). It was only in the 1970s that I discovered Robert Knight had resorted to the same sentence in the paper (published eight years before mine) which I cite in footnote 22 above.

· · · · · · · · · · · ·

wisdom, nor does his discipline teach it. Freedom, in Freud's terse but precise formulation, must embrace the option to make bad choices.

This much should now be plain. As long as mental forces that significantly affect human decisions are unconscious, they act as determinants that the person making the decision cannot take into account, cannot weigh or measure, let alone discard. And even if these forces enter consciousness, one's awareness of them must reach down to their roots, the very lair of repression. To make the unconscious conscious is to do more than provide intellectual food for thought. To put ego in place of id is hard and emotional work for analyst and analysand alike. It involves the shifting of mental energies to permit the patient not merely to assent to abstract propositions but to understand with his whole mind—and, I should add, with his body as well. Neurosis is, as I have suggested, a form of slavery. Symptoms may be compromises, but they are not compromises the neurotic has been free to negotiate. Lady Macbeth is not at liberty to take in and act on information provided by her senses that her hands are clean. And the symptoms of obsessive neurotics are only the most obvious instances of the unconscious as the source of compulsion; the symptoms of other mental disorders share the same quality. The Don Juan is the servant of appetites that he falsely believes serve him; the agoraphobic is forced not only to stay at home but to lead his crippled life under the sway of passions and fears he does not know and will refuse to recognize when a psychoanalyst first confronts him with them.

I have called neurosis a form of slavery, but this forceful characterization defines other human conditions as well. Infancy and childhood are slavery no less, more tolerable than neurosis only in that they include, in principle and fortunately often enough in practice, the prospect of manumission. Freud's scheme of maturation takes account of this by visualizing mental and emotional growth as a laborious, often disrupted, and never wholly completed attempt to escape from bondage. The glorious scenarios of omnipotence that the small child enacts in its fantasies are a profound irony, for they attest vividly to its impotence. Each stage of physical and mental development has its appropriate experience of servitude and its appropriate experiments in overcoming that servitude. The word *choice* in the technical psychoanalytic term *object choice* is as Pickwickian as the word *free* in *free association*. The child is not merely compelled to "choose" its love objects from a severely circumscribed field; it cannot evade the act of choosing. Only later, if it is fortunate, will it make choices that, rather than reflecting unconscious early memories and unappeased infantile desires, will be a play among possibilities. The unconscious is a necessary, permanent ingredient in human nature and remains, in the healthiest and best adapted of human beings, a repository of powerful irrational forces. It works at once as the supreme agent of and even more as the strongest fetter on human freedom. The wholly free human being is even more of a myth than the psychoanalyst's ideal, the fully analyzed patient.

The jargon of mental-health technicians and assorted publicists peddling infallible psychological cures has lent some plausibility to the notion that psychoanalysts are utopian dreamers about unfettered freedom. Freud's prescription, "Where id was, there ego shall be," has been less than felicitous, for it seems to hint at some higher, wholly rational self that emerges from analytic treatment. It would have been better, and a more accurate report on his purposes, if Freud had spoken instead of hoping for a lengthy truce among id, ego, and superego. For therapeutic optimism, certainly of an untrammeled kind, wholly misconceives the temperamental and intellectual direction of Freud's psychology. It may indeed be that the well-analyzed person has learned to "master" his impulses and is moving toward "realizing his potentialities." But this mastery and this realization are only correlates to the negative freedom—as it is called, freedom *from*—that the analyst has helped the patient to attain. Successful therapy will reduce anxieties, partially undo repressions, and correct distorted perceptions. The analyst has, to be picturesque for a moment, struck the shackles from his analysand's wrists. But as we have seen, he cannot and does not wish to dictate to that analysand how to use his hands. This is what Freud had in mind when he cautioned psychoanalysts against the ambition to become moral teachers or to fancy themselves models of maturity to be imitated by their adorers on the couch.

Some years ago, I had occasion to read an application for psychoanalytic treatment in which the applicant, unschooled in the jargon of the schools, put the matter with affecting simplicity: "If I undertake psychoanalysis now I think I will be able to make—although perhaps not immediately—some important decisions concerning my marriage, work, and future. And know why I make such decisions. I hope to achieve freedom from my own past." He was being overly sanguine: the utopia of so much elbowroom, I repeat, was not in Freud's gift. Nor did he ever promise it. But even if the past always retains some power over us, the program of this applicant was in Freud's spirit. Freedom is not total liberation from the yoke of cause, not the sovereign disregard of all predictability in life. To be free is to wield the weapon of reason against the blandishments and the terror of illusions.

4

Reading Freud Through Freud's Reading

Sometime in late 1906, the Viennese bookseller and publisher Hugo Heller asked a number of public figures—poets, novelists, critics, psychologists, and others—to enumerate "ten good books" for him. One of the prominent personages he addressed was Sigmund Freud. Inevitably so: Heller was an intellectual entrepreneur with a serious interest in psychoanalysis. He had joined Freud's Wednesday Psychological Society not long after its founding in 1902 and remained a member after that informal group transformed itself into the Vienna Psychoanalytic Society six years later.[1] A number of Freud's writings appeared under Heller's imprint, and Heller further ingratiated himself with Freud by undertaking such risky publish-

1. The full, conscientiously taken minutes (kept from the fall of 1906 on by Otto Rank) reveal that Heller was fairly faithful in his attendance and spoke occasionally. On October 23, 1912, he gave a short presentation, "Lou Andreas-Salomé as a Writer." *Protokolle* IV, 103. At other meetings, in the uninhibited manner of most members, Heller freely confessed to his youthful masturbation and his little boy's way of denying that he was playing with his penis. January 15 and March 4, 1908. Ibid., I, 266, 323.

ing ventures as the psychoanalytic journals *Imago* and the *Internationale Zeitschrift für Psychoanalyse.* Active and adroit, he ran a salon for artists, writers, and intellectuals; it was in his rooms, in December 1907, that Freud delivered his paper on the psychological links between the making of fictions and the dreaming of daydreams.[2]

Had it not been for Heller's cultivated style, wide acquaintance, and bustling energy his questionnaire would have received few answers. Contemporary culture, as some of his respondents complained, was awash in this sort of inquiry; they thought it vulgar and predictable and "American."[3] A few of Heller's respondents, in fact, had to be prompted before they bothered to reply. But eventually he managed to gather up thirty-two replies and collected them in a little pamphlet, *Vom Lesen und von guten Büchern,* prefaced by a letter from Hugo von Hofmannsthal.[4] And one of Heller's catches was identified as "Prof. Dr. Siegmund Freud." Misspelled first name notwithstanding, we are lucky to have Freud's letter. It opens a window into his mind, inviting us to read Freud through Freud's reading.

As one might expect, Freud introduced his list of books with some instructive distinctions; he analyzed Heller's question before giving his answer. "You ask me to name 'ten good books,' and refuse to add a single word of explanation," he wrote. "Hence you leave to me not only the choice of the books, but the interpretation of your request as well." Always ready to turn a public moment

2. "Creative Writers and Day-Dreaming" (1908), *SE* IX, 141–53.

3. Hugo von Hofmannsthal, expressing the facile anti-Americanism that was current among so many educated Europeans, thought that the gathering up of "a round number of 'best books' " was "a far from agreeable American enthusiasm." And Arthur Schnitzler had to be asked twice because he felt a deep "antipathy toward this whole practice of questionnaires." *Vom Lesen und von guten Büchern. Eine Rundfrage veranstaltet von der Redaktion der "Neuen Blättern für Literatur und Kunst"* (1907).

4. The pamphlet is exceedingly rare and virtually unobtainable. Fortunately, Hofmannsthal's introductory letter and twenty of the thirty-six replies (including Freud's, except for its concluding paragraph) were reprinted in *Jahrbuch deutscher Bibliophilen und Literaturfreunde,* ed. Hans Feigl, XVI–XVII (1931), 108–27. Hofmannsthal's comment is at p. 109, Schnitzler's at 124. Since Freud's contribution is docked of its conclusion, I shall cite it from *Briefe:* Freud to Heller, November 1, 1906.

into a didactic performance, he observed that he was "accustomed to take notice of small signs."[5]

The small sign that Freud found most striking in Heller's questionnaire was the adjective "good." He read it to mean that he was to stay away from "the ten most magnificent works" of world literature, those splendid monuments "Homer, the tragedies of Sophocles, Goethe's *Faust*, Shakespeare's *Hamlet, Macbeth,* etc."[6] Nor, he added, had Heller asked for "the 'ten most significant books,' " which would have elicited the writings of Copernicus, Darwin's *Descent of Man,* and other scientific classics. Nor, Freud continued his questioning of the questionnaire, had Heller asked for "favorite books," among which Freud would "not have forgotten to mention Milton's *Paradise Lost* and Heine's *Lazarus.*"[7] The vast repertory of books Freud swallowed in a lifetime of reading becomes clear from the books he would *not* list for Heller even more than from the ones he did.

That commonplace oral epithet "voracious reader" fits Freud to perfection. Citations and quotations in his published writings and his private correspondence attest to an unquenchable literary appetite: poets, novelists, playwrights, essayists, humorists, and on occasion even historians appear under his pen more frequently than psychologists. He can call with equal ease on DaPonte's libretti for Mozart's operas and Burckhardt's history of Greek civilization, on poets like Rückert, playwrights like Grillparzer, and novelists like Fontane. Goethe and Shakespeare are everywhere, at all times. Now, as Freud rehearsed his consumption of reading matter before composing his reply to Heller, he visibly weighed the works of these favorite authors. But Heller's wording seemed to exclude those books of which Freud stood most in awe, from which he had learned most, or which he loved best.

Instead, what the adjective "good" released in Freud was something rather unbuttoned. It reminded him of titles to which he stood,

5. *Briefe,* 267. Interestingly enough, several of the other respondents performed similar analyses, explicitly staying away from the obvious classics and from those masterpieces that had influenced them most deeply. (See the contributions by Marie von Ebner-Eschenbach and Auguste Forel. *Vom Lesen und von guten Büchern,* 116.)

6. *Briefe,* 267. In those days, of course, Freud still believed that Shakespeare had written Shakespeare.

7. Ibid. On *Paradise Lost,* see above, 68.

in his graphic analogy, "somewhat as one stands with 'good' friends, to whom one owes a portion of one's knowledge of life and one's world view." They were books "that one has enjoyed oneself and gladly commends to others" but that did not induce the "element of shy reverence, the sense of one's own smallness before their greatness." Finally, these subtle preliminaries and precautions out of the way, almost free-associating, Freud offered his list:

> Multatuli [Eduard Dowes Dekker], *Letters and Works*
> [Rudyard] Kipling, *Jungle Book*
> Anatole France, *Sur la pierre blanche*
> [Emile] Zola, *Fécondité*
> [Dmitri] Merezhkovsky, *Leonardo da Vinci*
> G[ottfried] Keller, *Leute von Seldwyla*
> C[onrad] F[erdinand] Meyer, *Huttens letzte Tage*
> [Thomas Babington] Macaulay, *Essays*
> [Theodor] Gomperz, *Griechische Denker*
> Mark Twain, *Sketches*

But Freud did not let this inventory speak for itself. Having enumerated his ten good books, those ten friends who did not intimidate him, he felt impelled to protect his selections with a few almost apologetic explanations. It was as though the whole process, perhaps his choices, had made him a little uneasy. "I do not know what you intend to do with this list. It appears quite peculiar to me; I really cannot let it go without comment." He had left out "works of purely poetical value," as though the request for "good" books had inhibited the recall of pure pleasure. Indeed, he told Heller that with one of his entries, Conrad Ferdinand Meyer's *Hutten,* he had felt obliged to "place its 'goodness' far above its beauty, 'edification' above aesthetic enjoyment."[8] This self-protective gloss was a sign that Freud's feeling for beauty had not been wholly dulled by years of concentrated scientific work.

In some obscure way, Heller had tapped hidden reservoirs in Freud's mind. This is no speculation; Freud said so himself: "With your request to name 'ten good books' for you, you have touched on something about which inevitably much could be said. Hence I close, not to become far more talkative even than this."[9] This is the Freud—

8. Ibid., 268.
9. Ibid.

half confessional, half reticent—we know from *The Interpretation of Dreams.* Musing on which books to include and which to exclude, he was hovering a little nervously on the edge of self-revelation, rather as he had done in interpreting the paradigmatic Irma dream he had dreamed in July 1895 and had subjected to an intense and lengthy, but deliberately incomplete, analysis in his dream book. He was sharing confidences but, pulling back from the abyss of intimate disclosures, selected them with some care. His list gives us Freud on holiday, the man very much himself, cigar in hand and, as it were, in his slippers, but with his dressing gown securely draped around him. It is this tantalizing, almost teasing, attitude which licenses the expectation that reading Freud through his reading may prove a promising experiment.

Together, Freud's ten good books add up to a most heterogeneous menu. They include two novels each loaded down by a thesis, a biography in fictional form, imaginary correspondence, a cycle of poems, expansive novellas, a collection of humorous sketches, inventive tales about savage animals and little less savage men, formal essays, and a whiggish, beautifully written history of Greek philosophy. The authors are Dutch, English, French, Russian, Swiss, Austrian, and American, the books in three different languages. To be sure, questionnaires such as Heller's exert a certain pressure on respondents to be as original, as unhackneyed in their choices, as possible. But since Freud, as we know from other evidence, was scarcely inclined to dramatize himself, at least consciously, we may take his catholicity as an index of his cultural range. Moreover, the very unpretentiousness of his choices virtually guarantees their authenticity. Freud reveled in the avalanche of diverse offerings that modern Western culture was pouring out year by year. We may safely assert that he never degenerated into what the Germans derisively call a *Fachidiot,* a narrow specialist reduced to idiocy by his professional preoccupations.

At the same time, we note that Freud's list also seems relatively conservative, in important respects rather conventional. Meyer's polished, formally perfect verse cycle about the last days and death of the German reformer Ulrich von Hutten and Keller's genial if pointed novella-length tales about a gallery of eccentric Swiss were likely candidates for any list of good books a cultivated German might compile. Leading spirits in what contemporaries called "poetic re-alism," Meyer and Keller escaped, yet in oblique ways portrayed, mundane realities, the first by placing his stories and poems in a remote and heroic past, the second by discovering general truths in his own life and the lives of his countrymen. It is significant that Freud was not the only participant in Heller's survey to find these two authors worth listing.[10] And Freud's omissions strengthen the impression his list gives of a safe set of favorites: although we know that he read controversial contemporary playwrights like Ibsen and Shaw, Wilde and Strindberg, he does not include them here. And avant-garde poets—like the French quartet Baudelaire, Mallarmé, Rimbaud, Verlaine—go unmentioned.

In fact, some of Freud's choices are not just exceedingly proper but highly debatable. Why not select, among Zola's works, one of his major novels—*L'Assommoir* or *Germinal,* or even *Nana*—from the Rougon-Macquart cycle rather than *Fécondité,* the least satis-factory, most didactic of his later fictions? After all, Freud's writings give ample evidence that he had traveled widely in Zola's vast output.[11] Kipling, too, seems at first glance an unadventurous choice: much read and much criticized in England, where his aggressive imperialist stance grated on civilized readers who preferred his less tendentious tales and poems, Kipling was an unfailing favorite on the Continent, and Freud simply followed the fashion. And what of Merezhkovsky's ambitious, oppressively written philosophical ro-mance of Leonardo da Vinci's life? Freud praised the book as a "great historical novel"[12] and drew on it heavily as he launched on his paper about Leonardo some three years later. His praise of Mer-

10. The Austrian poet and playwright J. J. David (an acquaintance of Freud who had been among the first to review *The Interpretation of Dreams* favorably) chose one of the tales from Keller's *Leute von Seldwyla* and a story by Conrad Ferdinand Meyer; Peter Rosegger, a prominent Austrian writer of humble peas-ant origins, picked Keller's *Leute von Seldwyla;* and Ludwig Thoma, a well-known humorist, listed "Master Gottfried Keller's works." *Vom Lesen und von guten Büchern,* 115, 124, 125.

11. In his published works alone, Freud refers to *Germinal, La terre, L'oeuvre, La joie de vivre,* and, with a casualness that bespeaks thoroughgoing familiarity, to "many of Zola's later works." "Der Dichter und das Phantasieren," *GW* VII, 221 / "Creative Writers and Day-Dreaming," *SE* IX, 151.

12. "Eine Kindheitserinnerung des Leonardo da Vinci" (1910), *GW* VIII, 139 / "Leonardo da Vinci and a Memory of His Childhood," *SE* XI, 73.

ezhkovsky's rhapsodic *Leonardo* seems unreflective, undiscriminating, almost philistine, for Merezhkovsky's very unconventionality was conventional for his age. Indeed, in the days of Heller's questionnaire, Merezhkovsky's reputation stood exceedingly high; Freud did not offend contemporary taste with his appreciation.[13]

Many of Freud's choices, then, remind one of the bourgeois Freud who thought philosophical investigations into ethical questions unnecessary, since it is perfectly obvious what is decent and what is not. They remind one, too, of the Freud who told his distinguished and influential American adherent James J. Putnam that he was interested in only one reform—a drastic loosening of restrictions on sexual conduct—and no other. We can hardly doubt it: if there was a bohemian streak in Freud, he resolutely suppressed it. He was and lived consistently as a good burgher, with his moral certainties, his commitment to family life, his cigars, his meticulously planned summer holidays.

And yet: if, as I once said long ago, if Freud was a good bourgeois, he was a bourgeois making explosives in his drawing room—or, better, his consulting room. It is, after all, no small matter to aim at subverting dominant respectable sexual mores. Once we study Freud's good books with some attention, we become aware that an undertone of rebelliousness, a kind of controlled radicalism, reverberates in his list for Hugo Heller.

I begin with Mark Twain's *Sketches,* an immensely popular collection of short early pieces which circulated in the United States and Europe for years. *Sketches* includes tall tales and humorous adventures, parodies and mock heroic dramas. Its most celebrated protagonist is the jumping frog of Calaveras County, but Mark Twain offers more than amusing vignettes about colorful American Westerners, something more weighty than slight anecdotes drawn from his experiences on the Mississippi River or his

---

13. Thus, among the respondents to Heller's questionnaire, several expressed their admiration for Merezhkovsky—Arthur Schnitzler tersely, by simply listing his *Tolstoi and Dostoevsky,* and Hugo von Hofmannsthal expansively, praising the same book: "It is infinitely more than its modest title proclaims. . . . It took a rare individual, at once Russian and European, to produce this book, an infinite tact, most happy flexibility, a strength of interest reaching to exaltation." *Vom Lesen und von guten Büchern,* 124, 112. Freud's tribute is cool beside this.

work as an editor. Slyly, and at times coarsely, Mark Twain defies authority and deflates respectability, cutting through politeness and cant and pompous pretense to less civilized pressures beneath. In his sketches good taste takes a holiday.

Evidently, Freud did not mind. Early in 1898—he was in the midst of hard labor on *The Interpretation of Dreams*—he allowed himself a rare luxury, attending a reading by "our old friend Mark Twain" in Vienna. It gave him, he reported to Wilhelm Fliess, "great pleasure,"[14] memorable enough to reappear more than thirty years later when he recalled that public reading and retold one of the amusing anecdotes he had heard on that occasion.[15] But Mark Twain's humor was not for the tender-minded. Consider "Riley—Newspaper Correspondent," one of the anecdotes in *Sketches.* Its hero, the author tells us with obvious relish, was equipped with "a ready wit." Riley listens, with a grave face, to the harrowing tale of a black woman burned to death, a tale delivered amid sobs by Riley's and the narrator's landlady. " "Ah, to think of it, only to think of it!—the poor old faithful creature. For she was *so* faithful. Would you believe it, she had been a servant in the self-same house and that self-same family for twenty-seven years come Christmas, and never a cross word and never a lick! And, oh, to think she should meet such a death at last!—a-sitting over the red hot stove at three o'clock in the morning and went to sleep and fell on it and was actually *roasted!* Not just frizzled up a bit, but literally roasted to a crisp! Poor faithful creature, how she *was* cooked! I am but a poor woman, but even if I have to scrimp to do it, I will put up a tombstone over that lone sufferer's grave—and Mr. Riley if you would have the goodness to think up a little epitaph to put on it which would sort of describe the awful way in which she met her—'

" 'Put it "*Well done,* good and faithful servant," said Riley, and never smiled.' "[16] Just in case the reader missed that appalling punch line, for whose sake Mark Twain had certainly invented the whole episode in the first place, he italicized "Well done." Mark Twain must have thought it all very funny, and there is no reason to assume that Freud failed to think it very funny too. There may be a hint in this little tale of Mark Twain's critical stance toward smug and

14. Freud to Fliess, February 9, 1898. *Freud-Fliess,* 327 (299).
15. See *Civilization and Its Discontents, SE* XXI, 126n.
16. Mark Twain, *Sketches* (1879), 175–76.

superior pieties, but the callousness of the ending drowns out all satirical intent.[17]

One more instance: recounting his falling out with a new coroner in some unspecified Western settlement, Mark Twain describes a trick he played on his enemy to make him look ridiculous and, given the paucity of entertainment in the wild and lonely West, keep him looking ridiculous in his neighborhood for years. To make his aggressive tale even more pointed, Mark Twain resolutely refuses to identify his victim by name and concludes rather complacently with a candid confession of the death wishes he harbored all along: "I hated ——— in those days, and these things pacified and pleased me. I could not have gotten more real comfort out of him without killing him."[18] An anecdote neither edifying nor elevating, but in its own crude way a blow in behalf of liberated impulse.

This search for emotional elbowroom supplies energy to all of Mark Twain's humor. Compiling imaginary answers to imaginary letters to the editor, he assails one purse-lipped writer who signs himself "MORAL STATISTICIAN" for being a hater of pleasure: "I don't want any of your statistics; I took your whole batch and lit my pipe with it. I hate your kind of people. You are always ciphering out how much a man's health is injured, and how much his intellect is impaired, and how many pitiful dollars and cents he wastes in the course of ninety-two years' indulgence in the fatal practice of smoking; and in the equally fatal practice of drinking coffee; and in playing billiards occasionally; and in taking a glass of wine at dinner, etc., etc., etc."

The whole reply turns into an ardent defense of hearty indulgence and of what Mark Twain calls "redeeming petty vices." Working himself into a fine state of outrage, he drowns out MORAL STATISTICIAN with a hymn to pleasure: "You never try to find out how much solid comfort, relaxation, and enjoyment a man derives from smoking in the course of a lifetime (which is worth ten times the money he would save by letting it alone), nor the appalling aggregate of happiness lost in a lifetime by your kind of people by *not* smoking."[19] Freud did not play billiards, but as everyone knows, he did smoke; one of the most defiant letters he ever wrote, I think, was a stubborn

17. On the harshness of the humor in those days, see below, 140–41.
18. Mark Twain, "The Petrified Man," *Sketches,* 275.
19. "Answers to Correspondents," ibid., 307–09.

note to his friend Fliess, after all an ear and nose specialist, who had forbidden Freud his beloved cigars: "I am not observing your ban on smoking; do you think it's such a glorious fate to live many long years in misery?"[20] Mark Twain's apparently logical but utterly irresponsible plea for the redeeming petty vice of smoking must have given Freud all the better grounds for taking pleasure in his favorite American humorist.

Kipling's *Jungle Books* fit into this pattern of barely suppressed insubordination against the respectable bourgeois world of which Freud was so visible—and so uneasy—a citizen. Freud valued Kipling highly: in the early nineties he recommended Kipling's tale "Phantom Rickshaw" and his novel *The Light That Failed* to Fliess and his wife, Ida.[21] His affection for the *Jungle Books* was quite as keen. The tales of Mowgli and his friends are, in their boyish simplicity, a critique of artificial culture somewhat in the tradition of Rousseau. This was a theme of considerable interest to Freud at all times, but quite conspicuously around the time he responded to Hugo Heller's invitation. In 1908, not long after drafting that reply, Freud published an important paper, pregnant with the germs of such later syntheses as *Civilization and Its Discontents,* on what he called, with marked reserve, " 'Civilized' Sexual Morality."

To be sure, the cultural criticism implicit in Kipling's *Jungle Books* should not be pressed too hard, though in his early years, before his fervent advocacy of war and empire made him the darling of the British establishment, Kipling was read as a modernist audibly discontented with the self-satisfied civilization around him. Writing of Mowgli's adventures with bears and snakes and monkeys, Kipling celebrated innocence, or what I might call honest guile. The only truly praiseworthy human being in the *Jungle Books* is Mowgli himself. Among the animals with which he lives, it is precisely the monkeys, closest to mankind of all the animal estate, that are most despicable: greedy, chattering, inconsequent, egotistical, foolish. The virtues that Mowgli's animal family, the wolves, and his teachers and friends, Beghera the panther, Baloo the bear, and Kaa the python, preach and truly embody—courage, fidelity, cunning in the service of survival—are military and aristocratic virtues. So are their

20. Freud to Fliess, November 27, 1893. *Freud-Fliess,* 54 (61).
21. See Freud to Fliess, October 21, 1892. ibid., 22 (34)

pleasures: the intoxication of revenge, the amusement an enemy's distress provides.

When Mowgli goes among men for a time, "he had to wear a cloth round him, which annoyed him horribly."[22] Kipling's lesson seems plain, almost obtrusive: men cover up their libido and their aggressiveness behind bland and mendacious surfaces; animals are superior beings, for they acknowledge their drives. They can hate and hate well, but, as Kipling explicitly and emphatically observes, they can love no less. The stories he wove around Mowgli, then, are intended to lift the reader above the humdrum, mediocre, middle-class world into the realm of candor, of free experience, of heroism.

An admiration for heroism—that, too, is what Merezhkovsky celebrates in his more-than-human protagonist, Leonardo da Vinci—is a very boyish ideal, one that never quite left Freud. It is on record that he envied Schliemann because in discovering Troy Schliemann had, as a grown man, realized a boy's dream of glory.[23] And glory is what Freud, in his leisured moments, dreamed on—dreamed on and realized (as he once said, not without a touch of complacency) by agitating the sleep of mankind.

But Freud's choice of Merezhkovsky's *Leonardo da Vinci* seems eccentric at best. Dmitri Merezhkovsky, born nine years after Freud, secured in his time a Europe-wide reputation as a perceptive literary critic, an imaginative poet and novelist, and, in his later work, a metaphysical-religious prophet. In his messianic writings, clothed in fictional garb, he preached a grandiose syncretic system in which the flesh and the spirit, science and religion, paganism and Christianity, would be reconciled. His best-known book (before his astonishing success, *Leonardo*) was a critical confrontation, *Tolstoi and Dostoevsky,* in which, as Renato Poggioli has put it, "the parallel criticism of their personalities, works, and beliefs unfolds into the metaphysical duel of two opposite archetypes."[24]

It is tempting to speculate that this kind of pugilistic dualism may have obscurely appealed to Freud by arousing presentiments of his later structural system in which libido and aggression, life and death,

22. Kipling, *The Jungle Books* (1894–1895; Signet Classics ed., 1961), 59.
23. See Freud to Fliess, May 28, 1899. *Freud-Fliess,* 387 (353).
24. Poggioli, *The Poets of Russia, 1890–1930* (1960), 72.

wrestle each other in solemn combat. Otherwise, how is one to explain Freud's evident tolerance for Merezhkovsky's muddy and pretentious metaphysics, precisely the kind of profound-sounding verbal game for which Freud had nothing but contempt? He never harbored the slightest doubt that religion and science must forever remain mortal enemies and that all efforts at making peace between them are bound to be futile.[25] What is more, one might have expected that Freud, with his curiosity about Leonardo, might turn to some more scholarly biographies of his favorite Renaissance man. It can only be that precisely this admiration blinded Freud's cool judgment. In his essay on a childhood memory of Leonardo, Freud would adopt Jacob Burckhardt's awed, almost worshipful appraisal of that enigmatic, uncannily versatile, and accomplished Renaissance man, painter, engineer, anatomist, architect—that "universal genius whose outlines one can only surmise, never fathom."[26] Merezhkovsky's book was, for Freud, precisely a "good" book, one vivid enough to foster, and not too sober to inhibit, the weaving of boyish fantasies around its hero.

Heroism, too, though of a rather different order, is the informing mood of Zola's *Fécondité:* the fertile family that act as its protagonists are powerfully—it is more precise to say, potently—committed to erotic love for the sake of procreation. Zola enlists sexual intercourse as the supreme weapon in the struggle of modern humanity for a

25. It is worth recalling that another enlightened spirit of Freud's time, Anton Chekhov, though he respected Merezhkovsky as a person and a critic, called him "supersmug" and "a resolute believer, a proselytizing believer." Chekhov to Victor Mirolyubov, December 17, 1901; Chekhov to Sergei Diaghilev, July 12, 1903. *Letters of Anton Chekhov,* tr. Michael Henry Heim in collaboration with Simon Karlinsky, ed. Simon Karlinsky (1973), 414, 453.

26. "Leonardo da Vinci," *GW* VIII, 128, 128n / "Leonardo da Vinci," *SE* XI, 63, 63n. As the editors of the Standard Edition rightly observe (*SE* XI, 61), Merezhkovsky's historical romance about Leonardo (1900), of which Freud owned the German version, *Leonardo da Vinci. Ein biographischer Roman aus der Wende des 15. Jahrhunderts,* tr. Carl von Gütschow (1903), was the source of much that Freud would put into his long paper on Leonardo. This included the fateful story of Leonardo's childhood memory (or fantasy) about the bird attacking him in his cradle, and the even more fateful mistranslation of Leonardo's "nibio" (kite) into "Geier" (vulture), on which Freud would build some wholly untenable constructions. (See his copy, p. 382, Freud Museum, London, which shows Freud marking this passage with an emphatic double line.)

larger and healthier population. More outspoken than many of his contemporaries but still observing most reigning literary taboos, he lyrically circumscribes but never graphically depicts the grand human act of making children. The principal pair, Mathieu and Marianne—the Evangelist and the emblematic embodiment of France—make love with "superb, divine improvidence. In their mutual possession, all low calculations foundered. All that remained was victorious love, with confidence in the life it creates without reckoning. If, in each other's arms, they had restrained the act, they would not have loved one another any more with all their being." Indeed, "giving themselves to the other wholly, with no restraint of heart or flesh, it was the task of life to do its work, if it judged that proper."[27] Thus the sexual drive compels Zola's lovers into the happy service of the human future.

Freud thought well of Zola, both for his exemplary courage in defending Captain Dreyfus in the exasperated political climate of late nineteenth-century France and for his sensitive understanding of human nature. He called Zola a connoisseur of men, a *Menschenkenner,* a desirable trait that Freud, the professional student of the human animal, feared he lacked.[28] Yet Freud could not have relished Zola's anti-Malthusian message in *Fécondité.* Even if he would have agreed that the practice of contraception is a generally unpleasant, neurosis-producing business, he would have dissented from Zola's forcefully offered argument that lovemaking which does not aim at procreation is an escape from sacred duty, a form of debauchery.[29]

With all its uncompromising, almost naive glorification of fertile love, *Fécondité* is what F. W. J. Hemmings, one of Zola's recent biographers, has called, rather too blithely, symptomatic of its author's "serene paganism."[30] The idea of sexual intercourse that creates a child with each exercise—that capacity for instant

27. Zola, *Fécondité* (1899; ed. 1957), 104.
28. For Freud on Zola's courage, see Freud to Fliess, February 9, 1898. *Freud-Fliess,* 326 (299). On Zola's understanding of humans, see *Drei Abhandlungen zur Sexualtheorie, GW* V, 141n / *Three Essays on Sexuality, SE* VII, 239n.
29. "All love that does not have the child as its aim is fundamentally just debauchery," Zola wrote in an article in *Figaro* on May 23, 1896. Quoted in F. W. J. Hemmings, *Emile Zola* (1953; 2nd ed., 1966), 291.
30. Hemmings, *Zola,* 257.

impregnation Greek myths lend the gods and their consorts—is bound to awaken wishful fantasies of amorous powers in male readers, whether, as good Christians, they believe procreation to be the only excuse for indulging one's sensual appetites or whether, as good pagans, they daydream about having extraordinary potency. Freud, of course, was a thoroughgoing pagan, though scarcely a serene one, and the mood, if not the message, of *Fécondité* must have appealed to him: sexual activity as heroism. He found the novel interesting enough to make it the subject of a lecture to his brethren at the Viennese lodge of B'nai B'rith he had joined in 1897.[31]

Zola's *Fécondité* makes a nonliterary point in scarcely literary guise. It was the first volume in what Zola planned to gather under the pointed collective title *Les quatre Evangiles.* The fundamental animus of Zola's four gospels was to be explicitly anti-Christian, even if some—though by no means all—of his ideas could be reconciled with the Christian social thought of the age. The quartet of novels was designed to preach large families; a just economic system reorganized along utopian Fourierist lines; a more satisfactory educational scheme that would be anticlerical, democratic, and difficult; and general disarmament to prevent all wars in the future. Together, *Les quatre Evangiles* were to stand as an exhaustive and solemn

31. See Freud to Fliess, April 24, 1900: "Yesterday I gave a lecture in my society on Zola's *Fécondité.* I always prepare myself poorly, actually only in the hour before—in the way one writes a German composition in school." *Freud-Fliess,* 450 (410). In an interesting brief treatment of the lecture, Dennis B. Klein argues that it was Zola's obsessive neurosis that "the book vividly clarified." *Jewish Origins of the Psychoanalytic Movement* (1981), 89–90. There is good evidence that Freud's interest in Zola's neurosis was more than casual. Discussing him with his colleagues and not concealing his admiration for him as a "great writer," he alluded to Zola as a "fanatic for truth" and an "obsessive neurotic" several times. (To mention only three such comments, see January 30, 1907; January 13 and April 7, 1909. *Protokolle* I, 95; II, 94, 183.) I am persuaded, however, that his fascination with Zola's *Fécondité,* which after all he listed as a "good" rather than just a "revealing" book, went beyond his clinical interest in Zola as a case history. Freud owned, and evidently found absorbing, the German version of Ernst Alfred Vizetelly's biographical study *Emil Zola. Sein Leben und Werk* (1904; tr. Heddi Möller-Bruck, 1905). He particularly noted passages commenting on Zola's pallor, nervousness, hypochondria, and fear of death. Yet Vizetelly concludes his biography with, and Freud took special interest in, a tribute to Zola's courage, a trait that Freud had also singled out. (See Freud's copy of Vizetelly, *Zola,* 48, 95–96, 115, 169, 362. Freud Museum, London).

secular parody of the Christian Word. *Fécondité* is, then, on whatever level one reads the book, a "philosophical" tale. What is interesting is that all this heavy baggage seems not to have disturbed Freud in the least.

He was just as indulgent with Zola's *Le Docteur Pascal,* the twentieth and concluding novel in his Rougon-Macquart cycle, which Freud had offered Heller as a possible substitute for *Fécondité.* Rounding out with rather incongruous cheerfulness a score of novels marked by somber tales of biological degeneracy, sexual lust, wanton adultery, unchecked greed, cruelty, and murder, *Le Docteur Pascal* expresses what Hemmings has called Zola's "optimistic pantheism." Its eponymous hero incorporates that strenuous doctrine to perfection: "Doctor Pascal had only one belief, the belief in life. Life was the unique divine manifestation. Life was God, the great motor, the soul of the universe."[32] This walking philosophy of existence pours all his capacity for love into affection for his niece, and the novel concludes, in a symbolic nudge that is a forecast of *Fécondité,* with the birth of a child. Thus the end of the Rougon-Macquart cycle throws a bridge to the opening of *Les quatre Evangiles.*

Zola's most uncritical readers have acknowledged that *Le Docteur Pascal* cuts the weakest figure in his stupendous collective portrait of France under the Second Empire. This raises yet another uncomfortable question about Freud's choices. Taking the opportunity to name not one novel of Zola's but two, he hit upon Zola's most conspicuous literary failures. And even as tendentious fictions, except in their anticlericalism, they do not speak for Freud's most fundamental convictions. Freud did not believe in a god, not even in a metaphorical one—except, perhaps, for his god *logos.* Nor did he really believe in a soul. His psychology, even at its most allusive, pointed in a very different direction.

Nor, for that matter, was Freud an optimist, certainly not, like Zola, a forced one. On the contrary, one might wonder why Freud did not diagnose Zola's "optimistic pantheism" as a defense against weariness and depression. Freud was after all convinced that the human animal is by its very nature delivered over to unresolvable conflicts. The basic institutions of the mind that he would come to call, after the First World War, the id, the ego, and the superego

32. See Hemmings, *Zola,* 257.

can at best conclude temporary, largely unreliable cease-fires. His perception of human nature was far closer to Kipling's dangerous jungle than to the luxuriant garden of Zola's late novels.

It seems most likely, then, that Freud's choices among Zola's prolific output hint at certain needs and certain limitations on his aesthetic imagination. They suggest a measure of identification with strong erotic heroes and a sneaking preference for fictions that make one think, for *littérature engagée*. Even at leisure, even in the Austrian mountains or in Roman museums, Freud was rarely far from his consulting room. It was a tendency that his friend the psychoanalyst Hanns Sachs amply confirms: it was hard to lure him to the theater or the opera, but once there, he would particularly enjoy the psychological insights he could gather in an evening away from his desk. "Freud's interest in books," Sachs observes, "was a part of his interest in the living human mind."[33] This was the Freud who confessed, anonymously, that he could derive far less pleasure from the formal properties of poetry, novels, and sculptures than from their subject matter—from what he could understand and (he might have added) what could teach him about the mind.[34] He told Fliess in the early 1890s that he was subject to a single tyrant, psychology, and he never liberated himself, or wished to liberate himself, from his exigent master.

Freud's choice of two among the authors on his list, Conrad Ferdinand Meyer and Gottfried Keller, suggests that it would be naive to attribute his selection of good books to a single overriding motive. Overdetermination reigned over his choices as it often does in so much of life. Freud's inclusion of these two established Swiss poets and storytellers on his list—I have called them

33. Sachs, *Freud: Master and Friend,* 102. There is a tantalizing hint in Freud's copy of Vizetelly's *Zola* (see note 31 above) that his dramatic structural theory of the drives, with the forces of life confronting the forces of death, may have begun to work in him more than a decade before he announced it in 1920 in *Beyond the Pleasure Principle.* Vizetelly reports that in the 1880s, when a group of literary men, including Zola, would meet monthly—this was after the death of George Sand and Gustave Flaubert—their conversation always turned, somberly enough, on "*death and love.*" This is the *only* passage (p. 169) that Freud underlined in *Zola.*
34. See "The Moses of Michelangelo" (1914), *SE* XIII, 211.

safe—exhibits Freud's aesthetic utilitarianism and, at the same time, his capacity for relaxed enjoyment, however beleaguered he might be by his sterner purposes. Indeed, his pleasure in Keller's two related cycles of novellas, *Die Leute von Seldwyla,* must have been quite unproblematic. In *The Interpretation of Dreams,* he cites a dream from Keller's famous autobiographical novel, *Der grüne Heinrich,*[35] and in discussions with his colleagues, he occasionally alludes to Keller's writings. But Keller's novellas were good, fairly undemanding friends, even if their penetrating psychology clearly bore on Freud's favorite preoccupation with the human mind in action. Inventing his Swiss countrymen and their adventures in his far from implausible Seldwyla, Keller ranges from the genre of the fairy tale to grotesque caricature to sturdy realism, and even, in his most famous novella, *Romeo und Julia auf dem Dorfe,* to tragedy. He traces psychological development, satirizes pretentiousness and affectation, laments snobbery and selfishness, and affectionately chronicles decency and measured reasonableness, always with humorous geniality—providing what today many call a good read.

Conrad Ferdinand Meyer, on the other hand, touched Freud at many levels. In two of his letters to Jung, Freud could conjure up some of Meyer's "fine verses" from *Huttens letzte Tage* and quote them, somewhat inaccurately, from memory.[36] Writing to Heller, he had characterized the cycle about Hutten's last days as elevating rather than aesthetically pleasing, but he did take aesthetic pleasure in reading Meyer's works. One of Meyer's novellas, *Die Leiden eines Knabens,* was bedside reading for him.[37] If, as he confessed, he had underestimated Meyer in his earlier years, his friend Fliess pushed him toward a juster appreciation. "I am reading C. F. Meyer," he told Fliess in June 1898, "with great enjoyment."[38] He was in the midst of Meyer's *Gustav Adolfs Page,* but, with the enthusiasm of a

35. See *Interpretation of Dreams, SE* V, 407. His familiarity with Keller's novel becomes clear from a casual reference to it in a letter to Fliess of March 1, 1896. See *Freud-Fliess,* 182 (174).

36. Freud to Jung, September 19, 1907, January 25, 1909. *Freud-Jung,* 97, 224 (87, 202).

37. See *Interpretation of Dreams, SE* V, 470.

38. Freud to Fliess, June 9, 1898. *Freud-Fliess,* 345 (316). For his indebtedness to Fliess for opening his eyes to Meyer, see Freud to Fliess, March 15, 1898. Ibid., 331.

convert, he was working his way through a collection of Meyer's novellas; the following month he praised *Die Hochzeit des Mönches* to Fliess as the "finest" of them all.[39] As if to offer tangible thanks to Fliess for providing this new pleasure, Freud sent him a brief psychoanalytic interpretation of Meyer's *Die Richterin*.[40]

This two-page tour de force, the first Freudian analysis of a literary work,[41] was a characteristic exploit. It was all the more characteristic for Freud in those heroic days, when he was calling on Sophocles and Shakespeare to help him visualize and explicate universal psychological conflicts. And his choice of a story by Conrad Ferdinand Meyer was appropriate because—it is at this point that overdetermination enters—Freud recognized in him a subtle psychologist. Depressive, suicidal, neurotically attached to his mother and his sister, Meyer was given to long spells of self-imposed isolation. His breakthrough to fame came in 1870, "the critical year," when, inspired by the "world-historical" spectacle of the Franco-Prussian War, he abandoned his French leanings. "Inwardly compelled," he became a German poet and wrote *Huttens letzte Tage*.[42]

It was not Meyer's patriotism, though, that attracted Freud but Meyer's awareness, almost celebration, of conflict. The much-quoted epigraph to *Huttens letzte Tage,* which Meyer borrowed from one of the poems in this cycle—"I am no cleverly contrived book / I am a man with all his contradictions—Ich bin kein ausgeklügelt Buch / Ich bin ein Mensch mit seinem Widerspruch"—expressed precisely the attitude toward human nature that Freud found most congenial.[43] Meyer's characters are obsessed, torn, saintly sinners and doomed saints, tormented by elemental passions. *Die Richterin,* the novella that Freud privately analyzed for Fliess, is an intricate, melodramatic

---

39. Freud to Fliess, July 7, 1898. Ibid., 349 (320).

40. See Freud to Fliess, June 20, 1898. Ibid., 347–48 (317–18).

41. Unless one awards this distinction to the couple of sentences with which Freud offers a psychoanalytic reading of Meyer's *Gustav Adolfs Page* in his preceding letter to Fliess of June 9, 1899. See *Freud-Fliess,* 345 (316).

42. See Meyer, "Autobiographische Aufzeichnungen" (1885), *Werke,* ed. Hans Zeller and Alfred Zäch, 15 vols. (1958–1985), XV, 134.

43. Freud was attached to this couplet enough to quote from it in a letter to Fliess on February 19, 1899 (see *Freud-Fliess,* 379 [346]) and in full in his case history of Little Hans ("Analyse der Phobie eines fünfjährigen Knaben" [1909], *GW* VII, 347n / "Analysis of a Phobia in a Five-Year-Old Boy," *SE* X, 113n).

story of deception, murder, and vindicated innocence in the time of
Charlemagne. Through a series of complicated events in their early
years, a young brother and sister meet only as adults. Palma, the
sister, has long idolized her unknown brother, but her love for him,
open and warm, is in its way pure; in contrast, Wulfrin's love for
his sister, as he comes to recognize with mounting horror, ripens
into an incestuous attachment. Yet in the end all is well: the presumed mother of the pair, a murderess who dies in a great public
scene, reveals that in fact Palma and Wulfrin are not siblings at all.
Nothing stands in the way of their being united.

It is easy to see why Freud should find this tale a classic account
of a neurotic family romance in action, a psychological stratagem
which, he suggested, serves one's need for grandeur and is a defense
against incest. In his novella, Freud told Fliess, Meyer had managed
to capture fantasies of punishment for the mother and rebellion
against the father and memories of childhood sexual play. Thus *Die
Richterin* is "identical in every feature with one of the novels of
revenge and exoneration" that Freud's hysterical male patients
wove around their mothers. In an ambiguous comment, Freud hints
that the erotic complications Meyer has transfigured into literature
had been taken from life—his own: "No doubt it is a matter of a
poetic defense against the memory of a love affair with the sister."[44]
Later, addressing his fellow members of the Wednesday Psychological Society, Freud, speaking of that very novella, grew quite
explicit on this delicate point: "Love for a sibling," he suggested,
"played a significant role in Meyer's life and was the principal cause
of his unhappy marriage; many of his finest love poems were addressed to his sister."[45] What made Conrad Ferdinand Meyer

44. Freud to Fliess, June 20, 1898. *Freud-Fliess*, 347–48 (317–18).
45. Meeting of October 24, 1906. *Protokolle* I, 19–20. Meyer had a curious career
as an obviously fascinating subject of psychopathography. Isidor Sadger, an early
though rather unpopular member of Freud's Wednesday Psychological Society,
gave a paper on Meyer in which he stressed Meyer's love for his mother and
other pathological elements. This aroused a storm of criticism among the other
members (see meeting of December 4, 1907. Ibid., 239–43), but Sadger nevertheless published his paper. When Karl Abraham, in a paper before the Society
for Psychiatry and Nervous Illnesses in Berlin, followed Sadger and mentioned
Meyer's love for his mother, a number of his listeners vigorously protested. One
of them patriotically objected that "German ideals are at stake." Abraham to
Freud, November 10, 1908. *Freud-Abraham*, 65 (55–56).

irresistible to Freud was not merely that he made poetry of man with all his contradictions but that he himself embodied these contradictions so poignantly.

Far more than Freud's two favorite Swiss writers, Anatole France and Multatuli throw a sharp light on the political ingredient in Freud's literary tastes. To be sure, both were little less safe than Gottfried Keller and Conrad Ferdinand Meyer. Traditional for all their experimentation, they played with their fictions in ways that nineteenth-century writers had been doing since E. T. A. Hoffmann, in ways that the reading public could appreciate without discomfort. They employed mystifying leaps in time, unreliable narrators, imaginary editors claiming to have happened upon the collection of letters they are now presenting to the public. In the years when Freud first read them, the reputations of Anatole France and Multatuli had risen to their zenith. It was the *kind* of reputation they enjoyed that made Freud's interest in them political: France was widely hailed as a modern Voltaire, while informed readers thought Multatuli the worthy rival of Nietzsche.

That Freud singled out *Sur la pierre blanche* from Anatole France's copious production is particularly piquant. Although an impassioned, articulate, and indefatigable Dreyfusard and fearless social critic, France made his points by amusing rather than straining his readers. The chief business of his life, he once said, was doing up dynamite in bonbon wrappers.[46] There was relatively little dynamite in *Sur la pierre blanche,* but Freud's choice reflects many of his most cherished concerns. He appreciated, and liked to quote, Anatole France as an ironist. More: Hanns Sachs reports that "among the modern authors of his choice—they are not modern any longer, but they stand up well—Anatole France was the one whom he discussed most often with me." Freud, it seems, was particularly struck with France's *La Révolte des anges,* which depicts civilization as a struggle between the divinity and the rebellious angels and on which he lectured to his B'nai B'rith lodge. Here was another foretaste, rather like Merezhkovsky's dualism, of that scheme Freud developed later

46. Cited in Edmund Wilson, "In Memory of Octave Mirbaud" (1949), *Classics and Commercials: A Literary Chronicle of the Forties* (1950), 473.

in which Eros confronts Thanatos.[47] When on May 6, 1926, Freud's closest associates gave him a set of Anatole France's complete works for his seventieth birthday, they knew what they were doing.[48]

France took the epigraph for *Sur la pierre blanche* from the dialogue "Philopatris," once attributed to the ancient satirist Lucian. It announces the text to come as a dream, a long dream in a short night. The rather undramatic dramatic characters populating the novel are a few cultivated French friends residing in Rome, endlessly talking. Prominent among their topics of conversation is archaeology, one of Freud's favorite metaphors and preoccupations—the archaeological fieldwork that Freud did was fieldwork in his mind and in the minds of his analysands. And Anatole France's French Romans dream about the ancient city and about the future. Rome, as Freud had revealed in his *Interpretation of Dreams,* had long been his dream city, one he did not dare visit until 1901, after he had analyzed his neurotic inhibitions against setting foot in it. Reading about thoughtful dreamers in Rome must have revived memories of his struggle, happily overcome at last.

All this should have made Anatole France's dream novel congenial to him. France's explicit philo-Semitism—or, at least, anti–anti-Semitism—made it more congenial still: "The antisemites," one character in *Sur la pierre blanche* declares, speaking for the author, "kindle the rage of Christian peoples against the Jewish race, and there is no Jewish race."[49] In those days, Freud was still using the popular nineteenth-century term *race* quite loosely, and thought that there was in fact some such thing as a Jewish race. But what mattered in Anatole France's well-meaning exclamation was its defiance of those fellow Frenchmen who had vilified the Jew Captain Dreyfus, that loyal French officer, and had resisted efforts at rehabilitating him in the teeth of overwhelming evidence in his favor.

47. See Sachs, *Freud: Master and Friend,* 103. In 1947 Edmund Wilson noted, with some disapproval, that Anatole France's "critical point of view" had become "unfashionable." It had been unfashionable for some time. "The Sanctity of Baudelaire," *Classics and Commercials,* 420.
48. *Jones* III, 125. "Of French authors," Jones records, "Freud chiefly admired Anatole France, his favorite of all, Flaubert for his imaginative insight, and Emile Zola for his realism." Ibid., 427.
49. France, *Sur la pierre blanche* (1904; ed. 1950), 25.

In the course of recounting involved dreams, and dreams within dreams, *Sur la pierre blanche* broods on a better future, one in which—as in the novel about a world without war that Zola projected but never wrote—armed conflict among nations has been abolished. There is, in France's utopia, a United States of Europe, and the old-fashioned family is no more. Women enjoy full equality with men. "We owe nothing to anybody," one of the emancipated feminists proclaims. "Formerly, a man would persuade a woman that she belonged to him. We are less simple-minded. We believe that a human being belongs to himself alone. We give ourselves when we please and to whom we please." What is more, "we feel no shame in yielding to desire. We are no hypocrites."[50]

This egalitarian brave new world has its moments of timidity. One way, to be sure, in which this imagined society regulates "the sex question" is by the refusal, at places of employment, to inquire after an applicant's gender. Still, "maternal love is a most powerful instinct in woman." Hence "there are among us many good companions and many good mothers. But there is a very large, steadily growing number of women who make do without men." This is so because the human animal has finally been recognized to be bisexual. There are indeed two sexes, as one character puts it, but it is a mistake to conclude from this "that a woman is absolutely a woman and a man absolutely a man."[51]

Even though Freud's assent to woman's full emancipation was severely limited, his interest was bound to be piqued by France's expansive vision of a bright future prudently hedged round. In a manner that Freud could appreciate, France placed the equality between men and women, and the recognition of human bisexuality, within the context of ineradicable differences and the recognition that many, if not all, women prefer a private, maternal role in life to an active, public one.[52] But above all, it was France's critique of hypocrisy that made him a welcome volunteer in Freud's army of candor. After all, Freud himself, as he once said, liked to call a cat a cat—even though he issued this little manifesto in behalf of frankness in French. Yet, as we have seen, Freud regarded himself as a

50. Ibid., 299–300.
51. Ibid., 301–2.
52. For a detailed exploration of the difficult topic of Freud's view of woman, see *Freud,* 501–22.

reformer precisely in the issue of sexual freedom. Anatole France's genial progressive compromises must have impressed Freud in their agreeable mixture of radicalism and good sense, especially as proffered in France's fluent, colloquial prose tinged with Voltairean skepticism. What made *Sur la pierre blanche* a "good book" in Freud's eyes, then, was that it played with and stimulated ideas about the relations of the sexes to each other and to society.

It is intriguing to know that Anatole France, that modern Voltaire, passed on this approving epithet to Multatuli: to France, Multatuli was the Voltaire of Holland.[53] This was a compliment that Multatuli did not reject. His appeal to Freud was one of shared experiences and common convictions, for all of Multatuli's self-pitying pseudonym, meaning "I have borne much." Born Eduard Dowes Dekker in Amsterdam in 1820, Multatuli made his career in the Dutch colonial service. But humane, eccentric, and not afraid of being insubordinate, he uncovered and publicly pilloried an appalling pattern of systematic exploitation to which the natives were subjected by his countrymen in the Dutch Indies. His tendentious novel of 1860, *Max Havelaar,* which exposed Dutch misrule in the colonies, made him famous, or, rather, notorious, overnight. The penalty for his inopportune frankness was severe: his career was ruined, and he died in 1887 in half-voluntary German exile. Here was a prophet whom his country had failed to honor, a man of courage with whom Freud could readily empathize.

Like Anatole France—and like Freud—Multatuli was an outspoken partisan of frankness. The supreme need to tell the truth is a pervasive theme in *Max Havelaar* and no less in his once-popular collections of imaginary letters, such as those Freud listed for Heller.[54] In these "letters," Multatuli writes as an informal moralist who employs aphorisms and anecdotes to mount his lifelong attack on hypocrisy, whether fostered by church, state, or family. The educator, he insists, is the nemesis of prejudices and of lies. One of his vignettes

53. See Peter Brückner, "Sigmund Freuds Privatlektüre, II," *Psyche* XVI (1962–1963), 731.

54. Freud owned not only Multatuli's *Briefe* and his novel *Max Havelaar* but also six other works by him. Since all of these are in editions dated 1900 and after, it is reasonable to conjecture that Multatuli was a recent enthusiasm for Freud, perhaps like Conrad Ferdinand Meyer. Information from J. K. Davies, personal communication, March 1, 1989.

sums up his method and his convictions: "O Father, tell me, why does the sun not fall? The father was ashamed because he did not know why the sun does not fall, and he punished his child because he was ashamed. The child feared the wrath of its father and never asked again why the sun does not fall, nor about other things it wanted to know. This child never grew up to be a man, although it lived for six thousand years."[55] This fanciful account of why and how adults foster repression in children is exemplary for Multatuli's way with psychology and pedagogy. No wonder that in his paper on the sexual enlightenment of children Freud quoted an extended passage from Multatuli to support his argument, a passage in which Multatuli argues for candor with small children about significant—which is to say, sexual—matters, lest the child's imagination, aroused and unsatisfied, be corrupted. No wonder that Freud called him in that paper "that great thinker and humanitarian Multatuli."[56]

I say "no wonder," and yet there is something to wonder about. Freud's commendation of Multatuli's educational ideals is perfectly in character. The god both men held up for admiration was the god of reason, *logos*. But Freud's evident sympathy with Multatuli's enthusiastic moralizing is something of a paradox, only deepened by the two works of discursive prose in his list of ten good books: Macaulay's *Essays* and Gomperz's *Greek Thinkers.* How can Freud regard a consistent and impassioned humanitarian as a truly great thinker? The Freud we believe we know is the stern, uncompromising stoic scowling at the photographer. He is the faithful reader of Heine, whose pathetic, late cycle of poems, *Lazarus,* Freud described to Heller as one of his favorite books.[57] He is the sardonic observer of the human animal who has exposed the principled pacifist as a reformed torturer of animals. He is the tough-minded realist who finds the Christian injunction to universal love not simply impractical but ridiculous. He is the pessimist who has freed himself from illusions, among which the belief in human goodness is only the most cherished—and the most illusory.

55. Brückner, "Sigmund Freuds Privatlektüre, II," 734.

56. "Zur sexuellen Aufklärung der Kinder (Offener Brief an Dr. M. Fürst)" (1907), *GW* VII, 20 / "The Sexual Enlightenment of Children (Open Letter to Dr. M. Fürst)," *SE* IX, 132.

57. *Lazarus* is a group of twenty short poems written by the bedridden, slowly dying Heine on his "mattress grave," lacerated by things left undone, love unrealized, unrelieved pain, and thoughts of death.

Nor is this sober perception we have of Freud a distortion: he lived his life despising most of his fellow humans and worked at rising above the general pitiful need for solace and soothing uplift. Would he not write late in the 1920s, after suffering bravely with his tormenting cancer for half a decade: "My courage droops to stand up before my fellow humans as a prophet, and I bow before their reproach that I do not know how to bring them consolation—for that is fundamentally what they all demand, the wildest revolutionaries no less passionately than the most conformist pious believers."[58] But while the portrait of Freud the grim master of reality is not inaccurate, it is not complete. Some stones are missing from our mosaic. Macaulay and Gomperz should supply them.

Macaulay is hard to place. While his relentless rhetoric and polished periods made his essays literary events and his *History of England* a best-seller, they grated on some of his more discriminating contemporaries. He was, at least in public, absolutely confident about his opinions and voluble in expressing them. Thomas Carlyle, no shrinking violet in the certainty department and no stranger to the secular sermon, said of him with a mixture of awe and irritation: "Macaulay is well for a while, but one wouldn't *live* under Niagara."[59] And Macaulay's programmatic cheerfulness, his compulsive need to sit in judgment on the past, his theatrical, primitive splitting of his cast of historical actors into heroes and villains, have compromised his work for posterity. Most readers have derided as naive and self-serving Macaulay's oft-reiterated opinion that his mid-nineteenth-century England was an infinitely better place than the England of two centuries earlier. Even his proverbial clarity has been accounted a vice: the world, his critics have never tired of saying, is too muddled and too desperate a place to warrant the categorical verdicts, the grand simplicities, that Macaulay permitted himself.

Yet, for all his obtrusive failings as a writer, Macaulay is a dazzling stylist in small doses, essay by essay or, even better, paragraph by

58. *Das Unbehagen in der Kultur* (1930), *GW* XIV, 506 / *Civilization and Its Discontents, SE* XXI, 145.

59. Extract from Carlyle's commonplace book, late 1830s. Sir T. Wemyss Reid, *The Life, Letters, and Friendships of Richard Monckton Milnes, First Lord Houghton,* 2 vols. (1890), II, 478. (See Peter Gay, *Style in History* [1974], 115.)

paragraph. Nor did his principled optimism make him aberrant in his time. Macaulay wrote in an age rich in hope; his view of long-range upward historical development had been anticipated, and domesticated, by Turgot and Condorcet in the eighteenth century and by Comte in Macaulay's lifetime. Closer to home, the English wit and novelist Thomas Love Peacock had a vision of reason tightening its hold on humanity: poetic expression and poetic beliefs, Peacock thought, were yielding to the beneficent reign of science and of fact. Macaulay, then, fitted into a tradition, a tradition that the scientists to whose views Freud was committed could only applaud and reinforce. Nor should it be forgotten—though it often is forgotten—that Macaulay qualified his hopes for humanity at decisive points. A few close readers have detected some becoming shadows of doubt, a measure of complexity, in his whiggish view of history, but only a few.[60] He was in fact persuaded that after ages of progress decay must set in. But in and for his time, his optimism was, he could argue with a good show of evidence, perfectly justified.

What is more, Macaulay was working to strengthen the positive forces he was celebrating; he did not just believe in progress, he served it. He was a willing and eloquent man of causes. He opposed entrenched superstition and Jewish legal disabilities. He was an indefatigable liberal reformer—a liberal but, since his faith in the multitude was qualified, not a democrat. All this suited Freud to the ground. In *Totem and Taboo* he committed himself to a Comtian scheme of progress, postulating an early animistic phase of human culture that had been superseded by a religious one, which, in turn, was giving way to an age of science.[61] And he was a self-described liberal, complete with disdain for the impulsiveness of the lower orders, a liberal (as he once told Arnold Zweig) of the old school.[62] Hence he could add Macaulay to that group of nineteenth-century English savants—Darwin, Huxley, Lyell—he vocally admired.

60. Freud was one of those readers, noting more than a touch of nostalgia in Macaulay. He shrewdly perceived Macaulay's *Lays of Ancient Rome* as idealizing, in criticism of his contemporaries, the "courage for self-sacrifice, the unity and the patriotism of their ancestors." *Der Mann Moses und die monotheistische Religion* (1939), *GW* XVI, 176n / *Moses and Monotheism, SE* XXIII, 71n.
61. See *Totem and Taboo* (1913), *SE* XIII, 90.
62. See Freud to Arnold Zweig, November 26, 1930. Sigmund Freud and Arnold Zweig, *Briefwechsel* (1968), 33 (21).

This fundamental congeniality with Freud's style of thought is as marked in Theodor Gomperz's *Greek Thinkers* as it is in Macaulay's *Essays.* In fact, in important respects, Freud's selection from Gomperz's work is the most telling of the ten good books Freud put on his list. Nowadays few classicists or philosophers go to the trouble of taking Gomperz's majestic four-volume history of Greek thought from the shelf.[63] His liberal interpretation of ancient ideas—Greek science, Greek medicine, Greek history-writing no less than Greek philosophy proper—has been shouldered aside by the cultural anthropologists' researches and the social historians' perspectives. Nor do his categorical judgments sit well with our disenchanted tentativeness: he was, in his way, the Macaulay of classical scholarship.

But in the Victorian years, Theodor Gomperz was honored at home and abroad and treated as the distinguished, erudite classical philologist and historian of ideas he was. Born in Brünn in 1832 to wealthy and cultivated Jewish parents, German in culture, he came under the spell of John Stuart Mill in 1853, a decisive encounter that governed his professional life from then on. As one student of Gomperz, Robert A. Kann, has put it: "Theodor Gomperz characterized the cosmological speculations of the early pre-Socratics as a dawning positivism, and viewed the later pre-Socratics and Sophists as representatives of a long-lived era of enlightenment."[64] Gomperz's emphatic secularism was the organizing principle of his history.

63. Some classicists right down to the 1930s and even into the 1950s, however, found Gomperz's scholarly work worth perusing and even arguing with. In 1928, Wilhelm Nestle, editing and revising the thirteenth edition of Eduard Zeller's classic outlines of Greek philosophy, thought well enough of Gomperz's *Griechische Denker*, 3 vols. (1893–1912), to give it room in the bibliography. (See Zeller, *Outlines of the History of Greek Philosophy* [13th ed., 1928; tr. L. R. Palmer, 1931], 317.) In his *Paideia*, Werner Jaeger respectfully took issue with certain views of Gomperz but called him "a distinguished modern historian of philosophy trained in the positivist school." Jaeger, *Paideia: The Ideals of Greek Culture*, 3 vols. (1934–1947; tr. Gilbert Highet, 1939–1944), II, 200. And Eric A. Havelock cites Gomperz appreciatively in *The Liberal Temper in Greek Politics* (1957), 408–09.

64. Kann, "Einleitung," in *Theodor Gomperz: Ein Gelehrtenleben im Bürgertum der Franz-Josefs-Zeit. Auswahl seiner Briefe und Aufzeichnungen, 1869–1912, erläutert und zu einer Darstellung seines Lebens verknüpft von Heinrich Gomperz*, revised and edited by Robert A. Kann (1974), 13.

Freud's appreciation of Gomperz, then, was grounded in their close intellectual affinity. It was also personal. As a young man, Freud recalled many years later, he had heard Gomperz lecture on dreams among the ancients, and in 1880 he had translated a volume of essays for the authoritative German edition of Mill that Gomperz was then compiling. Later Gomperz's wife, Elise, intelligent, labile, neurotic, enlisted herself among Freud's patients and, after that, used her considerable social prestige to help Freud secure the post of *ausserordentlicher Professor,* which he had long desired and which had long eluded him. What is more, their eldest son, Heinrich, himself on the way to becoming a respected historian of antique thought and a systematic philosopher, had some analytic treatment with Freud around 1900 and kept up with psychoanalytic developments.[65]

Freud, though, singled out Theodor Gomperz's *Greek Thinkers* not out of gratitude or as a friendly gesture but because he enjoyed reading it. Freud, as he never tired of saying, was no philosopher and no admirer of philosophers. But Gomperz's vigorous and lucid presentation of the emergence of reason's light from the dark night of universal superstition could only intrigue Freud as it gave him a rapid education in the style of critical thought of which he was a late self-conscious representative. Like a loyal son of the Enlightenment, Freud valued the ancients—some of the ancients—as intellectual precursors. It is not an accident, and it could only commend *Greek Thinkers* to Freud, that Gomperz should title a crucial section of the first volume, dealing with physicians, atomists, sophists, and historians, "The Age of Enlightenment."

A firm commitment to the thought of the eighteenth-century Enlightenment characterized all of Gomperz's historical writings. His esteem for John Stuart Mill was an integral part of that attitude. In 1912, on the occasion of Gomperz's eightieth birthday, his colleague the classicist Hans von Arnim cited three aspects of Mill's philosophy that Gomperz, though scrupulously independent and no one's blind disciple, had adopted and that made his synthetic history of Greek thought so attractive: "First, the rejection of all metaphysics and ontology, which is to say every effort at penetrating beyond the world of phenomena; second, in the moral-social sphere, utilitarianism"— in short, the serious attempt to derive practical ethical imperatives

65. Ibid., 15–20, 26; and see *Freud,* 136–38.

from purely human interests; and third, a strict determinism that "does not exempt the acts of the human will from the domain of sovereign causality."[66]

Anyone with the slightest grasp of Freud's style of thinking will recognize it in von Arnim's bald summary of Gomperz's debt to Mill. To begin with, while Freud did try to penetrate beyond surface phenomena by attending to the latent workings of mind hidden behind, and disclosed by, dreams, symptoms, verbal slips, and associations, the unconscious wishes, anxieties, and conflicts he uncovered were not metaphysical entities, not occult forces. They were, rather, elusive pieces of experience accessible to that technique of sounding the depths of the psyche that Freud had so laboriously developed. Moreover, by showing the human animal to be a wishing animal governed by an unstable compound of the pleasure principle and the reality principle, and by being skeptical about metaphysical and theological systems enjoining asceticism on man, Freud placed himself within the utilitarian ambience. No doubt, Jeremy Bentham's much-derided felicific calculus, that device for classifying and assessing quantities of pleasure and pain the better to secure the first and minimize the second, is far more rationalistic than Freud would have made it. Freud had too much wry respect for the tenacity of human irrationality to believe that calculation could overcome desire. But in its disarming way, Bentham's calculus foreshadows Freud's analysis of human behavior; it is a proposal designed to assist the pleasure principle by bringing the reality principle to bear on human experience. Finally, Gomperz's consistent determinism is the foundation on which Freud built his theory of mental structure and functioning.[67]

For Freud, then, to place Macaulay's essays and Gomperz's history of Greek thought on a list of companions he enjoyed was to signalize a meeting of minds. But this reached beyond a shared contempt for superstition, doubt of metaphysics, and commitment to the lessons of experience. It is worth stressing that the eighteenth-century philosophes wanted to do more than simply understand the world. To the extent that they thought action on the world practicable, they wanted to change it—or, to put it more precisely, they wanted to change the world through understanding it.

66. Kann, "Einleitung," 17–18.
67. See above, "Freud and Freedom," esp. 74–80.

The men of the Enlightenment were neither shallow optimists nor foolish rationalists. But they were men of goodwill and of good hope. At best, they led risky lives and could tolerate uncertainty, unresolved questions. Freud was in their mold: "Mediocre spirits," he once wrote Princess Marie Bonaparte, "demand of science the kind of certainty which it cannot give, a sort of religious satisfaction. Only the real, rare, true scientific minds can endure doubt, which is attached to all our knowledge."[68]

These bold words echo the accents of Diderot and Hume. Freud severely trimmed his budget of hope. In a late paper, "Analysis, Terminable and Interminable," he voiced grave reservations about the lasting curative effects of psychoanalytic treatment. And, as we know, his mature view of human nature was one of a continuing battle between the forces of life and the forces of death, with no guarantee that the party of life would eventually win out. The death drive, he told his Swiss friend the pastor and psychoanalyst Oskar Pfister, was not his "heart's desire"; it had simply become an "inescapable assumption on biological as on psychological grounds." Hence, he added, his own "pessimism appears to me as a result, the optimism of my adversaries as a presupposition."[69]

If, then, there was hope for the human animal at all, Freud sought it, as the Enlightenment had sought it, in scientific knowledge and in submission to reality. "No," he wrote in his celebrated closing paragraph of *The Future of an Illusion,* "our science is no illusion. But an illusion it would be to believe that we could get anywhere else what it cannot give us."[70] No irrational, infantile dreams of omnipotence here. But it seems that when Freud was reading for pleasure, as distinct from reading for information or edification, he allowed himself the luxury of fantasizing about a world less appalling than the world that the accident of birth in his time and in his place had compelled him to inhabit.

68. *Jones* II, 419.
69. Freud to Pfister, February 7, 1930. Freud Museum, London.
70. *Die Zukunft einer Illusion* (1927), *GW* XIV, 380 / *The Future of an Illusion,* *SE* XXI, 56.

II

. . . .
Entertainments

Introduction

In 1953, in a brilliant lecture entitled "Democracy and Anti-Intellectualism in America," Richard Hofstadter defined the intellectual as one who lives for ideas. But, he cautioned, the intellectual's piety before ideas "needs a counterpoise, something to prevent it from being exercised in an excessively rigid way; and this it has, in most intellectual temperaments, in the quality I would call playfulness."[1] This is a felicitous formulation. Piety without playfulness, we can see, invites dullness, pedantry, at worst fanaticism; playfulness without piety, for its part, invites flightiness, caprice, careless utopianism. The intellectual who lacks playfulness will never play host to an original idea; the intellectual who lacks piety will never do the necessary work to translate an intuition into a viable theory. Freud, in whom the qualities of piety and playfulness were happily combined, was rarely flighty and never dull. That is why I chose a title I borrowed from Goethe—"Serious Jests"—for my essay on Freud's jokes: to intimate that he made jokes while he was being serious and was serious about his joking.

Unlike Queen Victoria, Freud was amused—often. As I document in that essay, he found humor both an instrument of persuasion and a pleasure in itself. Yet with a few notable exceptions the scholarship piling up around him has been striking for its humorlessness. Sad to record, Freud the witty stylist has had no successor. To be sure, this unsmiling sobriety is perfectly understandable. The hard core of Freud's subject matter is, after all, forbidding in the extreme, so

1. Hofstadter, *Anti-Intellectualism in American Life* (1963), 30; the book grew from the essay of ten years earlier.

forbidding that much of it has been banished from awareness. It largely consists of the secrets we keep even from ourselves: conflicts of which we would be ashamed if we confronted them openly and selfish, lustful, murderous wishes, even against—especially against— loved ones. It is surely no accident that when Freud sought for instructive parallels in world literature to illustrate the mental conflicts he thought universal, he found them in tragedies.

Yet, for all the appalling news about human nature that Freud brought to the world, he did not succumb to solemnity. Discussing the phenomenon of blatant egotism—as exemplified in his own wishes—he resorts to the story of the loving husband telling his wife: "If one of us dies, I shall move to Paris." One significant piece of evidence that led Freud to speculate on the portentous repetition compulsion was a little entertainment that his infant grandson had invented for himself, the now famous "fort-da" game. Even in *Civilization and Its Discontents,* by all odds Freud's grimmest book, he found room for humor, or at least for sarcasm. Commenting on the way certain victims are selected as useful targets of aggression, he instanced the Soviet Union's campaign against the Russian bourgeoisie, designed to lend psychological support to the government's social experimentation. "One only asks oneself uneasily," he wondered dryly, "what the Soviets will do after they have exterminated their bourgeois." He was keenly aware that the disenchanted observer will see human life as a tragicomedy, presenting all too often the unlovely spectacle of unrelieved absurdity.

I wrote the four "entertainments" that follow in Freud's spirit. They are very different from one another; the rubric under which I have gathered them is a large umbrella indeed. Two of them, however diverting I hope they will prove, are perfectly serious in intent if not in execution. My analysis of Freud's jokes does more than provide me with opportunities for retelling some stories that Freud found funny; just like the four pieces in the first part of this book, this analysis, too, tries to reduce the blank spots on the map we now have of Freud's mind. And the principal amusement I have derived from raking up once again the hoary gossip about Freud's alleged affair with his sister-in-law Minna Bernays was the pleasure of hunting down elusive materials and trying to make sense of what I found. After all, there is nothing droll in an illicit love affair, either to the participants or the victims, particularly in a bourgeois culture that is determined to be censorious of such sport. But the issue permitted a less than portentous treatment because I recognized (unlike some malicious critics of Freud intent upon discrediting his ideas by discrediting his reputation) that the facts of Freud's life are irrelevant to the validity of his ideas. Freud's relations with his sister-in-law, whatever they were, certainly matter greatly to the biographer, for whom no intimate detail can be uninteresting or unimportant. But the Oedipus complex remains an essential human experience whether Sigmund Freud slept with Minna Bernays or not.

I should perhaps explain here why I did not use Freud's correspondence with his sister-in-law in my *Freud,* which I published with Norton in April 1988. While Anna Freud turned over a substantial cache of documents to the Manuscript Division of the Library of Congress in 1972, she could not bear to part with certain letters, above all those between herself and her father (which were, however, released in time for me to incorporate them in my biography) and those between Freud and his sister-in-law. These letters remained at 20 Maresfield Gardens, now the Freud Museum, Hampstead, London, until Harold Blum, executive director of the Freud Archives (which retains title and controls access to much Freud material), personally took charge of them. In due course, then, he transported them to be deposited in the Library of Congress. Once there, they were photocopied and scrutinized by two psychoanalysts to ink out patients' names and thus insure confidentiality. That task completed, the letters would be made available to the public. As I note below, in late 1987, when much of my *Freud* was already in galley proofs, I visited the Library of Congress once again and saw the bundle of Freud-Minna letters but was not permitted to read them. Hence I had to allow my biography to be printed without them. When, early in the fall of 1988, the correspondence was opened, I hastened to Washington to read them at last. The essay "The Dog That Did Not Bark in the Night" is the result.

All this is portentous enough. The two other "papers" are, however, wholly frivolous. That is why I have put quotation marks around the word "papers." And since one of them, my "review" of Freud's *Interpretation of Dreams,* has had an odd career since it was first published in 1981, I must dwell on its history for a moment. Late in 1980, Lewis Lapham (then, and now once again, editor of *Harper's* magazine) got in touch with me about contributing to a new department in *Harper's,* entitled "Revisions," in which major titles of the past would be lightheartedly revisited. We agreed that for me, Freud's *Interpretation of Dreams* would be ideal to write about, and I came up with the idea of adopting the persona of a contemporary of Freud, an Austrian physician sympathetic enough to give this strange scientific treatise a fair and extensive hearing but distant enough to wonder about its permanent value. Lapham was delighted with the idea. Accordingly, I invented a medical journal, the *Grazer Medizinische Vierteljahresschrift,* in which I had presumably found the review, equipped it with the grandiose claim of having made a real discovery in the field of Freud scholarship—fairly sensational in view of the fact that, after all, the field had been combed over and nothing of the sort had been found for decades—and added learned footnotes as commentary on the document that I, its discoverer, was now presenting to an astonished world.

I was, frankly, pleased with my effort, and remain pleased enough to reprint it here. It gave enjoyment not only to me but to numerous readers, who told me so. That it was a spoof was obvious, or should have been obvious: if I had really struck this sort of scholarly gold, I should have called a press conference and published the piece in a learned journal. But a small handful of readers—including some psychoanalysts, I regret to say—took the article at face value. Whenever I ran into someone who had taken my fiction for reality—which was exceedingly rare—I informed him, as kindly as I knew how, of the truth of the matter.

There my "discovery" rested until 1983, when my friend and colleague John Merriman asked me to contribute a piece to a volume of "humorous speculations" about the past. The project was designed to explore, as wittily as possible, Pascal's famous observation that if Cleopatra's nose had been shorter, the history of the world would have been different. The collection appeared after some delays in 1985 under the title *For Want of a Horse: Choice and Chance in History.* In my contribution, "A Gentile Science?," also reprinted below, I came back to my piece in *Harper's,* using as evidence for my fantastic rewriting of psychoanalytic history "an anonymous review of *The Interpretation of Dreams*" published in "the *Grazer Medizinische Vierteljahresschrift.*" At that point, I had playfully decided to give my creature, that anonymous Austrian physician, some further work to do. Early in 1984, *Harper's* and I agreed that I should make another discovery, this time a hitherto unknown review of Freud's *Three Essays on the Theory of Sexuality,* from the same imagined hand, published in the same imaginary journal. The editors gleefully recalled my piece of two years earlier and were only too pleased to lend my construction further life. But then more pressing work supervened, and I never wrote that second fictional review.

It was rudely recalled to me in the fall of 1988, when Daniel Goleman of the *New York Times* called me and told me that he wanted to write a story about the "flap" involving my piece in *Harper's,* now some seven years old. Somewhat amused but, even more than that, irritated by the gossip that seemed to be floating about New York psychoanalytic circles, I gave Goleman all the evidence I had. I recounted my memories of the episode and dug up my correspondence with *Harper's* editor Lewis Lapham. But I suggested to Goleman that he really did not have a story at all—or, rather, that it was a self-promoting story, like one of Andy Warhol's celebrities famous for being famous. Obviously he did not agree, and on January 22, 1989, his report appeared in the *New York Times* under the title "A Freudian Spoof Is Slipped Past Many Scholars." The word "many" was not the only misleading assertion in this non-story.

The sheer foolishness of the case did not stop Goleman. Nor did it stop one Maryon Tysoe, who called me from England and then published her piece about the affair in the London *Independent* on February 7, 1989. A sign that I had suddenly become a minor luminary was a story in a prestigious Yugoslav daily, which was for the most part copied from the *New York Times,* only with a few imaginative epithets added. By no means all the publicity was hostile. Interviewed by the *Times,* Lewis Lapham was quietly sensible in his defense of my piece, and I will not insult my reader's intelligence by quoting his reasoning. By the time the *Independent* got to Lapham, however, he was angry: "You have to remember the context in which the article appeared," he said. "It was intended to be seen as fiction. The American academic community is truly, in my view, appallingly earnest, solemn, humourless, dull-witted—I have no sympathy for them at all." I am glad to say that, judging by the mail and telephone calls I received during all this time of trial, Mr. Lapham was rather too pessimistic about the species Homo academicus. On the other

. . . .

hand, when I thought of those psychoanalytic candidates and their teachers in New York solemnly attempting to interpret my unconscious reasons for writing that piece for *Harper's,* I found myself sharing his annoyance.

In searching for opinions they could quote in their stories, Goleman and Tysoe rounded up the usual suspects, and the pious head-shaking they elicited would provide impressive material for an anthology of sanctimoniousness. I can only wonder what my late friend Richard Hofstadter, the historian who so beautifully defined the authentic intellectual, would have said about this episode. As for myself, I am reprinting the piece unaltered, only adding an epigraph from Friedrich Schiller. The brief conceit that follows it, "A Gentile Science?" should throw further light on my intentions.

5

· ·

Serious Jests

*To look at the
Medusa's head is
no parlour game.
—Hanns Sachs,*
Freud: Master
and Friend

In mid-June of 1897, while struggling with the manuscript of his *Interpretation of Dreams,* Freud informed his friend Wilhelm Fliess in Berlin: "I want to confess that I have recently started a collection of profound Jewish stories."[1] Three months later, on September 21, he dipped into that collection, significantly in one of the most important letters he ever wrote. He was announcing to Fliess that a lack of convincing evidence had compelled him to abandon his cherished seduction theory of neuroses, from which he had expected a modicum of fame and fortune. Feeling chastened, he communicated his mood in the characteristic way of intimates with the mere punch line of a "little story," a Jewish story, that Fliess had obviously heard before.[2]

Freud then dropped the intriguing subject of profound Jewish stories for some two years, until September 1899. Again writing to Fliess, he gave good reasons why humor in general, and jokes in

1. Freud to Fliess, June 22, 1897. *Freud-Fliess,* 271 (254).
2. The tantalizing punch line reads: "Rebecca, take off your dress, you aren't a Kalle—bride—any more." The joke has exercised students of Freud, but neither the story itself nor a convincing interpretation has turned up. See Freud to Fliess, September 21, 1897. Ibid., 285–86 (266).

. . . .

particular, are no laughing matter. Evidently Fliess, reading Freud's manuscript of the "dream book" chapter by chapter, had objected that the dreams Freud was reporting were just too funny. Freud acknowledged the charge: "That the dreamer is too witty is surely correct." But he disclaimed all responsibility for that. "All dreamers are equally intolerably witty, and they are so because they are under pressure; the straight path is barred to them." This observation gave Freud an opportunity for one of those bold generalizations about the mind that he was then pouring out to his confidant: "The apparent wit of all unconscious processes is intimately linked to the theory of the witty and the comic."[3] Much of Freud's theory of jokes, of wit and of humor, is adumbrated in these pregnant passages.

"I want to confess—*Ich will gestehen*": Freud's choice of words smacks of the apologetic, as though, in giving himself the pleasure of collecting Jewish jokes, he were taking an illicit holiday from his supreme duty of the moment, which was to complete *The Interpretation of Dreams.* Of course, since he could characterize the jokes he was gathering up as profound, their profundity might lighten his pangs of conscience. We have here, I think, yet another hint of Freud's compulsive need to work, his strong sense that he must not deviate from his life's assignment: solving great riddles.[4]

Yet, as those who came to know Freud agree, he enjoyed telling jokes and making pointed observations for their own sake. The British psychoanalyst Joan Riviere, an analysand of Freud in the early 1920s and an unsurpassed translator of his papers, speaks of the "inimitable dry humour of his writings," which "became in ordinary intercourse a charming gaiety and capacity for finding amusement in most situations."[5] Franz Alexander, the eminent Hungarian psychoanalyst, recalled that Freud "liked to illustrate a point with anecdotes and jokes, was an excellent raconteur, and even serious topics were robbed of the artificial austerity with which they are so

3. Freud to Fliess, September 11, 1899. Ibid., 407 (371). Freud did not write a great deal on the inviting topic of humor: only his book on jokes of 1905; an open letter in 1911 to the folklorist Friedrich S. Krauss, endorsing Krauss's contention that a collection of erotic jokes was of real interest to the psychologist; and much later, in 1927, a short paper on humor.
4. See above, 40–44, 50–52.
5. Riviere, "An Intimate Impression," *Lancet* II (September 30, 1939), 766.

frequently invested."[6] Freud was, in short, a witty man. For all his pessimism, his son Martin's characterization of him as a man with a merry heart seems not inappropriate.

In fact, when it came to jokes, he stooped to even the feeblest specimens. During the First World War, he jotted down a handful of appalling puns and jests that a bright schoolboy might have found juvenile: " 'Dear parents,' a Jew serving in the Russian army writes home, 'we are doing very well. We are daily retreating a few miles. God willing, I hope to be home on Rosh Hashana.' "[7] Freud's morale must have been very low in those days. But jokes meant much to him at all times. In the introduction to his book on the subject, he reminded his readers of the "peculiar, downright fascinating charm" that jokes exercised over his society: "A new joke works almost like an event of the most general interest; it is passed along from one to another like the news of the latest victory." Even eminent personages, he added, do not disdain retelling excellent jokes in their autobiographies, weighed down though these may be with graver matters.[8] Freud, making this comment, did not yet think himself an eminent personage, but he fully endorsed the interest and pleasure that the great took in perpetuating jokes.

At the same time, utilitarian that he was, Freud often enlisted varieties of humor, notably anecdotes, to illuminate a theory or strengthen an argument. Hanns Sachs, himself known for his ready wit, recalled that Freud's lectures at the university were anything but portentous: "The prevailing tone was a simple conversational one, often interspersed with witty or ironical remarks."[9] On one such occasion, Sachs remembered, in discussing with his audience the psychoanalytic theory of the neuroses, Freud had shown them a picture postcard depicting a rustic in a hotel room, trying to blow out the electric light as though it were a candle. "If you attack the symptom directly," Freud had glossed the scene, "you act in the same way as this man. You must look for the switch."[10]

6. Alexander, "Recollections of Berggasse 19," *Psychoanalytic Quarterly* IX (1940), 197.

7. From two sheets torn from a notebook, titled "Kriegswitze." Freud Collection, LC, uncatalogued. See *Freud,* 371.

8. *Der Witz und seine Beziehung zum Unbewussten, GW* VI, 13 / *Jokes and Their Relation to the Unconscious, SE* VIII, 15.

9. Sachs, *Freud: Master and Friend,* 43.

10. Ibid., 45.

Freud was equally trenchant in private conversations. On one of his long walks with Sachs and other adherents, Freud used a scatological anecdote—Sachs calls it "not 'quite nice' "—to explicate the startling phenomenon of individuals who have no scruple about contemplating their most unfortunate traits or actions but are at times upset by a trifle: Anatole France, Freud reminded his listeners, once told a story about the member of a most exclusive, exceedingly aristocratic club in Budapest who made a bet with a fellow member that he would "eat a goodly portion of fecal matter (monosyllabic among friends). It was served, of course, on a gold platter, and he fell to it with a will. Suddenly he paused, spluttered, and could not go on eating. He had found a hair in it."[11] Roy R. Grinker, an American analysand of Freud who knew him late in life, offered a far less revolting instance of Freud's telling stories "so sharply pointed that they accentuated the value of his interpretations." One of these, clarifying the notion of substitute gratifications, was about a man who took his little son to hear a marvelous mechanical device that could imitate musical instruments to perfection. After listening to its first notes, the father exclaimed, " ''There, doesn't it sound just as if it were playing a violin?' The little boy said, 'But Papa, why don't we go and hear a real violin played?' "[12] It was seriously playful, at times robust, illustrations of this kind that gave Freud's listeners access to esoteric psychoanalytic ideas.

Freud consistently enlivened his correspondence with pointed anecdotes or reminiscences. In mid-July 1934, some days after learning of the bloodbath that Hitler had visited on fellow Nazis whom he suspected of disloyalty—this was the only time Hitler ever gave him any pleasure—Freud wrote to Arnold Zweig: "Events in Germany remind me by way of contrast of an experience in the summer of 1920. It was the first Congress in the Hague, outside our prison. It still does me good today to recall how cordial our Dutch colleagues were toward the starved and seedy Central Europeans. At the end of the Congress, they gave us a dinner of authentic Dutch sumptuousness, for which we were not allowed to pay anything. But we had forgotten how to eat it. As the hors d'oeuvres were handed around, they tasted good to us all, and then we were done, we could

11. Ibid., 61–62.
12. Grinker, "Reminiscences of a Personal Contact with Freud," *American Journal of Orthopsychiatry* X (1940), 853.

not take any more. And now the contrast! After the news of June 30, I have only one sentiment: What! After the hors d'oeuvres, I should get up from table! And there is nothing more! I am still hungry."[13]

Not unexpectedly, Freud peppered his published writings in his persuasive way with jokes, lighthearted quotations, sarcastic remarks: in *Civilization and Its Discontents,* he underscores the absurdity of the Christian call for universal love with a caustic observation by one of his favorite writers, Heinrich Heine: "I possess the most peaceable disposition. My wishes are: a modest cottage, a thatched roof, but a good bed, good food, very fresh milk and butter, flowers before my window, a few handsome trees before my door; and if the good Lord wants to make me completely happy, he will let me live long enough to have the pleasure of seeing some six or seven of my enemies hanged on those trees. Before their death, with a tender heart, I shall forgive them all the wrong they did me in my life—yes, one must forgive one's enemies, but not before they have been hanged."[14]

Again, in one of his papers on technique, urging his fellow analysts not to compromise any of their severe, abstemious self-control during the analytic hour, Freud illustrates his prescription with a delightful story: A mortally ill insurance agent, a hardened atheist, allows his pious family to call in a pastor who might perhaps persuade the dying man to make his peace with God and win a chance for paradise. The private talk between the two men lasts so long that the family, waiting outside the closed door, takes heart. "At last, the door of the sickroom opens," Freud concludes. "The unbeliever has not been converted, but the pastor goes away insured."[15] And a final instance of palatable frosting on the heavy cake of theory: in his difficult essay *The Ego and the Id,* Freud recalls an old story to demonstrate the manner in which neurotics discharge their libidinal or aggressive energies with a sublime indifference as

13. Freud to Arnold Zweig, July 15, 1934. *Freud-Zweig,* 96–97 (86). See *Freud,* 596.
14. *Das Unbehagen in der Kultur, GW* XIV, 469–70n / *Civilization and Its Discontents, SE* XXI, 110n.
15. "Bemerkungen über die Übertragungsliebe" (1915), *GW* X, 314 / "Observations on Transference Love," *SE* XII, 165. I was unable to resist telling this story before; see *A Godless Jew: Freud, Atheism, and the Making of Psychoanalysis* (1987), 3.

to which targets they choose. After a capital crime has been committed in a Hungarian village, the mayor decides that one of the three local tailors, though completely innocent, must be hanged because the local blacksmith, actually the guilty man, is the only blacksmith in the village.[16] It is no wonder that Freud's conversation, like his writing, was punctuated with quotations from satirists like Georg Christoph Lichtenberg, scintillating stylists like Heinrich Heine, and popular humorists like Wilhelm Busch. Nor is it any wonder that Mark Twain was one of his favorites.[17]

"Jewish stories." Freud's relation to Judaism was subtle but not problematic—at least not to him.[18] He was born a Jew, lived as a Jew, died a Jew, and took public pride in his origins. Yet his attachment was not equally impassioned at all times. Rather, what I should call the temperature of his Jewishness exhibits a striking pattern. In times of troubles he would declare himself a Jew more assertively than in more placid intervals: he did so in 1873, when, entering the University of Vienna, he encountered anti-Semites; again in the late 1890s, when he dramatized himself as virtually alone in creating psychoanalysis just as the Jew-baiting demagogue Karl Lueger succeeded in becoming mayor of Vienna; once again after 1910, when he felt embattled in his growing tension with Jung and had to abandon his hopes of making Jung, the non-Jew, his scientific heir; and finally in the late 1920s, when the emergence of Hitler and his Austrian followers began to loom as an ominous threat to Jews in Europe. In 1926, he bluntly told an interviewer, the journalist George Sylvester Viereck: "My language is German. My culture, my attainments are German. I considered myself German intellectually, until I noticed the growth of anti-Semitic prejudice in Germany and German Austria. Since that time, I prefer to call myself a Jew."[19] Actually he had called himself that all his life.

16. See *Das Ich und das Es, GW* XIII, 274 / *The Ego and the Id, SE* XIX, 45. Economical with his material, Freud had already told that joke in his book. See *Jokes, SE* VIII, 206.

17. For Mark Twain, see above, 101–04.

18. Since I have explored Freud's Jewish identity at considerable length elsewhere (in *A Godless Jew,* esp. ch. 3, and in *Freud,* esp. 597–610), I shall be summary here.

19. Viereck, *Glimpses of the Great* (1930), 34. The interview had been published earlier, in 1927. See *Freud,* 448.

For Freud, as an unrepentant Lamarckian convinced that acquired characteristics can be inherited, the essence of Jewishness is some undefinable ancient quality that had persisted through the ages and was not yet—not yet, but some day might be—accessible to psychoanalytic investigation. Before the First World War, as he was battling Jung and when, as we have seen, imprecise talk about race was only too common—Freud indulged in it as much as many others—he claimed a certain "racial kinship" with Karl Abraham and his other Jewish adherents.[20] His sense of solidarity with his fellow Jews never faded, and the mystery of Jewishness never ceased to haunt him. In 1922, he told Sándor Ferenczi of "strange secret longings" rising up within him, "perhaps from the heritage of my ancestors, from the Orient and the Mediterranean."[21] His last sustained work, *Moses and Monotheism,* testifies to the persistence of this enigma and its importance for him.

The repertory of Freud's published jokes, though, shows a measure of barely concealed hostility against some Jews—the Jews of Eastern Europe. "Two Jews run into one another near a bath house. *'Have you taken a bath?'* asks one. *'Why,'* asks the other in return, *'is one missing?'* "[22] Evidently Freud relished this crude caricature of the unwashed Jew, clearly of East European vintage, enough to repeat it with only a slight variation. "Now once again the two Jews in front of the bath house. *'A year gone by again already!'* sighs one of them."[23] These are by no means the only specimens of the aggressive, tendentious jokes he retails: Freud tells others about Galician or unspecified eastern Jews, about men unkempt, all of them strangers to comb, soap, and refined manners.

It is hard to fathom Freud's need for these stabs at low-grade wit except to say that his culture was overrun by them. To be sure, analyzing his jokes, Freud principally offered these feeble efforts, as he did more respectable ones, as evidence for a scientific theory. He was studying and illustrating techniques of joke construction and linking the making of jokes to the rest of mental work. But why choose stories that could only support the malevolent clichés against

20. See Freud to Abraham, May 3, 1908. *Freud-Abraham,* 47 (34).
21. Freud to Ferenczi, March 30, 1922. Freud-Ferenczi Correspondence, Freud Collection, LC.
22. *Der Witz, GW* VI, 50 / *Jokes, SE* VIII, 49.
23. Ibid., 84 / 78.

Jews current in Freud's day? His explanation for including them in his treatise is—for Freud—exceptionally unconvincing: Jews, he argues, excel in humorous self-criticism. "The jokes that outsiders make about Jews are for the most part brutal farcical tales," but the jokes that Jews make about themselves censure real faults and, at the same time, establish "their connection with their merits."[24] But what is meritorious about bathing just once a year, or showing in one's matted beard the remnants of what one had for supper two days before? In his monograph on Freud's jokes, Elliott Oring speculates that while Freud sought to establish a safe distance between himself and the uncouth, uncivilized Jewish immigrants who had been crowding into Vienna from Eastern Europe for decades, he may have felt uncannily like them. "Did he sense an element of this dirtiness and untidiness in himself as well?" After all, his father and mother were both Jews from Galicia, and his mother was anything but ladylike. Freud "seems compelled to see a potential Jew concealed behind the most unlikely of façades, and his Jew always stands ready to reveal himself in the language of the Ostjude."[25]

But Oring fails to see the share of Freud's culture in Freud's sense of humor. After all, Freud lived among Austrians and Germans, most of them assimilated Jews, all perfectly prepared to make crude remarks at their own expense—or at least at the expense of East European Jews. It was a culture that, far from objecting to the coarsest ethnic humor, the most cutting ethnic slurs, reveled in them. In 1884, Hermann Levi, the famous conductor at Munich's opera and an abject admirer of that vociferous anti-Semite Richard Wagner, celebrated the twenty-fifth anniversary of his career as a *Kapellmeister*. His friends gave him a fond celebration and published for the occasion a festive little newspaper filled with laudatory doggerel. On the front page there was a hideous caricature of a Jewish high priest, complete with dark, kinky beard, heavy-lidded eyes, prominent, protruding nose, and sly, wicked smile. There is no evidence that either Levi or any of the other celebrants found this caricature in poor taste. True enough, Levi, longing to be a Christian, was afflicted with an exquisite case of self-hatred. But there was nothing out of the ordinary for his time in this drawing. It was, after all, a

24. Ibid., 123 / 111.
25. Oring, *The Jokes of Sigmund Freud: A Study in Humor and Jewish Identity* (1984), 44, 51.

time in which Jewish publishers could make money with little pamphlets collecting jokes that made the most derisive points about their
nouveau riche Jewish protagonists, including their repellent appearance, ludicrous names, commercial greed, and total lack of cul-
tivation.[26] In such a culture a joke about a Jew not bathing for a year
was a commonplace, even among Jews.

Nor is it necessary to invoke abject Jewish self-hatred to explain
Freud's affection for these malicious witticisms. Feeling himself, all
his life, distant from the flood of Jewish immigrants, no matter what
his father's and mother's family history, he did not need to work at
creating that distance. At sixteen, on a train returning to Vienna
from a visit to his native Freiberg, he ran into a Jewish family,
unmistakably Ostjuden, whom he savagely sketched in a letter to a
school friend, a Jew like himself. The father, he wrote sarcastically,
was "a highly honorable old Jew" with wife to match, "a corre-
sponding old Jewess complete with melancholic, languishing little
daughter and an impudent, promising son." He found their company,
he wrote, "more intolerable than any other" and took particular
exception to the son. "He was of the kind of wood from which fate
carves the swindler when the time is ripe: crafty, mendacious, encouraged by his dear relatives that he has talent, but without principles or a view of life."[27] Reading such snobbery through the terrible
history of the last fifty or sixty years, we are likely to make more of
it than was at work in Freud's conscious, or even his unconscious,
mind. There is not a trace of anxiety in this assault, no fear that he,
young Freud, might be in any respect like the targets of his scorn.
In his book on jokes, telling yet another Jewish story, he paused to
comment that "only the trimmings are Jewish; its core is general
human."[28] And the core is, by definition, the heart of things. What
mattered most to Freud was a theory of mind, not merely of the
Jewish mentality—whatever that might be.

         "The apparent wit of all unconscious processes is
intimately linked to the theory of the witty and the comic." The

26. See Peter Gay, "Hermann Levi: A Study in Service and Self-Hatred," in
Freud, Jews, and Other Germans: Masters and Victims in Modernist Culture
(1978), 189–230; the front page is shown on p. 201 and the covers for the
pamphlets on pp. 210–12.
27. Freud to Emil Fluss, September 18, 1872. *Freud,* 19.
28. *Der Witz, GW* VI, 51 / *Jokes, SE* VIII, 49.

Freud whom the educated public knows, or thinks it knows, is a therapist specializing in the neurotics whom he places before him on the couch and listens to intently. There is no reason to contest this portrait, but by itself it is partial, sadly incomplete. From his school days on, Freud was engrossed by what tormented him as the riddles of the world.[29] As he matured, he concentrated his fascination with the unknown, with the secret behind the curtain, on the human mind. It is true that he gathered his evidence first and foremost from his analysands. His consulting room was his laboratory. But he aimed at more than a reputation for being the first to elucidate certain types of mental distress: he aspired to become nothing less than the founder of a psychology whose laws, or at least secure conjectures, would explain the workings of the human mind, whether neurotic or normal. That is why he was not taking a detour from his principal concerns when he ventured, in the first decade of the twentieth century, into cultural subjects like art, literature, folklore, anthropology, education, law, religion, politics. And that is why he wrote his first book as a psychoanalyst not about his neurotic analysands but about the phenomenon of dreams, a phenomenon within the experience of everyone. *The Interpretation of Dreams* is many things, but Freud distinctly designed it to buttress his claim that the psychoanalytic view of mind has universal applicability. It is no accident that the book opens with a highly specialized bibliographical survey of the literature on dreams and rises, in the notoriously demanding seventh chapter, to a general theory of mental functioning.

Freud's book on jokes makes a very similar claim, if in rather less ambitious form. "Is the subject of jokes worth all this trouble?" Freud asks rhetorically, and answers: "I think there can be no doubt about it. . . . I can appeal to the fact of the intimate connection among all mental happenings—which guarantees that a psychological discovery even in a far-away field will be of value for other fields, not calculable in advance."[30] Indeed, in his book on jokes, Freud linked the dream work he had elucidated in his *Interpretation of Dreams* to what he now called the "joke work." These two types of mental activity perform very much the same sort of task, and by very much the same means: "The interesting processes of condensation with substitute formation, which we have recognized as the core of the

29. See above, 40–44.
30. *Der Witz*, GW VI, 12–13/*Jokes*, SE VIII, 15.

technique of verbal jokes, pointed us toward the formation of dreams, in whose mechanism the same mental processes have been uncovered. Indeed, the techniques of conceptual jokes—displacement, faulty reasoning, absurdity, indirect representation, representation by the opposite, which appear one and all in the technique of the dream work—also point in the same direction."[31] In *The Interpretation of Dreams,* Freud had analyzed one of his dreams that largely turned on a single made-up word, *Autodidasker,* which wittily combined the term *autodidact* with the name of a German-Jewish politician, Lasker, as well as concealing other meanings beneath its baroque surface. Jokes, he now observed, work in precisely the same way.[32] Hence the chance for a general theory of humor, enriched by theoretical insights into other aspects of mental functioning. While earlier students of wit and humor, Freud noted, had shrewdly identified most of the elements that go into making things funny—playfulness, the use of dissimilarity and contrast, economy of expression, and the rest—their work had remained anecdotal, fragmentary: "these elements are *disjecta membra,* which we should like to see fitted together into an organic whole."[33] What Freud confidently offered was that organic whole, a theory. It was a theory that he hoped not only seized the essence of wit and humor but also, in the process, elucidated the essence of mental work as such.

In pursuing this theoretical enterprise, Freud paid a steep price. Humor is perhaps the only mental activity that is destroyed by analysis. A poem studied word for word and a symphony studied bar by bar may yield keener, better-informed enjoyment than naive reading or listening can provide. But a joke analyzed is a joke ruined. Wordsworth's famous line "We murder to dissect" applies supremely to the whole realm of the funny. Freud was fully aware of this peril. He quotes Ludovic Dugas's *Psychologie du rire* to the effect that the skeptics were probably right: might it not be best just to laugh and give up trying to find out why? After all, reflection kills laughter.[34] Taking the risk, Freud plunged ahead, joining a small tribe of nineteenth-century philosophers and psychologists intent upon penetrating to the heart of laughter. He cites and quotes several of his

31. Ibid., 95 / 88.
32. See *Interpretation of Dreams, SE* IV, 298, and *Jokes, SE* VIII, 29.
33. *Der Witz, GW* VI, 11 / *Jokes, SE* VIII, 14.
34. See ibid., 163 / 145–46.

predecessors and contemporaries, including Jean Paul Richter, Theodor Lipps, Herbert Spencer, Franz Brentano, and Henri Bergson—he might have added Charles Baudelaire and George Meredith—to show that he appreciates them but is confident that he has gone beyond their studies.[35] Jokes, he had little doubt, are sturdy enough to survive even psychoanalysis.

"Profound—*tiefsinnig.*" In the last letter Goethe ever wrote, five days before he died at the age of eighty-two, he spoke to his friend Wilhelm von Humboldt about the second part of *Faust,* which had preoccupied him for sixty years, and called it "these serious jests." For Freud, too, jests, especially Jewish jests, were serious. More than just widening his horizons, they deepened his vision. The striking, unexpected adjective with which Freud characterized the Jewish stories he was beginning to collect— "profound"—attests to the weight he attached to this particular brand of humor, and by extension to humor in general. In his book on jokes, he cites Goethe's saying about Georg Christoph Lichtenberg that in his jokes and verbal play a problem lies concealed.[36] More, Freud adds: at times Lichtenberg's wit concealed solutions as well. Nor had Lichtenberg been alone in pointing to the problematic, the exceedingly serious, nature of the funny.

For Freud, the most serious uses of the joke are fairly obvious. Apart from the naive humor, mainly of children, that derives sheer pleasure from verbal play, jokes are acts of aggression, though not necessarily of destructiveness. Jokes, he writes, "make possible the satisfaction of a drive (whether lustful or hostile) in face of an obstacle standing in its way; they circumvent this obstacle and thus draw pleasure from a source of pleasure the obstacle had made

35. The theorist of the comic who probably taught Freud most was Theodor Lipps, whose much marked-up *Komik und Humor. Eine psychologisch-ästhetische Untersuchung* (1898) was in his library. (Freud Museum, London). A philosopher like Lipps who insisted that "psychology is, after all, not a field for blind speculation" (p. 8) could only be congenial. It was in Lipps's *Komik und Humor* that Freud could read of the power of brevity in wit; and while Freud doubtless knew his Heine inside and out, it may be that the theoretical possibilities of Heine's joke about the "famillionär" baron Rothschild first dawned on him in reading this treatise (see Lipps, p. 87).
36. *Der Witz, GW* VI, 101 / *Jokes, SE* VIII, 93.

inaccessible."[37] Freud's parenthesis should not be overlooked: the drive a joke permits to be satisfied is either libidinal or aggressive. The polite late-Victorian middle-class society of Freud's day sought, and often managed, he believed, to repress such impulses. "Through the repressive activity of civilization primary possibilities of enjoyment, now repudiated by the censorship in us, are lost." This is a hard psychological burden to bear: "Every renunciation is so very difficult for mankind's psyche, and so we find that tendentious jokes provide a means of undoing the renunciation, of retrieving what was lost."[38] By retreating from the blunt utterance of feelings and wishes and substituting an indirect outlet, the joke manages to outwit the censorship under which all civilized persons labor, whether in the form of social constraints upon one's freedom to speak and act or prohibitions that have been internalized and are so intractable because they are largely unconscious. A joke, then, speaks the unspeakable: "A joke will allow us to exploit something ridiculous in our enemy which, because of obstacles standing in the way, we could not express openly or consciously." What is more, a joke will "further bribe the hearer with its yield of pleasure into siding with us without any very strict examination."[39] I might note that while Freud does not put it that way, a joke is something of a paradox. Though an economical form of expression, it is at the same time a detour around social, cultural, religious restrictions. The shortest way to the pleasure a joke yields is not through the straight line of open sexuality or aggression.

This is not the only paradox that Freud leaves unaddressed. Humor has a curious double-sided political aspect on which Freud does not comment. He pays homage to the first of the Janus-faced qualities of jokes: whether they are obscene or hostile or cynical, they strike, however subtly, a blow for freedom. "Tendentious jokes are used with particular relish to make aggressiveness or criticism possible against exalted personages who claim authority. Jokes, then, represent a rebellion against that authority, a liberation from its pressure."[40] True: tendentious jokes may covertly assail political leaders, moral dogmas, sexual hypocrisy, the institution of marriage.

37. Ibid., 110 / 101.
38. Ibid., 111 / 101.
39. Ibid., 113 / 103.
40. Ibid., 114–15 / 105.

That much Freud sees and pursues vigorously. But there is another side to the matter. Jokes may not only subvert authority with a laugh but prop it up. To begin with, they may, and often do, aim not at the mighty but at the defenseless. A joke at the expense of a dictator or of entrenched professions like law or medicine is one thing. A joke at the expense of some relatively impotent social group— whether blacks or gypsies or Jews—is quite another. Moreover, a joke may trivialize serious abuses or reduce the listener's sympathy for victims. Freud had some inkling of what he calls "saved compassion," so typical of Mark Twain's stories. Thus Mark Twain tells a pathetic tale about his brother working on a major road-building scheme and being blown up into the air by the premature explosion of a mine, coming down far from where he had been working. In consequence, Mark Twain's brother was docked half a day's pay for being absent from his place of employment. The rage one may feel against the rapacious, careless employer has its sting drawn by his absurd if self-serving action.[41] By making something unfunny appear funny, a joke can diffuse justified indignation and slacken the energy needed to rectify a wrong. Thus a smile or the benign explosion of a laugh can take the place of action.

Of course (and totalitarianism has taught the world that old lesson all over again), there are situations and societies in which political protest is imprudent or guaranteed to be futile—the very thought of such protest only an invitation to frustration and rage. One group of Freud's favorite jokes, those dealing with the *Schadchen*, the Jewish marriage broker, derive much of their point, and much of their poignancy, from a sense of helplessness in such a world. The theme of the Schadchen jokes is virtually always the same: the marriage broker, presenting a hopeful bride to a prospective husband, works to convince him that she is supremely eligible; but, alas, she is unappealing, with visible and unpleasant defects: she is hunchbacked, lame, over the hill, not as rich as touted. "The future bridegroom is most disagreeably surprised upon the introduction of the bride"— runs one of Freud's Schadchen jokes—"and draws the broker aside to communicate his objections in a whisper: 'What have you brought me here for?' he asks him reproachfully. 'She's ugly and old, she is

41. Ibid., 262 / 230. For another instance of Mark Twain's humor, see above, 102–03.

cross-eyed and has bad teeth and runny eyes'—"You may talk out
loud,' the broker interjects, *she's deaf too.'* "[42] Another of these
stories is no less unsettling: "The future bridegroom, accompanied
by the broker, is paying his first visit to the bride's house, and while
they are waiting in the salon for the family to appear, the broker
draws attention to a vitrine in which the finest silver plate is exhibited. 'Look at that! You can see from these things how rich these
people are.'—"But,' asks the suspicious young man, 'might it not be
possible that these fine things have only been borrowed for the
occasion, in order to give an impression of wealth?'—"What are you
thinking of!' replies the broker coolly. *Who would lend these people
anything?'* "[43]

The most obtrusive feature of these stories is their heartlessness.
The matchmaker faces a desperate task: the women he represents,
his "merchandise," are unappetizing, and their families are shabby
behind their glittering façade. The marriage broker himself is a far
from alluring figure. In the Middle Ages and the early modern era,
respectable community figures, scholars and rabbis, had figured as
matchmakers and conscientiously sought to mate honorable couples.
"When you are arranging a marriage between two parties," one
seventeenth-century injunction laid it down, "never exaggerate, and
always tell the truth."[44] By the time Freud recorded his marriage-
broker jokes, and for some time before that, a far more raffish kind
of salesman had taken the scholar's place. The Schadchen character
in these jokes was of course a caricature, but it contained more than
a kernel of truth. In this half-fictional version, the Schadchen is a
professional liar who deals every day in the grossest misrepresen-
tations. Then something happens—and this is the joke—that sur-
prises him into truthfulness. He confesses more than the victim he
is trying to ensnare had asked for: the bride is not only ugly and
squint-eyed but deaf as well; the bride's family enjoys far less credit
than the wary suitor ever suspected.[45]

42. Ibid., 68 / 64.
43. Ibid., 68 / 64–65.
44. "Shadkhan," Cecil Roth et al., eds., *Encyclopaedia Judaica,* 17 vols. (1972–
1982), XIV, 1255.
45. If the Schadchen does tell the truth, he does so while conveying an impression
that amounts to a lie: when a potential bridegroom complains to the marriage
broker that the woman he is being introduced to has one leg shorter than the

. . . .

But the cruelty of Freud's jokes goes beyond casual indifference to the lot of some miserable, unmarriageable woman: the culture in which he lived, and whose values he in large measure shared, was not disposed to be compassionate to unattractive spinsters. What his jokes about the Schadchen point to is the cruelty of the world in which East European Jews were caught. It was a world of bigoted, callous, oppressive Russians, Poles, and Ukrainians, a world where poverty, stultification, and mistreatment were endemic and pessimism was realism.[46] In a ruminative essay, "On the Nature of Jewish Wit," Theodor Reik, one of Freud's most loyal later admirers, generalized from this world of pogroms and persecution to the Jewish world as a whole. Recalling a much-quoted line from Goethe's *Torquato Tasso* about the tormented poet divinely inspired to make poetry from his inner misery, he writes grimly: "Jehovah has forbidden the Jew of our time to speak His word to cajole the hostile world. But by giving him the gift of wit, his God has conferred on him the power to say what he suffers." We laugh at Jewish humor, "but usually it is not comical. In the best examples of this humor there lurks behind the comic façade not merely something serious, as in other witticisms, but something horrible."[47] Freud, too, had a vivid sense of the somber realities underlying many of the funny stories he enjoyed telling. He recognized that if frequently jokes are

---

other and limps visibly, the salesman of marital bliss endorses the description but argues forcefully that the woman's lameness is a great advantage—if the young man were to marry a healthy woman, he would only be nervous all his days that she might fall and break a leg, thus causing him suffering and large medical expenditures. Being lame, the woman would spare him all this worry. She is a fait accompli. (*Der Witz, GW* VI, 66 / *Jokes, SE* VIII, 62–63.) This is the world upside down. In dreams and slips of the tongue appearance hides— or, to the consummate investigator, reveals—reality, but with such sophistry that the frank acknowledgment of reality only creates illusion.

46. In analyzing Heinrich Heine's character Hirsch, a Jewish lottery agent and extractor of corns from Hamburg who changes his name to Hyacinth, Freud observes that this is a self-portrait which, amusing as it is, barely conceals the "serious bitterness" that the poverty-stricken Heine had experienced at the table of his rich and imperious uncle Salomon. Ibid., 158 / 141.

47. Reik, "On the Nature of Jewish Wit," in *From Thirty Years with Freud,* tr. Richard Winston (1940), 190. Reik was writing, of course, with the Nazis' persecutions of the Jews in mind, even though their full horror had not yet been revealed.

acts of aggression, they are also ways of self-protection, defenses against anguish and heartache. With others, he understood that only too often one laughs that one may not cry.

But Reik's dark vision is too unrelieved to be wholly representative of Freud's pleasure in—or for that matter, his theory of—jokes. As a cultivated European, Freud could recite with ease Virgil's famous plaint in the *Aeneid* for the tears in the nature of things: "sunt lacrimae rerum." But he preferred a more combative line from the same epic poem, in which Virgil invokes—or, I cannot help feeling, celebrates—the rebellious energy of the passions: "If I cannot bend the higher powers, I will move the Infernal Regions—Flectere si nequeo superos, Acheronta movebo." Freud liked that line well enough to choose it as the epigraph for his *Interpretation of Dreams.* There is indeed a nocturnal kind of humor, gallows humor, that wrests a modicum of amusement from utter hopelessness. But in general, jokes navigate in a broader, somewhat brighter twilight zone between hope and despair.

Another class of Freud's favorite jokes, about Jewish beggars—the *Schnorrer* joke—exemplifies this somewhat less portentous vision of the world in the most gratifying way. Freud enjoyed these jokes in part because he could at times identify with the Schnorrer. As a young man he had been poor; even after his marriage, he lived on borrowed money. And there were moments when he felt like an intellectual Schnorrer whose capital of scientific ideas was exhausted.[48] Schnorrer jokes, too, as Freud does not neglect to observe, are deeply pessimistic, recalling the "manifold, hopeless misery of the Jews."[49] Certainly this type of joke, confronting the rich and the poor, does nothing to alleviate, let alone eliminate, the age-old and painful problem of economic inequality. In fact, there are some Schnorrer jokes in which the rich take revenge on their disturbing visitors. Freud tells the story of the baron—a Rothschild, no doubt—who is moved almost to tears by a Schnorrer's tale. And he calls for his servants: "Throw him out; he is breaking my heart!"[50] The Schnorrer had done his work too well.

48. "Perhaps it is better if I save and collect," instead of writing a long letter, "so that at our Easter congress I won't again stand before you as a poor Schnorrer." Freud to Fliess, January 16, 1899. *Freud—Fliess,* 372 (340).
49. *Der Witz, GW* VI, 126 / *Jokes, SE* VIII, 114.
50. Ibid., 125 / 113.

The Schnorrer was a beggar and more than a beggar. In the isolated, tedious village life of the East European Jew he was an ambiguous, often a welcome visitor, virtually an institution. He brought news from the outside world and entertained his hosts with stories, and when he migrated to western cities he transferred his rhetorical pathos intact. At his best, he spun ingenious, masterful tales of his neediness that extracted funds from his generous patrons. "A poverty-stricken man has borrowed 25 florins from a well-to-do acquaintance with many protestations of his needy situation. On the very same day, the benefactor encounters him in a restaurant with a plate of salmon with mayonnaise before him. He reproaches him: 'What! You borrow money from me and then order salmon with mayonnaise for yourself. That's what you needed my money for?' 'I don't understand you,' replies the accused. 'When I have no money, I *can't* eat salmon with mayonnaise; when I have money, I *may not* eat salmon with mayonnaise. *So when should I eat salmon with mayonnaise?*' "[51] The brazen illogic, Freud notes, is delightful. And it is true: the man knows his rights!

Freud enjoyed this bit of brash impudence sufficiently to repeat this joke in a different setting: "A Schnorrer asks the rich baron to grant him some subsidy for a trip to Ostend; his physicians have recommended sea-baths to him for the restoration of his health. 'All right, I shall give you something toward it,' the rich man says. 'But do you have to go of all places to Ostend, the most expensive of all the sea resorts?'—'Herr Baron,' is the rebuke, 'as far as I am concerned, for my health nothing is too expensive.' "[52] As Freud observes, the Schnorrer treats the baron's money as virtually his own, giving a communistic twist to the traditional sacred Jewish obligation to succor the unfortunate. But apart from some glorious moments, as these jokes leave little doubt, the poor remained poor.

Yet there is, in such jokes, in addition to melancholy, a touch of rebelliousness, not only against one's economic plight but also against time-honored beliefs. Freud recalls the blasphemous remark reported of the dying Heinrich Heine, who had been confined to his bed for years, to a well-meaning priest who commended him to divine grace and held out hope that God would mercifully pardon

51. Ibid., 51 / 49–50.
52. Ibid., 58 / 55–56.

his sins: "Of course, he will pardon me!" Heine replied. "That's his job"—"Bien sûr, qu'il me pardonnera; c'est son métier." This means, Freud comments, that Heine was at least dimly aware that he, presumably the creature, was really the creator who himself had made God.[53] The joke, at the moment of death, becomes a supreme act of defiance.

And this is how Freud, not far from death, dealt with the Nazis: with a defiant joke, almost calling the implacable wrath of his captors on his head. His son Martin recounts the story: just before the Austrian—now German—authorities permitted Freud to leave the country, they insisted that he sign a statement affirming that he had not been ill-treated. Freud agreed to sign, and added the gloss: "I can most highly recommend the Gestapo to everyone—Ich kann die Gestapo jedermann auf das beste empfehlen."[54] I have speculated elsewhere why Freud should have taken such a risk on the verge of liberation. Did he unconsciously want to provoke the Nazis and thus die in Vienna, the city in which he had lived for nearly eighty years and which he had professed to hate but had never before seriously wanted to leave?[55] Or was his vitality, and with that his sense of humor, irrepressible? We may never know. But it is precisely this unresolvable ambiguity that lies at the heart of jokes.

53. Ibid., 126 / 114–15.
54. Martin Freud, *Sigmund Freud: Man and Father*, 217. In her autobiography, Helene Deutsch recalls this incident slightly differently, insisting that Freud *said* this rather than writing it. (*Confrontations with Myself: An Epilogue* [1923], 170.) Whichever version is correct, it seems likely that Freud made the risky remark.
55. See *Freud*, 628.

6

. . . .

Mind Reading: The Forgotten Freud

*Mit der Dumm-
heit kämpfen
Götter selbst
vergebens.
—Friedrich
Schiller,* Jung-
frau von
Orléans

*I discovered the unsigned review that follows in
an obscure Austrian medical journal, the* Grazer
medizinische Vierteljahresschrift *XVIII, 3 (July
1900), 139–48. As far as I can discover, it has been
wholly overlooked in the voluminous literature on
Freud and appears here in English, in my translation and with my annotations, for the first time.*

This is a brilliant, disturbing, and, for all its
suavity, difficult book. Dr. Sigmund Freud is a
noted, somewhat controversial Viennese neurologist who first established his reputation in medical circles with a monograph on aphasia nine
years ago. Since then, in private practice as a specialist in nervous disorders, he has recorded some
spectacular cures for hysteria. But his unorthodox
methods of treatment, which conform to what he
calls the "cathartic technique," have aroused
some skepticism. In 1893, Dr. Freud hinted at the
directions his medical thinking was taking by pub-
lishing a "Preliminary Communication" with a distinguished Viennese specialist, Dr. Josef Breuer;
two years later, he and Dr. Breuer offered further
theoretical considerations and five new case histories in *Studies on Hysteria.* Since then, as those

who follow the Viennese professional journals will know, Dr. Freud has taken his ideas far beyond the *Studies.* There, affronting the orthodox wisdom that nearly all mental aberrations are hereditary or signs of physiological degeneration, he argued that mental aberrations are more often (though, to do him justice, by no means always) psychological in origin. Hysterics, Freud and Breuer put it bluntly, "suffer mainly from reminiscences." These heresies now prove to be but a pale prologue to Dr. Freud's most recent notions, as expansively presented in *The Interpretation of Dreams.*

In several recent papers, notably "Sexuality in the Aetiology of the Neuroses" (1898), Dr. Freud has proposed an erotic origin for several forms of nervous disorder, thus inviting charges of reductionism and, from some readers, of downright obscenity. In the present book, he attaches these theories to an entirely different field of mental activity. Dr. Freud's ambition, to judge especially from the last (and most difficult) section of his new monograph, is to provide an explanation not merely for some nervous illnesses but for *all* mental functioning. The book's last section, complete with some indecipherable diagrams, offers nothing less than a sketchy outline of a theory of mind. Evidently, Dr. Freud, the nerve specialist, is setting up as a general psychologist. He is not the first physician of the mind to have been lured by the siren of universal mental knowledge.[1]

To unlock the mysteries of the mind, Dr. Freud has chosen a strategy that must strike the informed reader as venturesome, if not perverse. "In the pages that follow," he promises in the opening sentence, "I shall bring forward proof that there is a psychological technique which makes it possible to interpret dreams, and that, if that procedure is employed, every dream reveals itself as a psychological structure which has a meaning and which can be inserted at an assignable point in the mental activities of

1. In view of how little this anonymous reviewer could have read of Freud by 1900, and since none of Freud's confidential correspondence with his colleague Wilhelm Fliess was available to him, this is a prescient observation. Freud certainly saw all his specialized work, whether with dreams or with patients, as an aspect of a larger ambition to produce a general theory of the mind.

waking life." Dr. Freud confidently presents himself as a serious researcher, and his book displays all the stigmata of the scientific monograph: a review of the literature, footnotes, bibliographies. In the preface he explicitly calls himself "a man of science and not a poet." The reader may wonder.

After all, by fastening on dream interpretation as his master guide to mental life, Dr. Freud has entered a realm normally occupied by superstitious servant girls who keep "dream books" on their bedside tables. Dr. Freud is aware of the rather bizarre company he is keeping: "I have been driven to realize," he writes, "that here once more we have one of those not infrequent cases in which an ancient and jealously held popular belief seems to be nearer the truth than the judgement of the prevalent science of today." It remains to be seen whether this conviction reveals exceptional daring or merely exceptional gullibility.

If the choice of subject makes Dr. Freud's claim to science problematic, the almost obtrusive literary form and devices he employs make it more problematic still. For all his denials, he is something of a poet. In one of the case histories he published in 1895, he said, a little pathetically, "I have not always been a psychotherapist. Like other neuropathologists, I was trained to employ local diagnoses and electro-prognosis, and it still strikes me myself as strange that the case histories I write should read like short stories and that, as one might say, they lack the serious stamp of science." This book does not dissolve Dr. Freud's dilemma. The very shape of his new monograph—with its intimate anecdotes, tantalizing glimpses of autobiography, scattering of *bons mots,* and disarming disclaimers—places it in a class by itself, making it part novella, part essay, part special pleading. If it remains a difficult book, that is precisely because Dr. Freud presents an extremely complex argument—about how dreams work—and, beyond that, as I say, reaches for a complete theory of mind.

The logical form of *The Interpretation of Dreams* is, I believe, that of a circle, with the long concluding chapter returning to the comprehensive bibliographical survey of the opening chapter. Dr. Freud restates his precursors' theories about dreams in order to argue that while many of them have something to offer, all of them are ultimately wanting and must be replaced by his own psychoanalytic theory. This sustained dramatic logic of the circle firmly undergirds the entire structure of *The Interpretation of Dreams,* despite its glittering decoration.[2]

The book's anecdotal, witty, and confessional character is unorthodox, to say the least, but its purpose is persuasion. Whatever future scientific researches will prove, we must now concede that Dr. Freud is an advocate of the greatest skill. I suspect that if there should ever be a need for popular versions of his ideas Dr. Freud will be the one to provide them.[3]

Such popularization will undoubtedly be made easier by his autobiographical bent. Certainly few writers laying claim to the name of scientist have made as free, and as profitable, a use of self-disclosure as Dr. Freud. In discussing the "Dream of Irma's Injection," for instance—the so-called "specimen dream," which he reports at some length and then analyzes in great detail to reveal his method—Dr. Freud enters into some intimate, and by no means always savory, detail about his personal life. The dream, of course, is his own.

At the same time, Dr. Freud teases his readers rather unfairly: he breaks off in what appears to be the middle of his revelations, suddenly overcome by an attack of reserve. "Considerations which arise in the case of every dream of my own restrain me from pursuing my interpretative work. If anyone should feel tempted to express a hasty condemnation of my reticence, I would advise him to make the experiment of being franker than I am."

This reviewer feels tempted to express just such a condemnation of the author's reticence, and does not think it hasty. Dr. Freud's defense seems disingenuous: no one had asked him to draw on his own dreams as scientific material.

It seems oddly conventional, in this most unconventional of neurologists, to stop the flow of disclosure just when it promises to

2. While there is no evidence that Marcel Proust ever heard of Freud's *Interpretation of Dreams,* it is tantalizing to conjecture whether he, that psychologist among novelists, perhaps did read this book. The famous circular line of *A la recherche du temps perdu,* with the narrator's decision, at the end of the work, to devote himself to writing a novel—the novel that the reader has just read—bears a more than casual resemblance to what the reviewer calls, perhaps a little pretentiously, Freud's dramatic logic.

3. Right once more: Freud in fact published a number of popularizations, from the comprehensive *Introductory Lectures* to brief articles for encyclopedias, all of them models of lucidity.

. . . .

become really interesting. On Dr. Freud's own showing, a more penetrating analysis of this "Irma" dream would have led him, and his readers also, straight into his sexual life.[4]

It is Dr. Freud's insistence on the centrality of sexual passion in the making of men's minds that will prove most offensive, yet perhaps—if we may be allowed the pun—most fertile. The connection between dreams and sexuality, if we follow his reasoning correctly, is provided by the crucial role of the *wish* in mental life. In fact, Dr. Freud defines the dream one recalls on waking (and all that stands behind it to make the dream possible in the first place) as desire, and desire gratified. *"Its content was the fulfillment of a wish,"* he writes, *"and its motive was a wish."*

The argument that he leaves here largely implicit—and one can only wish that he had made it explicit, for reviewers, too, have wishes—seems to run as follows: man is a wishing animal. Beginning in earliest childhood, a phase of human development to which Dr. Freud evidently assigns considerable importance, the little boy (to concentrate solely on males for the moment) wants to love his mother undisturbed by rivals, and finds his father in the way of his desire.

According to Dr. Freud, "Being in love with the one parent and hating the other are among the essential constituents of the stock of psychical impulses which is formed at the time. . . . It is the fate of all of us, perhaps," he goes on to say, "to direct our first sexual impulse towards our mother and our first hatred and our first murderous wishes against our father." We take it that the "perhaps" in this statement functions as a piece of self-protection, since the assertion is, even with the qualification, really rather appalling. Dr. Freud tries to buttress his extraordinary imaginative portrayal of amorous and murderous little boys by leaning, a little quaintly, on the authority of Sophocles' tragedy *Oedipus Rex*. He also professes to find the same incestuous triangle at work in *Hamlet*. Why not, we may ask, in *The Brothers Karamazov?*[5]

4. True enough, as we know from other evidence. But there were other reasons for Freud's deliberately incomplete interpretation, including his desire to protect his close friend Wilhelm Fliess from the justified charge of incompetence.

5. Freud did, in fact, have some analytical words to say about *The Brothers Karamazov*, a novel he immensely admired. See "Dostoevsky and Parricide" (1928).

Dr. Freud argues that although these wishes cannot be fulfilled, they persist, soon appearing immoral and indecent to the child who holds them. And so they are pushed out of awareness—"repressed," in Dr. Freud's term—and prevented from reaching consciousness by what Dr. Freud calls, in one of his many felicitous metaphors, the "censorship." At night, when the censorship itself is somewhat somnolent (like an armed border guard dozing while on duty), the repressed wishes, still alive later in life and often urgent, struggle toward consciousness. In this way they are the true, or ultimate, cause of the dream.

What Dr. Freud is asserting here is nothing less than staggering, and the skepticism he is sure to encounter in the medical profession should come as no surprise to him. First, he claims that there is a part, a very important part, of our minds of which we are wholly unaware, and which acts behind the scenes, alert, powerful, insatiable. Some modern thinkers, notably Eduard von Hartmann, have developed veritable philosophies of the unconscious, but for Dr. Freud, no philosopher, the unconscious appears to be a concrete psychological structure, laid down in childhood and never dissolved. Surely this is the most radical possible version of a dubious romantic idea. Dr. Freud, for all his debt to positivist thinking, may be the last romantic.[6]

No less radical is Dr. Freud's assertion that sexuality shows itself first not at puberty, as all our best physicians and alienists have maintained, but soon after birth. "A child's sexual wishes—if in their embryonic stage they deserve to be so described—awaken very early," he writes. Once again we may note Dr. Freud's tactical caution. The implication of all his thinking is that embryonic or not, a child's wishes for love can only be described as sexual.

At the same time, we note that Dr. Freud's argument on this important point is neither complete nor consistent. He can write, surprisingly enough: "We think highly of the happiness of childhood because it is still innocent of sexual desires." And yet in our judgment his theory calls for infantile sexuality, nothing less. If he rather ob-

6. If this is the first appraisal of Freud as a late romantic—in my judgment unwarranted—it was not to be the last; Lionel Trilling would express the same view half a century later.

scures the issue with such asides, we can only explain his hesitation as a residual embarrassment in the face of a proposition that shocks even its author. No less than the rest of us, Dr. Freud is a citizen of the nineteenth century—he is, we are told, in his mid-forties—and while he seems perfectly willing, almost eager, to offend the Podsnaps of our time, and bring blushes to the cheeks of the young, he is properly a little dismayed by his own theories.

For all his preoccupation—some would say obsession—with sexuality, infantile or adult, Dr. Freud must be acquitted of the charge of pan-sexualism.[7] After all, the little boy in Dr. Freud's "oedipal" phase does not only love. He also hates. And it seems inescapable, on Dr. Freud's own showing, that the latter emotion is as fundamental a human impulse as the former. But on this important point, which bears on the nature of man's instinctual equipment, Dr. Freud is lamentably inconclusive. We may note in his defense that other scientists, psychologists and biologists alike, remain confused over man's instinctual drives. But it would have been useful if Dr. Freud had described the dimensions of the problem that he and all other students of the mind confront when they approach its essential building blocks.

In Dr. Freud's theory, then, the dreamer dreams all his life of infantile wishes. Why then are dreams so hard to read? Why do they not simply and invariably show a little boy in bed with his mother, his father lying on the floor, dead? It is in order to answer these reasonable questions that Dr. Freud has felt obliged to make his book so long. Part of the answer we have already supplied: the condition of sleep is, by definition, one of reduced vitality. True, the "censorship" that protects waking humans from impermissible wishes, both sexual and hostile, is also in a state of somnolence; but it remains alert enough to force the wishes to take on disguises, to steal across the frontiers of consciousness in a variety of masks. (The sole exception, Dr. Freud notes, is the dreams of small children, in which desires for forbidden foods and other gratifications are directly represented as fulfilled.)

7. If this review had entered the mainstream of early discourse about psychoanalysis, perhaps Freud would have been spared some of the accusations that the reviewer here disposes of so briefly.

This almost universal procedure of disguising wishes (he calls it "dream work") has a complex logic of its own, just as the language of dreams has its own grammar, and Dr. Freud devotes much time to both. In the course of his exposition, he shows how the dreamer picks up the materials for his dream from recent, often quite neutral, experiences ("day's residues"), and how long trains of thought have a peculiar order imposed on them by what Dr. Freud describes as "condensation" and "displacement." He adds a catalogue of dream symbols standing for such phenomena as sexual intercourse, and life and death. It is here, of course, that *The Interpretation of Dreams* most resembles the dream books of servant girls. Considerations of space prevent me from going into details here; suffice it to say, Dr. Freud amply documents his dream symbols with dreams drawn from his own life, those of his friends, and from literature. Dreams appear finally as the true guardians of sleep, employing tactics of great ingenuity as they forge a compromise between wishes and defenses against wishes in order to keep the sleeper at rest.

Far-reaching as these elucidations of dreams certainly are, what we must call Dr. Freud's enormous scientific effrontery emerges most plainly in the concluding chapter, in which he attempts, as we have noted, to generalize beyond dreams to a universal theory of the human mind. But that theory remains intertwined with, and dependent on, his narrower, though still very bold, interpretation of dreams. Whether together they will stand or fall is a question that must await the kind of empirical research that we, as medical scientists, accept as our only road to conviction. As it stands, this monograph depends more heavily on assertion and sheer wit than on proof, though we must confess that we think it more likely that Dr. Freud will prove to be a genius than a charlatan. If Dr. Freud should be proved right, this monograph will stand as a scientific achievement of impressive dimensions. But since it has its origins in a highly technical field, interest in which is severely limited, we think we can safely predict that *The Interpretation of Dreams* will find few readers.

In fact, in its first six years, The Interpretation of Dreams *sold only 351 copies; a second edition was not called for until 1909.*

7

. . . .

A Gentile
Science?

*Be assured, if my
name were Ober-
huber, my inno-
vations would
have found, de-
spite it all, far
less resistance.*
*—Freud to Karl
  Abraham, July
  27, 1908*

In November 1899, Professor Dr. Sigmund Oberhuber published his *Interpretation of Dreams*
and instantly captured the attention of the learned
world. Well he might, for his book was most startling, especially from so unimpeachable a source.
Equipped with all the panoply of modern psychological science, it delved into a subject, dreams,
which few serious researchers had ever troubled
to investigate and demonstrated, in a manner usually reserved to servant girls, that dreams have
meaning. With this sensational manifesto, psychoanalysis was launched.

The principal reason why Dr. Oberhuber's astonishing, unprecedented, indeed often rather obscene assertions gained such rapid acceptance
among the most skeptical of medical inquirers was
precisely the author's solid and unblemished reputation. He was widely known as a sound physician, reliable researcher, and loyal patriot. A
devout Roman Catholic, he was highly valued by
his colleagues at the distinguished University of
Vienna, an intimate of Dr. Karl Lueger, Vienna's
popular anti-Semitic mayor, and recipient of signal honors and decorations at the hand of Em-
peror Franz Joseph. Hence any new publication

by Dr. Oberhuber was bound to be received with utmost seriousness, no matter how astonishing its assertions. Dr. Oberhuber was in fact fully aware that it was his prestige and his person that had given his unsettling new science, psychoanalysis, so unanimously respectful a hearing. He was heard to say more than once, while crossing himself: "If my name had been Rapaport, my innovations would have encountered far more resistance." He was proud to claim psychoanalysis as a gentile science.

The history of psychoanalysis, from this auspicious beginning, promised to be a sequence of triumphs. In the wake of *The Interpretation of Dreams,* which was reprinted several times in the space of one year and enthusiastically reviewed in the medical press and in alert literary periodicals, Dr. Oberhuber felt encouraged to prepare some of his other psychoanalytic work for publication. These included a penetrating case history of an adolescent hysteric with a very complicated erotic life and a set of essays on sexuality that bade fair to be, if anything, more radical and uninhibited than his book on dreams. But then an ominous series of events, still incompletely explained, cast a shadow on his plans. An impecunious and erratic, though undoubtedly brilliant, Jewish Viennese physician named Sigmund Freud laid claim to priority, indeed to the discovery of psychoanalysis itself. Muttering darkly in coffeehouses frequented by students, addressing obscure conclaves of medical men, and descending to several scurrilous pamphlets, Dr. Freud reiterated to anyone willing to listen that he in fact was the first psychoanalyst and that the dreams in the text that Dr. Oberhuber had "arrogated" and gradually drawn to himself were really his own.

No one in Vienna was at first inclined to take such scandalous claims seriously. Who, after all, was Dr. Freud? He had earlier published, hiding behind the reputation of an esteemed nerve specialist, a series of case histories on hysteria in which he had deliberately falsified some important information. He had "experimented" with cocaine, giving rise to unconfirmed rumors that he was a drug addict. And, though a member of a profession that prided itself on its moral probity—an example to the public it was sworn to serve—he lived in a *ménage à trois* in a none too fashionable neighborhood, giving house room to his wife's lively and attractive sister, with whom, reports had it, he was carrying on an illicit love affair. His preoccupation with the seduction of little girls by their fathers—he had

. . . .

in fact three daughters of his own—was also causing some comment. It would be just like such an adventurer to dispute Professor Dr. Oberhuber's right to call himself the discoverer of psychoanalysis. At the same time, he was not the kind of scientist to have the unclouded intelligence, and the patience, to have *made* such a discovery. Dr. Oberhuber's colleagues, profoundly impressed with his imaginative research, which they firmly—and rightly—believed could change the face of Western culture, leaped to his defense. The dynamic unconscious! The Oedipus complex! Infantile sexuality! Dream work! Repression! Regression! Such magnificent insights into the workings of the human mind could never be the fruit of Jewish science!

But Dr. Freud proved adroit and tenacious. He continued to press his claim with a persistence worthy of a better cause. He went so far as to submit an anonymous review of *The Interpretation of Dreams* to the *Grazer medizinische Vierteljahresschrift* in which he coolly and expertly discussed himself as the author of this epoch-making masterpiece.[1] It was a clever bit of writing in which Freud steered clear of any fulsome self-praise but hinted at the possibility that he—Dr. Freud!—might be a genius. And he left open the possibility (thus unconsciously revealing, to all who could read between the lines, his true nature) that he might be a charlatan. In this review, perhaps the most substantial and intelligent of the many that the book was to receive that year, the name of Oberhuber was not even mentioned.

Freud pushed his impudent campaign further than this. He founded a journal, assiduously corresponded with innocent interested physicians abroad, and gradually drew to himself a number of disciples, dupes all of them, who hailed him as their master. Their distance from the Vienna medical scene doubtless contributed to their gullibility. And a linguistic accident was to help Dr. Oberhuber's unscrupulous rival to gain the upper hand in this odd and terrifying duel. Irritated, dismayed, but undeterred, Dr. Oberhuber continued his psychoanalytic researches and his publications. In one popular work devoted to demonstrating the lawfulness of mind in daily life, he established the proposition that slips of the tongue and similar common errors were not accidental but deeply caused and proposed

1. See above, 152–59.

to give such bungled actions the name of Oberhuberian slips. However persuasive his demonstration that such slips were indeed ubiquitous and wholly explicable on psychoanalytic grounds, the public would not follow this great medical innovator largely because it found the locution awkward somehow. And the prospect that deviants would have to be called neo-Oberhuberians, or Oberhuberian revisionists, contributed to the master's decline in the general esteem. His publisher, grasping as all publishers are, quietly substituted the name of the impostor, making his own and Freud's fortune at the same time.

The rest is history. Dr. Freud's schemes bore fruit, and in the course of years, the gentile science of Dr. Oberhuber was transformed into what its adversaries liked to call a Jewish science. One can only speculate how much its eventual failure to capture psychological science and the popular imagination had to do with its transformation. But the psychoanalytically informed historian, who knows his Oberhuber well, cannot stop here. He must ask why Freud persisted in his self-destructive course. Why did he not leave the credit to a respected physician who could have given psychoanalysis the success it so richly deserved? Freud, we know from a letter to one of his disciples, wanted to *be* Oberhuber, not to *have* Oberhuber as a lover, but to identify with him. Now, what is an Oberhuber? On the showing of Dr. Oberhuber's *Psychopathology of Everyday Life* nothing, certainly not a name, is accidental. Why did Freud fasten on Oberhuber? It was not Dr. Oberhuber's triumphant discovery that made Freud want to identify with him. It was his name. Now, an "Ober" is a headwaiter; it is the name that any ordinary waiter is called in Germany and Austria, from a residue of politeness. He is a man of authority, normally dressed in impressive black cloth. And what is a "Huber"? He is a heaver, a lifter up. An Oberhuber, then, is a chief raiser. And what is raised in a man? The answer should be obvious; such association to bodily parts is only too familiar to the psychologist steeped in Oberhuber's writings.

The unconscious meaning of Freud's most ardent wish should thus be plain. He wanted to be first in potency. Thus, in his neurotic need to acquire that potency, he tore down a great scientist and, with him, his science. It is one of the tragedies of modern culture, for, had Oberhuber been allowed to go his way, psychoanalysis would have triumphed as it deserved.

8

. . . .

The Dog That
Did Not Bark
in the Night

My sister-in-law Minna . . . my closest confidante.
—Freud to Fliess.
May 21, 1894

As every biographer of Freud must ruefully acknowledge, Freud left behind some intriguing private mysteries. Probably the most titillating of these, which has been generating gossip for perhaps seventy-five years, is his relationship with his sister-in-law Minna Bernays. Did he have a love affair with her or did he not?

Jung, it seems, started it all. He recalled that on his first visit to Freud, in March 1907, a year after he had launched a correspondence with him, Minna Bernays took him aside. In deep distress she confessed to him that Freud was in love with her and that "their relationship was indeed very intimate." Jung professed to remember, half a century later, the "agony" he had felt at this revelation.[1] Since then the rumor, fed by gossip, by

1. See Jung's interview with John M. Billinsky in 1957, published by Billinsky a dozen years later: "Jung and Freud (The End of a Romance)," *Andover Newton Quarterly* X (1969), 39–43, esp. 42. C. A. Meier, a longtime intimate of Jung and an eminent professor of psychiatry in Zurich, has confirmed the accuracy of Billinsky's recollection: Jung had told Meier precisely the same thing years before. (Personal communication, February 15, 1989.)

ingenious readings of Freud's dreams and papers, even by a diagram of the Freud family's apartment at Berggasse 19, has not died down.[2]

Almost from the moment Freud took a passionate interest in Martha Bernays in April 1882, he was drawn to her younger sister Minna, intelligent, lively, and caustic. He wrote her intimate, almost amorous letters, called her "My Treasure" and "sister."[3] For a time, she was engaged to Ignaz Schönberg, a scholarly friend of Freud. But Schönberg died of tuberculosis in 1886, the year Freud married, and Minna apparently resigned herself to her single state. She took care of her mother in Hamburg, then worked intermittently as a lady's companion until she came, in 1896, to live with the Freuds at Berggasse 19, a welcome permanent guest enjoying considerable authority. "Aunt Minna" chose to live through her nephews and nieces, taking them to spas in the summer and suffering (she once told Freud) from "obligatory migraines."[4]

In writing my biography of Freud, I could of course not ignore the provocative Minna question. I knew that Freud's possible love affair was immaterial to any appraisal of the validity of his ideas. Nor could it be relevant to my placing Freud's thought in the twentieth-century mind. But as a biographer I found myself, somewhat to my surprise, an insatiable voyeur. Working to put together an intricate mosaic from vast numbers of scattered pieces—I estimate that my book contains nearly two thousand previously unpublished passages—I

2. The diagram is shown in *Berggasse 19: Sigmund Freud's Home and Offices, Vienna 1938*, introduction by Peter Gay (1976), 73. The Freuds' apartment was large and sprawling, with Minna Bernays's bedroom at one end. That room had no independent entrance of its own; she had to go through the bedroom of her sister and brother-in-law to reach it. While the evidence concerning this unconventional arrangement is incomplete, I can throw light on it: in 1920, Anna Freud asked her father to arrange it that she might trade one of her two rooms at Berggasse 19 so that they would be adjacent to each other. Freud, though sympathetic, demurred: in such matters, he told her, her mother was in charge. "I cannot force her," he told his daughter on October 12, 1920. "I have always let her have her way in the house." In the end, Anna had her way. This suggests that the bedroom Minna Bernays occupied in the last years of the Freuds' stay in Vienna had originally been Anna's. See *Freud*, 428n.
3. Freud to Minna Bernays, October 12 and August 18, 1884. Sigmund Freud Copyrights, Wivenhoe.
4. Minna Bernays to Freud, September 25 (1910), postcard. Freud Collection, LC.

wanted them all. Here was a persistent story that Freud, the good bourgeois, had committed "incest" with his "sister." And he was on record, in a much quoted letter to the eminent American neurologist James J. Putnam, that while he stood for greater sexual freedom than bourgeois society thought proper, he himself had taken very little advantage of it. Was Freud, the truth teller, lying?

Obviously it was not my task to moralize. But I found the scenario absorbing. Ernest Jones's emphatic, almost nervous disclaimers in his classic three-volume biography of Freud only piqued my interest. Freud, Jones insisted more than once, was "monogamic in a very unusual degree."[5] Indeed, the "strange legends" circulating about Freud's erotic escapades were absurd: his wife "was assuredly the only woman in Freud's love life." And, evidently responding to the rumors floating about concerning Minna Bernays, Jones added that "her caustic tongue gave rise to many epigrams that were cherished in the family. Freud no doubt appreciated her conversation, but to say that she in any way replaced her sister in his affections is sheer nonsense."[6] In view of Freud's strong, often expressed feelings for his sister-in-law, Jones's impassioned denials sounded more protective than persuasive. Yet in the end, having reviewed all the evidence, I concluded tentatively that the rumors about Freud's illicit affair were probably untenable. Not, I must confess, without some regrets: such an amorous intrigue would have added another lively touch to my biography. But I found witnesses unreliable; the flights of conjecture, though ingenious, inconclusive. After rehearsing my reasoning in some detail, I concluded: "Freud *may* have had an affair with Minna Bernays," and I added that if convincing independent evidence should come my way, "I shall revise my text accordingly."[7]

Some of that independent evidence might be in the letters that Freud and Minna Bernays exchanged throughout their long lives. Realistically, whatever my luxuriant fantasies, I expected no incriminating passages: these letters were part of an impressive mass of correspondence and manuscripts that had to be packed and shipped from Berggasse 19 when the Freuds left Vienna

5. *Jones* I, 139.
6. *Jones* II, 386–87.
7. *Freud*, 753.

in the spring of 1938; Freud himself, in April of that year, had tried to dispose of papers in his wastebasket, and Anna Freud and Princess Marie Bonaparte, seeking to rescue what they could, did not save all of them; once in England, the Freuds moved again, in September 1938, to Freud's last dwelling place, 20 Maresfield Gardens in Hampstead. Such vicissitudes alone virtually guaranteed some losses. And after his death, Freud's surviving papers were affectionately combed over by those jealous for his reputation. What is more, I recognized that the absence of erotic material in whatever correspondence might have survived could allow no conclusive demonstration one way or the other: how does one prove a negative?

Still, if any of their letters *had* escaped destruction, they were likely to prove interesting. And, it turned out, at least some of them indeed defied the ravages of time and of well-meaning protectors. Near the end of 1987, when my biography of Freud was in galley proofs, I was notified that the correspondence between Freud and Minna Bernays was on deposit in the Manuscript Division of the Library of Congress. But it was not yet accessible—not yet. Accordingly, when I published *Freud: A Life for Our Time* in April 1988, still skeptical about the story of Freud's secret affair, I was compelled to draw this provisional conclusion without them.

In September 1988, I was informed that the Freud–Minna Bernays correspondence was open to inspection at last. At long last, in Washington, I had the exquisite pleasure—every scholar will know what I felt—of exploring the precious bundle. There I was in the large, peaceful manuscript room of the Library of Congress, sitting at the familiar table where I had sat so often before. Freud's handwriting by now, after years of acquaintance an old companion, offered me no resistance. In contrast, Minna Bernays's was somewhat more problematical: she often dashed off notes in pencil, quickly informing Freud of train schedules and the children's well-being. But before long her handwriting, too, yielded to me.

The cache was fragmentary. It consisted of clusters of letters but displayed sizable gaps. Thus a dozen or so letters from Minna Bernays to Freud dating from the summer of 1910 were obviously replies to messages from Freud—which were missing. Still, what I found was interesting enough. It substantially confirmed, and sometimes elaborated the portraits I had drawn of Minna Bernays, of Martha

. . . .

Freud, of Freud himself in my biography. While in these letters Minna Bernays rarely gave vent to the wit which was proverbial in the family, she showed her claws once or twice. In the Freud household, she was a manager, a privileged nurse, a house sitter. In one letter, dated only "Tuesday," from the summer of 1910, she showed herself in charge while the rest of the Freud family was scattered across the map. "Condition of piggishness—*Schweinerei*—has reached its climax," she informed her brother-in-law in the intimate telegraphic style family members will use with one another. "We had Jewish electricians who were naturally too refined to remove the filth they had left."[8] Such domestic authority was not as good as being married, but it helped a little.

In my biography of Freud I had much to say about his financial straits in the first two decades of his marriage and his pervasive anxiety over his family's future. Several letters in this collection eloquently attest to these worries. He wrote about them frankly, almost obsessively, and normally addressed his mother-in-law as well as his sister-in-law in his communiqués. In early 1887, when the Freuds had been married for just a few months, their poverty threatened a cherished plan to have Minna for a long visit. Freud passes along details about his income, the number of new patients coming in and those deserting him, always with Minna's prospective visit in mind. He could be wryly humorous about his impecuniousness. At the beginning of January 1887, he listed three eventualities that would permit the Freuds to invite Minna to Vienna: a stunning scientific discovery, a marked increase in the roster of his patients, or a lucky hit in the Vienna lottery.[9]

In this letter we see Freud the scientist wrestling, as he always would, with the healer. When in February 1887 his paternal and munificent friend Josef Breuer gave him a microtome, "the most important piece for a domestic laboratory," an expensive scientific instrument that Freud could not possibly have afforded, he was happy. "My style of life," he proudly reported on receiving Breuer's generous present, "stands before a great upheaval."[10]

8. Minna Bernays to Freud, "Tuesday," summer 1910. Freud Collection, LC.
9. Freud to Minna Bernays and Frau Bernays, January 2, 1887. Ibid.
10. Freud to Minna Bernays and Frau Bernays, February 21, 1887. Ibid. The original microtome now stands in the Freud Museum at Berggasse 19.

Several weeks before, on January 19, Freud had notified his correspondents in Hamburg that "since January 1, a fresh wind is blowing through my practice, so that [last] summer's position"—the first summer of his private practice—"has been reached. True, since then two patients have left me, but," he added with sham piety, "God now performs a miracle every day so that we are earning a few Gulden, and it would be very nice of him if he continued to act this way." There is a malicious point to Freud's mockery: Frau Bernays, Minna's mother, was as devout a Jew as Freud was aggressively irreligious. Just five days later, his good cheer irrepressible, he left God aside to report that his practice had only been suffering under a "seasonal depression."[11]

Characteristically, he took pride in his independence: "To be sure, the practice is quantitatively as well as qualitatively quite shabby, still, for a beginner quite promising. To which should be added that it is all my own." In those hard years, the word "shabby" imaginatively varied—including "shabbification—*Verschäbigung*"—was frequently under his pen. Freud's former professor Hermann Nothnagel, who had undertaken to send him patients, had sent only one; his good friend Breuer had sent none: "I stand on my own feet, and will owe my livelihood to myself alone."[12]

Yet this letter of January 24 demonstrates that Freud's confidence as the ambitious research scientist was mingled, even in these youthful days, with a sense of isolation, sometimes of bitterness. He reported that he had some patients "suitable to experimentation," that "literary works" were overwhelming him, that he was making good progress with a lecture he was drafting. "For the rest it is a matter of waiting and keeping prepared." Then he added more somberly: "One finds scientific support nowhere; rather, there is an effort 'not to give you a chance,' which you feel as very disagreeable." An instance: "It is probable that I will lose a second case of male hysteria I discovered in the hospital, only because the chief physician concerned will not permit the case to be published."[13]

This is a revealing passage in more ways than one. In my *Freud*, I noted that Freud's sharp-tongued, sharp-witted sister-in-law had

11. Freud to Minna Bernays and Frau Bernays, January 24, 1887. Ibid.
12. Freud to Minna Bernays and Frau Bernays, February 21, 1887. Ibid.
13. Freud to Minna Bernays, January 24, 1887. Ibid.

. . . .

been his confidante in psychoanalytic matters far more than his wife, even though he did not initiate her into all his intimate medical concerns. Their correspondence offers inklings of their confidential, if in the end appropriately reserved, relationship. Traveling to France in the summer of 1889 to study hypnotic techniques with leading practitioners like Hippolyte Bernheim at Nancy, Freud mainly complained to Minna Bernays, in a rapid-fire series of notes, just how bored and lonely he was. Still, he told her a good deal, then and later. On April 27, 1893, banished from the bedroom while his wife was recovering from giving birth to their daughter Sophie, he wrote Minna Bernays: "I am now using my sleeping in the library room to note down my dreams," and he added in a burst of optimism that in ten years this enterprise would yield "a fine piece of work" and some money as well.[14] This early record of Freud's preoccupation with dreams anticipates his classic *Interpretation of Dreams* not by ten but by six years.[15]

In short, Freud confided in Minna Bernays—about many things, much of the time. A letter she wrote him on August 6, 1910, from Hamburg, where she was caring for her aged and ailing mother, demonstrates how much Freud shared with his sister-in-law—and how much he withheld. Some days before, Freud, on holiday in the Netherlands, had granted Gustav Mahler, a troubled husband, a four-hour psychoanalytic interview. Evidently Freud reported on this consultation to Minna Bernays, because she wrote in reply: "The case of Mahler is very amusing. Perhaps he wanted your advice whether he should return to the Vienna Opera." Nothing about Mahler's severe sexual problems here—Freud could be indiscreet, but he was not about to inform Minna Bernays of the delicate issues the two men had canvassed.

Many of Minna Bernays's letters and hasty postcards circle around the six Freud children. This, as Freud's letters to Fliess of the 1890s

14. Freud to Minna Bernays, April 27, 1893. Ibid.
15. As Ernest Jones has rightly noted in his biography, Freud's interest in dreams extends all the way back to his youth. His letters to his fiancée contain some interesting accounts of his dreams, and a long footnote in his case history of Frau Emmy von N., published in 1895 and evidently written the year before (referring to a session of May 15, 1889), contains the first *published* reference to what was to develop into his full-fledged dream theory. (*Jones* I, 351–53.)

show, had been true for a decade and more.[16] She was inclined to hover over the "rabble," taking a close, intrusive interest in every detail of their lives. In a letter of July 1910, she gently scolded Freud for being too indulgent, especially with his sons: "I'm afraid, *mein Alter,*" she wrote, "you spoil the bad boys too much."[17] That summer, she vacationed with the three Freud daughters at Bistrai, a resort in Austrian Silesia. She found it overcrowded and vulgar but kept her eye on her charges: "Annerl," then going on fifteen, "has in the last few days again gained 80 deca[grams]," over two pounds, "which does not prevent her from being a little *meschuggene.*" Yet the doctor in whose sanitarium they were staying, Ludwig Jekels, was crazy about Anna. Freud always enjoyed hearing such news: Anna was a somewhat troubled youngster who complained to her father in candid letters how all sorts of unreasonable thoughts and feelings plagued her. In postscripts to her aunt's letters, she voiced her longings for intimacy with him and described her state of mind. On July 25, writing to her father from Bistrai, she exclaimed, "Would like to ride, too!!! and play Tarock!"—the card game her father invariably played on Saturday nights in Vienna. By September 4, writing from the delightful Dutch resort of Nordwijk am Zee, she reported that she had enjoyed horseback riding, far more than swimming. She added, "I am now reasonably sensible." Eight years later, though still reasonably sensible, she entered psychoanalysis with her beloved, tarock-playing father.

By that time, Freud was, and would remain, Minna Bernays's "Beloved Old Man—Mein gel. Alter," an affectionate appellation which had also become his wife's name for him. While Freud was traveling through Italy with his new Hungarian friend, Sándor Ferenczi, Minna Bernays was in the Netherlands with all but the eldest of the Freud brood. All, she wrote him reassuringly, were flourishing. One of

16. For an instance, see Freud's jocular note to Fliess, May 25, (18)97: "Last night, my gang—*Gesindel*—left with Minna for Aussee and arrived, according to report, in the finest weather." *Freud—Fliess,* 261 (245). For another, Freud to Fliess, May 28, 1899: "On Friday, they're off (Minna with the children except for Mathilde) to Berchtesgaden." Ibid., 387 (353). Indeed, Freud could refer to his wife and his sister-in-law as "the two mothers." Freud to Fliess, November 9, 1899. Ibid., 423 (385). These are abiding refrains.
17. Minna Bernays to Freud, July 23 (1910). Freud Collection, LC.

· · · · · · · · · · · · · ·

them, Sophie, added a cheerful postscript in a charming mixture of German and approximate Dutch: "Es ist herrlich, prächtig, gemoekelik, lekker etc.—It is magnificent, splendid, jolly, pleasant, etc."[18] Minna confessed herself extremely fond of the Netherlands: "Berlin is a monster," she wrote Freud after visiting that city on her way home, "though one before which we must have the greatest respect." But if she could choose, she added, "I would only want to live in Holland."[19]

Almost incidentally and quite informally, this collection of letters, however fragmentary, sheds light on the characters of other members of the Freud household. In my *Freud,* I acknowledged with some regret that Martha Freud remains a shadowy figure. Only a few of her letters are extant—or accessible—and the observations that visitors to Berggasse 19 made about her are relatively scarce and sometimes contradictory. One of her traits, her compulsive orderliness, of which I have given an instance or two in my biography of Freud, is amply confirmed in one of Freud's letters to his sister-in-law after a few months of marriage. Clearly, this was a lifelong characteristic. In late January 1887, Freud, half amused and half exasperated, told Minna Bernays: "My wife scolds only when I spill something or leave something lying about in disorder, or when I lead her across a filthy spot on the street. It is generally said that I am henpecked. What should one do against that?"[20] A dominant paterfamilias in the classic nineteenth-century bourgeois mold, Freud was grousing good-humoredly, and Minna, who knew him well, understood that perfectly.

The two were close enough, in fact, to exchange a few letters in secret, keeping them from Minna Bernays's mother. "Dear Minning," Freud wrote fondly in April 1887, "my effort to appear as an affectionate son-in-law, in addition to my lack of time, has led to the cessation of our private correspondence." He wanted to resume it, especially since he sensed that she was in a bad mood "for which I do not want to be even partly responsible." Again he canvassed the possibility of her visit, which both Freuds so cordially desired. As a matter of fact, he told her in confidence, they wanted more: "We

18. In a letter by Minna Bernays to Freud, September 7 (1910). Ibid.
19. Minna Bernays to Freud, September 16 (1910). Ibid.
20. Freud to Minna Bernays, January 24, 1887. Ibid.

firmly intend to keep you with us until you establish your own household or after you, following our previous discussions, begin studying at the university at thirty." And so, he urged, "dear child, don't be grumpy. Come to us and let us consider together, how we can move Mama here."[21] These were not matters the two could discuss openly, since Frau Bernays, exacting and pious, would feel uncomfortable in the secular Freud household. He concluded with a tantalizing private reference: "Do you still remember our novel, Book the Second, Riches?" This casual allusion to Dickens's *Little Dorrit* speaks, as they say, volumes. It speaks of closeness and fond hopes, of novels shared and of wealth out of reach.

These early letters yield yet another glimmer of light on Martha Freud's character, on her reserve: "All sorts of circumstances and conditions, among them a few in the morning, indicate," Freud told Minna Bernays in early March 1887, genteelly notifying her that his wife was pregnant, "that our loneliness will come to an end this very year, let us say: in October. My wife does not want me to notify you of this, but I consider concealment wholly useless."[22] He was soon to found a profession that would show concealment to be far worse than useless.

But if Martha Freud cultivated symptoms of gentility, she did not push them to extremes. "Martha," Freud proudly reported to Hamburg in mid-October after the birth of their first child, Mathilde, "was so well-behaved, so courageous and amiable the whole time. Not a sign of impatience or foul mood, and when she had to scream, she would apologize to the physician and the midwife."[23] Indeed, after it was all over, Martha Freud did not object to discussing corporal details with her sister. "Everyone tells me," she wrote in mid-November, "that I look better than before my pregnancy, my body has once again regained its girlish slenderness."[24] Whatever she was, Martha Freud was not the shrinking, fainting female that legend has foisted on middle-class Victorian women.

Then there is a long break in the letters now opened, from the summer of 1910 to the spring of 1938. Obviously,

21. Freud to Minna Bernays, April 28, 1887. Ibid.
22. Freud to Minna Bernays, March 9, 1887. Ibid.
23. Freud to Minna Bernays and Frau Bernays, October 16, 1887. Ibid.
24. Martha Freud to Minna Bernays and Frau Bernays, November 10, 1887. Ibid.

much happened in those twenty-eight years, both to the world and to the Freud household: a devastating world war, postwar misery and furious political struggles in Austria, the Nazis' rise to power in Germany, and then, in early March 1938, Austria's absorption into Hitler's Thousand-Year Reich. Both Minna Bernays and Freud had long been in ill health. Minna had grown increasingly invalid, seeking relief in spas and coping with deteriorating eyesight; Freud was living with the aftermath of drastic operations for cancer of the palate, diagnosed in April 1923. Yet the last series of letters, a set of six dating from mid-May to early June 1938, show a Freud, at eighty-two, as forceful, as much of a stylist, as ever. He wrote them while he was tensely waiting for permission to leave Nazified Austria.

Minna, seriously ailing and almost blind, was no longer in Vienna. She had been taken to London by Anna Freud's intimate, Dorothy Burlingham, on May 5 that year, ahead of the others. There are no replies to Freud's letters to her, but this is not surprising: she was in no condition to write letters, perhaps even to read them. But Freud wrote to her nonetheless, on his large stationery in a firm and vigorous hand, mainly to beguile the time. After the Nazis had taken over Austria, he had declared himself too old, too ill, to leave Vienna. Ernest Jones, who had flown to Vienna soon after the *Anschluss* to persuade Freud that emigration was not desertion, had found him stubborn, if wavering. But one particular event proved more persuasive than Jones's eloquence: Anna, Freud's Antigone, was summoned to Gestapo headquarters on March 22, and Freud spent the most anxious day of his life, fearing the worst, pacing up and down in his study, smoking incessantly as he waited for her release. Now he wanted only one thing: "to die in freedom" in England. Yet the Nazis were exigent, unwilling to issue Freud the *Unbedenklichkeits-erklärung*—the "certificate of innocuousness"—attesting that he had paid all his taxes and met all the extortionate exactions that Nazified Austria had imposed on Jews aching to depart.

"You owe today's letter," Freud wrote Minna Bernays on May 14, "to the circumstance that I am sitting in my room inactive and useless" while "the women" were "working and packing." The sentence vividly conveys Freud's impatience, his almost intolerable frustration with his helplessness. He had always taken pride in his independence and had detested passivity, especially enforced passivity. He informed Minna that he, his wife, and his daughter Anna were "anxiously" waiting for that *Unbedenklichkeitserklärung.* "Anxiously" was not a word he had often applied to himself in his long life. As usual, he went on, Anna was everyone's mainstay. Every other day she reported to police headquarters that they were still in the country. "Almost everything that had to be done Anna has taken care of." He added acidly that "the men"—he himself, his son Martin, and his son-in-law Robert Hollitscher—"were of no use, half mad." In addition to running distasteful and exhausting errands for her own family, Anna was doing the same for others, mainly for Viennese psychoanalysts and their families. "Kris, Wälder, Bibring, Lampl," Freud wrote, "are already out of the country, and this has eased Anna's activity, but she always finds others as substitutes."[25] With almost audible envy, he congratulated Minna for missing all the turmoil and agitation: "Be glad both of you, that you and Dorothy are out of this."[26]

What made all this waiting particularly stressful for Freud was his uncertainty about his cherished little private museum of antiquities. "In the fateful first days of next week," he told Minna, "the commission on which the fate of the collection depends is supposed to come here. The shipper is lurking in the background."[27] Given the sheer calculated mean-spiritedness of Austria's new rulers, he could not be at all confident that they would allow his silent companions to accompany him into exile.

Writing to Minna again on May 20, he mused on the curious turn that events had taken: "You have wished so often to get to England. Now you are there; these are new situations one would have thought

25. There is an interesting discrepancy between Freud's remark about his fellow analysts having left the country and the firm memory of Mrs. Heinz Kohut, who was there at the time. She writes, "Freud was wrong in thinking that at least the Waelders had left Austria before he did. . . . The Waelders left in June— unfortunately I don't know the exact date, but it was my understanding that most of the analysts stayed in Vienna until Freud was safely out of Austria." She speculates that "perhaps Anna told him that [they had already left] so that he wouldn't worry about all she was doing to help people emigrate." Personal communication, February 1, 1989. Since Mrs. Kohut's memory is evidently well founded, her speculation seems to me wholly reasonable and extremely probable. Her comment throws more light on the protective attitude that Freud's younger colleagues and his favorite daughter took toward him.
26. Freud to Minna Bernays, May 14, 1938. Ibid.
27. Ibid.

extremely improbable only a few weeks ago." His desk was empty except for a few sheets of stationery just in case he wanted to write such letters as this. "These are only reports on our moods—*Stimmungsberichte.*" She was, after all, being kept informed by telephone, and some matters, Freud added, "cannot be communicated." Freud's gift for original turns of phrase was unimpaired: "We are between door and hinge," he wrote—quoting a saying conveying a sense of being in a great hurry—like "someone who wants to leave the room but finds that his coat is caught." While his daughter Mathilde and her husband, Robert, he went on, had permission to leave Austria, he was still embroiled with the tax authorities. Again Anna was proving indispensable: "She works, with great skill and good-humoredly, to get us free. She manages things far better than Martin would have succeeded in doing. She gets on good terms with people, becomes popular with them and gains influence over them." The family's situation was unenviable, almost literally painful: "It is said that when one leg of the fox is caught in a trap, he bites off the leg and limps away on three legs. We will follow his example and, I hope, soon get free, if limping." He told Minna that "twice this week" he had taken a drive through the city "to say farewell to Vienna." He remained, as he had been for so long, susceptible to the charm of flowers and commented on their "first spring glory."[28] I am haunted by those two unpretentious, poignant sentences about his farewell to the city he had hated and loved for almost eighty years and imagine Freud in the back of the car, prudently slumped back in his seat, his legs covered with a plaid shawl.

Writing again a few days later, he dwelled on the intense mood of imminent departure. On May 23, he had splendid news: "My collection has been released. Not a single confiscation, a minimal levy of RM 400"—about $100. Fortunately, Director Dehmel of the Vienna museum who had appraised his holdings had been very "merciful." He had estimated the value of Freud's ancient statuettes at RM 30,000—a substantial sum, but far below the limit that would have compelled Freud to leave his collection behind. And so, wrote Freud triumphantly, "the shipper can start with the packing without delay." There was lively traffic at Berggasse 19: "very affectionate farewell visits" from "old friends" and from Mrs. Wiley, the wife of

28. Freud to Minna Bernays, May 20, 1938. Ibid.

the American consular official in Vienna who had been so helpful to the Freuds since the Nazi invasion. A bookseller stopped by, offering to buy the books Freud would not want in England—a business call that reminded Freud of a saying attributed to Francis Bacon which, he notes, he had often quoted in English: "I won't be plucked of my feathers."[29]

That was on May 23. Three days later, Freud reports that there are daily telephone calls to London and Paris and inquiries from journalists as to whether the Freuds are still there. There is even time for a game of tarock. It seems a ghostly card party, worthy of a scene in an Ionesco play: old friends together fighting anxiety in an emptying apartment once full of life, in a crazy and deadly city. In that letter of May 26, Freud shrewdly observes a pervasive dream-like atmosphere in the household: "Everything is in a certain sense unreal, we are no longer here and not yet there."[30] The sentence is a testimonial to the intimacy that Freud and his daughter Anna had achieved; the day before, Anna Freud had expressed this very feeling in almost the same words: "One would not be surprised if the whole affair continued this way for a hundred years. We are no longer quite here and not yet there at all."[31] By this time the two, father and daughter, had virtually merged into a single being.

Two days later, on May 28, the suspense continued. Freud reports that "there is of course nothing new from headquarters." His physician, Max Schur, who was in the hospital with a badly timed attack of appendicitis, was doing well and assured the Freuds that he would be able to accompany them abroad as planned. "The question is," Freud noted, now prepared to see only difficulties, "whether we will be ready."[32]

But relief was in sight. By June 2, when Freud wrote his last letter to his sister-in-law, everything had been settled. Only the date of departure remained in question. Princess Marie Bonaparte, that indispensable, immensely wealthy friend, had come to the rescue. "It seems," Freud notes, "that we have now succeeded in satisfying the tax people with the aid of the princess. There are still lots of for-

29. Freud to Minna Bernays, May 23, 1938. Ibid.
30. Freud to Minna Bernays, May 26, 1938. Ibid.
31. Anna Freud to Jones, May 25, 1938. Jones papers, Archives of the British Psycho-Analytical Society, London. See *Freud,* 628.
32. Freud to Minna Bernays, May 28, 1938. Freud Collection, LC.

malities to be taken care of, one encounters the whole unwieldiness of the official apparatus." Having been overly sanguine before, Freud now showed himself excessively cautious. His lawyer thought the Freuds could "leave as soon as the day after tomorrow," June 4, but Freud conjectured that it would be the following Tuesday, June 7. The lawyer proved right. In any event, Anna had gone to Cook's to buy railroad tickets, and once again Freud took the opportunity to applaud her. "You cannot imagine the role that trivialities now play, and everything, the most important as well as the insignificant, Anna must take care of on her own. She has no help to relieve her of anything just once, and with all this she is steadily pressured and besieged by friends." He was stern about the burdens she was obliged to bear: "It was unjust to leave Anna alone. I am naturally wholly useless." He had taken another excursion, but it only showed how little he could trust himself to do. Finally, in a single reference to his wife, then seventy-eight, he praised Martha Freud for her courage.[33]

This last letter yields another striking, if surprising, image. Freud tells Minna Bernays that he and his family had not been at Berggasse 19 in June for so many years that he was "unprepared for how dark it can be during the day." Ten days earlier, he had reported that the trees in the courtyard on which his study gave were in full leaf. Now he added that he had turned on the electric light only to discover that the shadow of his hand on the paper disturbed him. Hence he was writing this letter in half-darkness. This is a moving revelation, reporting far more on Freud's state of mind than on the light in his study. The darkness was within, for the fact is that, across the years, Freud had spent much of June in Vienna. Here was the investigator committed during all his career to bringing clarity disturbed by what he perceived as shadowy twilight. Night was falling over his life as he wrote a last letter to his beloved sister-in-law in London.

But how beloved? The question remains open. I said earlier that I was not surprised to find only a fragmentary exchange of letters. Still, there was something odd about the missing portions. Someone had numbered the letters consecutively, in pencil. I recognized these numbers: I had seen them before on Freud's

33. Freud to Minna Bernays, June 2, 1938. Ibid.

letters to Karl Abraham and other correspondents. Someone, then, during the London years after Freud's death, had taken the trouble to put Freud's correspondence more or less in order.[34] But, I asked myself, why should there be a gap in the numbering of this collection between a letter of April 27, 1893, and one of July 25, 1910? The letter of 1893 bears no number, but since it follows letter 93 by a single day, it was evidently letter 94 in the series. And the next number is 161. What happened to letters 95 to 160? If someone found good reason to conceal or destroy letters with "forbidden" content—say, unrestrained declarations of love—why not renumber the remaining lot? Or why not destroy them all? The years 1893 to 1910 were the very years when an affair between Freud and his sister-in-law would have taken place, if it did.

But did it? The missing letters are like Sherlock Holmes's famous dog that did not bark in the night. It is most likely that those missing letters no longer exist and that all those who could testify to the tampering, if there was tampering, are dead. Still, if those letters ever do show up, I believe it is exceedingly improbable that they would substantiate the rumor that Jung was apparently the first to float. There are suggestive passages in Freud's writings about coming to terms with the thought of incest with one's mother or sister. But these refer to fantasies rather than to actions. I have noted that Freud was very fond of Minna Bernays from the beginning, even while he was passionately courting her older sister. How fond he remained of her is proved by the talks they had and trips they took, at times alone. But a love affair between them seems to me out of character, for her as much as for him. Jung is too unreliable a witness; the conjectures of others are more ingenious than persuasive. It is not impossible; nothing in human relations is impossible. But there are times when dogs do not bark because they have nothing to bark about.

34. I say "more or less" because whoever did the numbering at times violated the obvious chronological order.

Bibliographical Essay

1: Freud and the Man from Stratford

The literature on Shakespeare is, as everyone knows, already mountainous and growing more so virtually every day. All I can list and comment on (skimpily) here are the titles most relevant to my special concerns and those that stimulated my thinking about the sweet swan of Avon.

Norman H. Holland has a spirited, comprehensive, and beautifully informed account of Freud's views toward Shakespeare (including his Oxfordianism) in *Psychoanalysis and Shakespeare* (1966), esp. ch. 6; it covers some of the ground I have explored. See also the sensible if scattered pages in Jack J. Spector, *The Aesthetics of Freud: A Study in Psychoanalysis and Art* (1972), and Harry Trosman, "Freud and the Controversy over Shakespearean Authorship," *J. Amer. Psychoanal. Assn.* XIII (July 1965), 475–98.

The array of competing claims to Shakespeare's mantle has been examined in S. Schoenbaum's exhaustive, at times devastating and quite pitiless *Shakespeare's Lives* (1970), esp. in part VI, "Deviations," 529–629, which includes several pages on Freud among the Oxfordians. R. C. Churchill, *Shakespeare and His Betters: A History and a Criticism of the Attempts Which Have Been Made to Prove That Shakespeare's Works Were Written by Others* (1958), is a lively dissection of the revisionists, while George McMichael and Edgar M. Glenn, eds., *Shakespeare and His Rivals: A Casebook on the Authorship Controversy* (1962), though slender, collects a diversified anthology of rival claims and includes a helpful bibliography. Two competent professional cryptographers, William F. and Elizebeth S. Friedman, have authoritatively surveyed the history and studied the methods of the games imaginative readers have played with Shakespeare's identity in their fascinating and appropriately skeptical *The Shakespearean Ciphers Examined* (1957).

. . . .

The most convincing (or least unconvincing) advocates of Oxford as Shake-speare are Dorothy and Charlton Ogburn in their extremely bulky *This Star of England* (1952) and their son Charlton Ogburn's only slightly less bulky *The Mysterious William Shakespeare: The Myth and the Reality* (1984). I have listed the pro-Oxford titles Freud owned (and he owned many of them) in the text, pp. 11–13. For these and all other volumes on and by Shakespeare in Freud's library, see J. Keith Davies, N. J. Lockley, and S. D. Neufeld, compilers, *Freud's London Library: Preliminary Catalogue* (typescript, 1988). James Lardner, "Onward and Upward with the Arts: The Authorship Question," *New Yorker* (April 11, 1988), 87–106, is a characteristically in-formal but well-researched report of the "trial" of the Oxford question in Washington on September 25, 1987.

Practically all responsible literary scholars have agreed that Shakespeare wrote Shakespeare. But they have not simply taken his identity for granted; rather, they have patiently amassed evidence in the Stratford man's behalf. See again the titles by Churchill and by McMichael and Glenn cited above, and the most dependable modern life, complete with virtually all available supporting material, S. Schoenbaum, *William Shakespeare: A Documentary Life* (1975). (A revised compact edition of this attractive behemoth was published in 1977.) Schoenbaum has compressed what we have come to know in "The Life of Shakespeare," in Stanley Wells, ed., *The Cambridge Companion to Shakespeare Studies* (1986), 1–16. T. W. Baldwin, *William Shakspere's Small Latine & Lesse Greeke*, 2 vols. (1944), is an exhaustive justification of the Stratfordians' case.

On the powerful nineteenth-century tradition of biographical criticism, see the chapters on Sainte-Beuve, Bagehot, Taine, Brandes, and others in René Wellek's informed, nuanced, masterful *A History of Modern Criticism, 1750–1950*, esp. vol. III, *The Age of Transition* (1965), and vol. IV, *The Later Nineteenth Century* (1965). For James Joyce's Shakespeare, there is, for a start, ch. 2 in Richard Ellmann's *The Consciousness of Joyce* (1977). On the failure of the Germans to be the first to write a major biography of Goethe, see Wolfgang Leppmann, *The German Image of Goethe* (1961), and the earlier, still useful H. Maync, *Geschichte der deutschen Goethe-Biographie* (1906; 2nd ed., 1914).

While psychoanalytic criticism, whether of Shakespeare or of any other writer or artist, cannot help being in some way biographical, modern literary assessments have, of course, made much of the shaping power of the literary imagination and the *distance* of writers from their creations—creations which are, in any event, not living human beings with psyches of their own. "Shakespeare wrote *Hamlet*," the late Robert Penn Warren has said, speak-ing for the dominant consensus, "he was not Hamlet." Among the most assertive literary historians of that school, the prolific Elmer Edgar Stoll stands out; see, above all, *Art and Artifice in Shakespeare* (1933) and *Shake-speare and Other Masters* (1940). "It is not justifiable," Stoll wrote in *From Shakespeare to Joyce: Authors and Critics, Literature and Life* (1944), 1, "to treat literary or dramatic art as a document, a record or relic of the time, on the one hand, or of the author's life, on the other." (In this last-cited volume, he has a long chapter, "Psychoanalysis in Criticism: Dickens, Kipling, Joyce," in which he takes Edmund Wilson's *The Wound and the Bow* [1941; rev. ed., 1952] severely to task for psychologizing literature.) A key document in the revolt against biography, inevitably (and justly) cited, is L. C. Knights, "How Many Children Had Lady Macbeth? An Essay in the Theory and Practice of Shakespeare Criticism" (1933), conveniently available in *Explorations: Essays in Criticism, Mainly on the Literature of the Seventeenth Century* (1946), 1–39.

Psychoanalytic critics have not fully come to terms with this disjunction between creator and creation, though Meredith Anne Skura, *The Literary Use of the Psychoanalytic Process* (1981), makes a valiant attempt, while Elizabeth Dalton, *Unconscious Structure in "The Idiot": A Study in Literature and Psychoanalysis* (1979), bravely treats Dostoevsky's characters *as* human beings.

Surveying the psychoanalytic reading of Shakespeare, by Freud and other analysts, Holland, in his *Psychoanalysis and Shakespeare,* already cited, is entertaining and informative, being both general and particular—play by play—and offering an exhaustive bibliography down to 1964. David Willbern has taken relevant titles (articles, portions of books, and books—461 of them) forward from that date in "A Bibliography of Psychoanalytic and Psychological Writings on Shakespeare: 1964–1978," in Murray M. Schwartz and Coppélia Kahn, eds., *Representing Shakespeare: New Psychoanalytic Essays* (1980), 264–86. Other papers in that volume include theoretical pieces (notably Norman H. Holland, "Hermia's Dream," 1–20, and Murray M. Schwartz, "Shakespeare Through Contemporary Psychoanalysis," 21–32, attempting to move beyond "traditional" to more "modern" Freudian readings) and a clutch of papers on Shakespearean plays and themes. (I should note parenthetically—though this deserves more extended treatment elsewhere—that I am somewhat skeptical of the "progress" that a number of recent psychoanalytic critics see in an increasing preoccupation with the critic's own mind as over against the "old-fashioned" preoccupation with the work under review.) One of the editors, Coppélia Kahn, has also published an interesting feminist study, *Man's Estate: Masculine Identity in Shakespeare* (1980). Among other anthologies, Edith Kurzweil and William Phillips, eds., *Literature and Psychoanalysis* (1983), ranging from Freud to Kristeva, Fromm to Hartmann, is perhaps the most versatile. Probably the most venturesome recent speculative psychoanalytic interpretation of

Shakespeare is Stanley Cavell, *Disowning Knowledge in Six Plays of Shakespeare* (1987), including a short essay on *Hamlet* which resorts to the technical psychoanalytic notion of the primal scene to explicate the play. I should also mention some of the fine work by C. L. Barber, who, though no psychoanalytic critic, was open to Freud's ideas; see, notably, *Shakespeare's Festive Comedy: A Study of Dramatic Form and Its Relation to Social Custom* (1959) and "The Family in Shakespeare's Development: Tragedy and Sacredness," in Schwartz and Kahn, *Representing Shakespeare,* 188–202.

But to the two plays I concentrate on in my essay: *Macbeth* and *Hamlet.* For the psychoanalysis of *Macbeth,* apart from the Freudian texts discussed in my essay, see Ludwig Jekels, "The Riddle of Shakespeare's *Macbeth*" (1917; tr. 1943), in *Selected Papers* (1952), 105–30. Isadore Henry Coriat, an early American follower of Freud, published a slim volume whose thesis is contained in its title, *The Hysteria of Lady Macbeth* (1912; 2nd ed., 1920). The New Haven psychoanalyst Henry Wexler had a brief paper on the knocking at the gate, "Fate Knocks," *Int. J. Psycho-Anal.* XL (1959), 232–37, while one of Freud's original adherents, Isador Sadger, devotes part of his monograph *Sleepwalking and Moonwalking* (1914; tr. Louise Brink, 1920) to Lady Macbeth. Freudian readings apart, the study by Henry N. Paul, *The Royal Play of Macbeth: When, Why, and How It Was Written by Shakespeare* (1950), is exhaustive on the dynastic and political details of this *"pièce d'occasion."* See also Roy Walker, *The Time Is Free: A Study of Macbeth* (1949); the introductory essay and commentary on *Macbeth* by G. K. Hunter in *The New Penguin Shakespeare* (1967); William Empson's quirky and suggestive *"Macbeth,"* in *Essays on Shakespeare* (1986), 137–57; Cleanth Brooks, "The Naked Babe and the Cloak of Manliness," in *The Well-Wrought Urn: Studies in the Structure of Poetry* (1947), 22–49, an elegant, still stirring essay in the old new criticism concentrating on the imagery in the play; the relevant section (part II, ch. 5) in E. M. W. Tillyard, *Shakespeare's History Plays* (1944); not to forget the pioneering, still-stimulating, and still-controversial chapters in A. C. Bradley, *Shakespearean Tragedy* (1904; 2nd ed., 1905), lectures IX and X.

On the psychoanalytic reading of *Hamlet,* there is principally the much-debated study of Hamlet's motives for hesitating to kill King Claudius by Ernest Jones, *Hamlet and Oedipus* (1949), which began as a short article some four decades earlier. Holland, in *Psychoanalysis and Shakespeare,* has a valuable lengthy bibliographical account (pp. 373–77) of the way that Jones's thesis has been accepted, adapted, enlarged, and rejected. Among a vast outpouring of nonpsychoanalytic literature on *Hamlet,* I have found most impressive (and this is a subjective set of choices if ever there was one) L. C. Knights, as magisterial an authority as we have had in this century, *An Approach to "Hamlet"* (1960); another late essay by William Empson,

"Hamlet," in *Essays on Shakespeare,* 79–136; Helen Gardner, *"Hamlet* and the Tragedy of Revenge" (1959), W. H. Clemen, "The Imagery of *Hamlet"* (1951), and above all Maynard Mack, "The World of *Hamlet"* (1952), all three conveniently available in Leonard F. Dean, ed., *Shakespeare: Modern Essays in Criticism* (1957; rev. ed., 1967), 218–26, 227–41, 242–62; and once again Bradley, *Shakespearean Tragedy,* lectures IV and V. Arthur McGee, *The Elizabethan Hamlet* (1987), ingeniously puts the play into its original ambience. J. Dover Wilson, *What Happens in "Hamlet"* (1935), remains worth reading. André Green, *Hamlet et "Hamlet"* (1982), is a brilliant, speculative essay by a French psychoanalyst. See also the psychoanalytic reading by Theodore Lidz, *Hamlet's Enemy: Madness and Myth in "Hamlet"* (1975).

2: Six Names in Search of an Interpretation

Since Freud's six children were born between 1887 and 1895, the most informative source for his attitude toward naming them is his correspondence with Wilhelm Fliess, to be eked out with some revealing comments Freud makes in *The Interpretation of Dreams.* For Freud's attitudes toward his parents, which necessarily influenced his perception of his own paternal role, see the important papers by George Mahl: "Father-Son Themes in Freud's Self-Analysis," in Stanley H. Cath, Alan R. Gurwitt, and John Munder Ross, eds., *Father and Child: Developmental and Clinical Perspectives* (1982), 33–64, and "Freud, *Father* and *Mother:* Quantitative Aspects," *Psychoanalytic Psychology* II (1985), 99–113.

Unfortunately, historians of Jewish culture have had very little to say about the custom of bestowing names on children. But see J. (Joseph Jacobs), "Names (Personal)," in Isidore Singer et al., eds., *The Jewish Encyclopedia,* 12 vols. (1901–1905), IX, 152–60, a concentrated but helpful entry; the authoritative pages in Jacob Z. Lauterbach, *Studies in Jewish Law, Custom and Folklore,* selected by Bernard J. Bamberger (1970), 30–74; Solomon B. Freehof, *Reform Jewish Practice and Its Rabbinic Background* (1944); and Herman Pollack, *Jewish Folkways in Germanic Lands (1648–1806): Studies in Aspects of Daily Life* (1971), esp. p. 25. For the Ephraim family, see the brief entry "Ephraim," complete with an informative family tree, in Cecil Roth et al., eds., *Encyclopedia Judaica,* 17 vols. (1972–1982), VI, 810–12.

For Freud's intellectual style as developed in his early years, see *Jones* I, 40–41; Siegfried Bernfeld, "Freud's Earliest Theories and the School of Helmholtz," *Psychoanalytic Quarterly* XIII (1944), 341–62; Bernfeld, "Freud's Scientific Beginnings," *American Imago* VI (1949), 163–96; and *Freud,* 30–36, with the relevant bibliographical indications. For Freud's medical Vienna, George Rosen's brief "Freud and Medicine in Vienna," in

Jonathan Miller, ed., *Freud: The Man, His World, His Influence* (1972), 21–39, is authoritative. E. Th. Brücke, *Ernst Brücke* (1929), and Max Neuburger, *Hermann Nothnagel. Leben und Wirken eines deutschen Klinikers* (1922), are informative but should be supplemented with Erna Lesky's compendious and reliable *The Vienna Medical School of the Nineteenth Century* (1965; tr. L. Williams and I. S. Levij, 1976).

Leonard Shengold, "Freud and Josef," in Mark Kanzer, ed., *The Unconscious Today: Essays in Honor of Max Schur* (1971), 473–94, says the essential about one of Freud's most significant identifications, and well.

3: Freud and Freedom

The debate over determinism and freedom is both ancient and apparently unending. What I have attempted to do in my essay on Freud's deterministic psychology of freedom is to place Freud in the continuing discussion, largely to improve, once again, my opportunities for mapping Freud's mind. In my reading among philosophical texts on freedom and determinism (scattered but, I trust, not casual), I have particularly benefited from the following titles—arranged not in order of importance but, for convenience, alphabetically: A. J. Ayer, "Freedom and Necessity" (1946), in *Philosophical Essays* (1954), 271–84; Donald Davidson, "How Is Weakness of the Will Possible?" (1970), 21–42, in *Essays on Actions and Events* (1980), and "Freedom to Act" (1973), ibid., 63–82; Ilham Dilman, *Freud and the Mind* (1984), a careful survey of the issues Freudian thought presents to the philosopher, including two chapters (9 and 10) on determinism and freedom; Harry G. Frankfurt, "Freedom of the Will and the Concept of a Person," *Journal of Philosophy* LXVIII (January 14, 1971), 5–20, which lucidly takes on P. F. Strawson's definition of a person in *Individuals* (1959), and "Alternate Possibilities and Moral Responsibility," ibid., LXVI (December 4, 1969), 829–39; Stuart Hampshire, "Spinoza and the Idea of Freedom," a British Academy Lecture for 1960, in P. F. Strawson, ed., *Studies in the Philosophy of Thought and Action* (1968), 48–70, with a pair of stimulating pages on Freud (66–68), and *Freedom of the Individual* (1965); Thomas Nagel, *The View from Nowhere* (1986), a most congenial essay, with ch. 7, "Freedom," particularly relevant here; Brian O'Shaughnessy, *The Will: A Dual-Aspect Theory*, 2 vols. (1980), a sustained argument that draws on Freud frequently; Bernard Williams, *Ethics and the Limits of Philosophy* (1985), esp. ch. 4, "Foundations: Practical Reason." I single out Isaiah Berlin, who was after all the occasion for my writing this paper in the first place: *Four Essays on Liberty* (1969), esp. the long paper "Historical Inevitability." (For some trenchant criticisms of Berlin's thesis, however, see Ernest Nagel's classic text on which many of us grew up and which remains valuable, *The Structure of Science: Problems in the Logic of Scientific Explanation* [1961], esp. 599–606.) Nagel's treatise ends with this stirring call: "However acute our awareness may be of the rich variety of human experience, and however great our concern over the dangers of using the fruits of science to obstruct the development of human individuality, it is not likely that our best interests would be served by stopping objective inquiry into the various conditions determining the existence of human traits and actions, and thus shutting the door to the progressive liberation from illusion that comes from the knowledge achieved by such inquiry" (606). Nagel was no Freudian, but this closing sentence simply paraphrases the famous last paragraph of Freud's *Future of an Illusion,* which I quote twice in the text of this book.

There are useful papers and comments gathered in Sidney Hook, ed., *Determinism and Freedom in the Age of Modern Science* (1958), including presentations by Brand Blanchard, Max Black, H. L. A. Hart, and Paul Edwards, as well as particularly interesting responses by Carl G. Hempel and Ernest Nagel; one paper I found especially rewarding is John Hospers, "What Means This Freedom?" (pp. 126–42), which argues the issue of determinism from a psychoanalytic perspective. In contrast, for the widespread hostility of outspoken philosophers to psychoanalysis (which, to their minds, is unscientific because it does not offer—they say—falsifiable propositions) see a number of the contributions to a symposium edited by Sidney Hook, *Psychoanalysis, Scientific Method, and Philosophy* (1959).

The uses of psychoanalysis for philosophy (or vice versa) have been little explored; such cross-fertilization as exists has been sparse, informal, and inconclusive. Only a few philosophers have gone to school to Freud; a small handful of psychoanalysts have tried to think philosophically in their theoretical papers. (Freud's own contemptuous attitude toward philosophy and philosophers has not helped.) For the first group, the philosophers Brian O'Shaughnessy and Richard Wollheim are particularly noteworthy; for the second group, the psychoanalysts, see Ernest Jones (grappling with the central issue in a paper delivered in 1924, "Free Will and Determinism," in *Essays in Applied Psycho-Analysis,* 2 vols. [1923; ed. 1951], II, 178–89), Roy Schafer (especially his attempt to translate technical psychoanalytic lingo into ordinary language in *Language and Insight* [1978]), and Heinz Hartmann (a philosophically trained analyst, as his masterly essay *Psychoanalysis and Moral Values* [1960], attests). In this drought, the volume of essays edited by Wollheim and James Hopkins, *Freud: A Collection of Critical Essays* (1983), which sports a variety of philosophical papers on psychoanalytic topics, is all the more welcome. It may seem invidious to single out some contributors to this collection at the expense of others, but I found partic-

·ularly instructive B. R. Cosin, C. F. Freeman, and N. H. Freeman, "Critical Empiricism Criticized: The Case of Freud," 32–59; Brian O'Shaughnessy, "The Id and the Thinking Process," 106–23; Richard Wollheim, "The Bodily Ego," 124–38; Thomas Nagel, "Freud's Anthropomorphism," 228–40; David Pears, "Motivated Irrationality, Freudian Theory and Cognitive Dissonance," 264–88; and Donald Davidson, "Paradoxes of Irrationality," 289–305.

In addition, I call attention to some informal lectures by John Wisdom, "Philosophy, Metaphysics and Psycho-Analysis," in *Philosophy and Psychoanalysis* (1969), 248–82, which keep less than the title promises. And see the engaging, in some ways naive but still pioneering essay in psychoanalyzing a philosopher by John Oulton Wisdom (not the same man): *The Unconscious Origins of Berkeley's Philosophy* (1953). This refreshing perspective has long been the hallmark of Morris Lazerowitz. See his "The Relevance of Psychoanalysis to Philosophy," ch. 6 in *Studies in Metaphilosophy* (1964), 236–56; "Understanding Philosophy" and, less directly, "Philosophy and Illusion," chs. 4 and 5 in *Philosophy and Illusion* (1968); and his comparative paper "Freud and Wittgenstein," ch. 2 in *The Language of Philosophy: Freud and Wittgenstein* (1977). The idea underlying Lazerowitz's attempt to ally psychoanalysis with philosophy is to see the latter as a kind of therapy, exposing illusions. David Pears, a philosopher open to psychoanalytic ideas, has used them in *Motivated Irrationality* (1984), which, though, to my mind, does not go far enough in its uses of Freudian categories. Donald Davidson's paper "Paradoxes of Irrationality," cited just above, is on the other hand exemplary.

On free association, see in addition to the passages from Schafer quoted in the text, Anton O. Kris, *Free Association: Method and Process* (1982).

For the physiological bent of nineteenth-century psychiatry, see *Freud*, 119–24, and, above all, William F. Bynum, Jr., "Rationales for Therapy in British Psychiatry," in Andrew Scull, ed., *Madhouses, Mad-Doctors, and Madmen: The Social History of Psychiatry in the Victorian Era* (1981), 35–57, as well as Michael J. Clark, "The Rejection of Psychological Approaches to Mental Disorder in Late Nineteenth-Century British Psychiatry," ibid., 271–312.

The central issue of my paper, freedom, has been discussed by at least two psychoanalysts: Robert Waelder, "The Problem of Freedom in Psychoanalysis and the Problem of Reality Testing," first published in German in 1934, *Int. J. Psycho-Anal.* XVII (1936), 89–108; and Robert P. Knight, "Determinism, 'Freedom,' and Psychotherapy" (1946), in Stuart C. Miller, ed., *Clinician and Therapist: Selected Papers of Robert P. Knight* (1972), 131–48. I did not discover until the 1970s that Knight had used the sentence about freedom from Freud's *The Ego and the Id* some eight years before I did so in "The Enlightenment in the History of Political Theory," *Political*

Science Quarterly LXIX (1954), 374–89 (quotation at 379n), a paper in which I first characterized Freud as a belated child of the Enlightenment. (On this characterization, see the bibliographical notes for chapter 4.)

4: Reading Freud Through Freud's Reading

In writing this paper, I found myself on relatively virgin ground. The only scholar to have studied Freud as a reader seriously (in addition to the comments that such biographers as Ernest Jones or memoirists like Hanns Sachs have necessarily scattered through their writings on Freud) is Peter Brückner, whose articles "Sigmund Freuds Privatlektüre," *Psyche* XV (1962), 881–902; XVI (1962–1963), 721–43, 881–95, he slightly recast and enlarged into a book: *Sigmund Freuds Privatlektüre* (1975). Brückner concentrates on some ten or more of Freud's favorite authors, like Milton and Cervantes and Dickens, and has much of interest to say. On the other hand, three excellent studies of Freud as a writer say virtually nothing about him as a reader: Walter Muschg, "Freud als Schriftsteller," in *Die Zerstörung der deutschen Literatur* (1956; 3rd ed., enlarged, 1958), 303–47, a splendid pioneering appreciation; Walter Schönau, *Sigmund Freuds Prosa. Literarische Elemente seines Stils* (1968), a technical study including remarks on Freud's metaphors, citations, even epigraphs; and Patrick J. Mahony, *Freud As a Writer* (1982; expanded ed., 1987), more informal but quite as informative.

Not all of the ten authors of the "good books" Freud listed have been studied thoroughly. Dmitri Merezhkovsky, for one, might benefit from more thoroughgoing critical attention. Meanwhile, there are some illuminating pages in Renato Poggioli, *The Poets of Russia* (1960), passim, esp. 71–83. See also C. Harold Bedford, *The Seeker: D. H. Merezhkovsky* (1975), and Bernice Glatzer Rosenthal, *Dmitri Sergeevich Merezhkowsy and the Silver Age: The Development of a Revolutionary Mentality* (1975). W. H. Bruford, *Chekhov and His Russia: A Sociological Study* (1948), sets the stage well. As for "Multatuli," there is now an abundant Dutch literature, but in English there is principally Peter King, *Multatuli* (1972), a terse but convenient study of a writer and reformer once famous but now (outside his homeland) almost forgotten (Brückner also has some helpful comments).

Most of the other writers suffer from, if anything, an abundance of studies, and I list here only those that have made a difference to me. To begin with, the literature surrounding Mark Twain is threatening to become ungainly. Van Wyck Brooks, *The Ordeal of Mark Twain* (1920), was a once-sensational disenchanted treatment of Samuel Clemens as a tragic case of selling out to mass culture; though now partly dated, it retains more than mere period charm. Bernard De Voto, *Mark Twain's America* (1932), offered a vigorous response. Justin Kaplan, *Mr. Clemens and Mark Twain: A Biography* (1966), is a full and thoughtful life resting on wide research. Among modern students, Henry Nash Smith has been particularly authoritative. See his *Mark Twain: The Development of a Writer* (1962); *Mark Twain's Fable of Progress: Political and Economic Ideas in "A Connecticut Yankee"* (1964); "That Hideous Mistake of Poor Clemens's," *Harvard Library Bulletin* IX (1955), 145–80, a hilarious and, at the same time, highly instructive account of Mark Twain, the rambunctious Westerner as after-dinner speaker in the East, offending the brahmin establishment with his sense of humor; and "Guilt and Innocence in Mark Twain's Later Fiction," ch. 6 in *Democracy and the Novel: Popular Resistance to Classic American Writers* (1978).

The literature on Kipling is quite as large as that on Mark Twain, and growing as rapidly. I single out Edmund Wilson's classic essay, "The Kipling That Nobody Read," ch. 2 in *The Wound and the Bow*. Charles Carrington, *Rudyard Kipling: His Life and Work* (1955), is a substantial, rather protective biography. J. M. S. Tompkins, *The Art of Rudyard Kipling* (1959), is an original study of the writer. Roger Lancelyn Green has edited *Kipling: The Critical Heritage* (1971), which, in revealing fashion, collects the reception. Andrew Rutherford, ed., *Kipling's Mind and Art: Essays* (1964), gathers together some important statements (including Edmund Wilson's, cited above, Lionel Trilling's sensitive "Kipling" [1943], and George Orwell's well-known "Rudyard Kipling" [1946]); the anthology, though, is valuable in addition for its more recent papers on the controversial aspects of Kipling's ideas on war and empire, such as Noel Annan, "Kipling's Place in the History of Ideas," Andrew Rutherford, "Officer and Gentlemen," J. H. Fenwick, "Soldiers Three," and, above all, George Shepperson, "The World of Rudyard Kipling." See also J. I. M. Stewart, *Rudyard Kipling* (1976).

For Zola, there is F. W. J. Hemmings, *Emile Zola* (1953; 2nd ed., 1966), well informed on the life but a little superficial (it seems to me) on the thought. Hemmings, *Culture and Society in France, 1848–1898: Dissidents and Philistines* (1971), more satisfactory, provides the relevant social and political background, especially in the later chapters. The splendid five-volume Pléiade edition of the Rougon-Macquart cycle, edited by Armand Lanoux (1960–1967), boasts a magnificent apparatus. Angus Wilson, *Emile Zola* (1952), is the interesting appreciation of one novelist for another. The treatment of Zola (ch. 6) in Harry Levin, *The Gates of Horn: A Study of Five French Realists* (1963), is somewhat pretentious in tone but valuable in judgment.

For Gottfried Keller and Conrad Ferdinand Meyer, two mainstays of nineteenth-century German-language literature, see, for the first, J. M. Lindsay, *Gottfried Keller: Life and Works* (1968), rather pedestrian but thorough and with an extensive bibliography, essential for those who have no German.

Adolf Muschg, *Gottfried Keller* (1977), is an original, venturesome essay complete with long quotations from others and commentaries on pictures. Hermann Boeschenstein, *Gottfried Keller* (1969), offers a succinct summary of life and work; his longer study, *Gottfried Keller: Grundzüge seines Lebens und Werkes* (1948), is a fine exploration. The key study, including letters and diaries, on which much later commentary has been based, is Emil Ermatinger, *Gottfried Kellers Leben, Briefe und Tagebücher,* 3 vols. (1915–1916). For a reading of one novella in Keller's *Leute von Seldwyla,* "Die drei gerechten Kammacher," see Martin Swales, *The German "Novelle"* (1977), ch. 8. Marianne Burkhard has performed a service for English-speakers with her brief yet dependable *Conrad Ferdinand Meyer* (1978). Among many interpretations, I found particularly instructive Günter H. Hertling, *Conrad Ferdinand Meyers Epik. Traumbeseelung, Traumbesinnung und Traumbesitz* (1973), with separate treatment of *Huttens letzte Tage* and *Die Richterin* (chs. 2 and 11). See also Heinrich Henel, *The Poetry of Conrad Ferdinand Meyer* (1954).

For Anatole France, Nobel Prize–winner for literature whose star has long been waning, there is the sensible study by Carter Jefferson, *Anatole France: The Politics of Skepticism* (1965). Micheline Tison-Braun, *La Crise de l'humanisme,* vol. I, *1890–1914* (1958), offers an interesting interpretation of the age. And for a look back at Anatole France's debt to the French Enlightenment's greatest wit, see Jean Sareil, *Anatole France et Voltaire* (1961).

For Macaulay, we have John Clive, *Macaulay: The Shaping of the Historian* (1973), a valuable and appealing biography of his early years which goes beyond its self-imposed limits. My "Macaulay, Intellectual Voluptuary," in *Style in History* (1974), 95–138, seeks the man in the style (see also the bibliographical indications in that book, pp. 227–30). Both Clive (pp. 77–78, 107) and I (p. 131) comment on the limits of Macaulay's optimism. Among many studies, the old biography by G. O. Trevelyan, *The Life and Letters of Lord Macaulay,* 2 vols. (1876; enlarged one-vol. ed., 1908), a monument to Victorian thoroughness, retains much of its value.

For Gomperz, there is the authoritative collection of documents with rich commentary by his son, *Theodor Gomperz: Ein Gelehrtenleben im Bürgertum der Franz-Josefs-Zeit. Auswahl seiner Briefe und Aufzeichnungen, 1869–1912, erläutert und zu einer Darstellung seines Lebens verknüpft von Heinrich Gomperz,* revised and edited (with a good introduction) by Robert A. Kann (1974).

As for the Enlightenment and its thought, I want to note that I devoted some twenty years of my professional life to that intellectual and political movement, attempting to show (among other things) that the philosophes were not, their reputation to the contrary, mindless optimists, superficial rationalists, or unhistorical journalists. See my collection of essays *The Party of Humanity: Essays in the French Enlightenment* (1964); my longer reading *The Enlightenment: An Interpretation,* vol. I, *The Rise of Modern Paganism* (1966), and vol. II, *The Science of Freedom* (1969); and my brief, informal set of dialogues summarizing my argument, *The Bridge of Criticism: Dialogues Among Lucian, Erasmus, and Voltaire on the Enlightenment—on History and Hope, Imagination and Reason, Constraint and Freedom—and Its Meaning for Our Time* (1970).

5: Serious Jests

Considering the attractiveness of the theme, it is astonishing how thin the literature on Freud and humor continues to be. The most sustained effort, a well-informed monograph from which I have learned despite considerable disagreements on interpretations, is Elliot Oring, *The Jokes of Sigmund Freud: A Study in Humor and Jewish Identity* (1984). I do not share Oring's admiration for John Murray Cuddahy's *The Ordeal of Civility: Freud, Marx, Lévi-Strauss, and the Jewish Struggle with Modernity* (1974), which cites some of Freud's jokes. Theodor Reik has been earnest, even tragic, in his paper "On the Nature of Jewish Wit" (1954), in *From Thirty Years with Freud* (tr. Richard Winston, 1940), 185–96. The same holds true of Reik's longer treatment, *Jewish Wit* (1962). See, in addition, Kurt Schlesinger, "Jewish Humor as Jewish Identity," *International Review of Psychoanalysis* VI (1979), 317–30, and Alexander Grinstein, *On Sigmund Freud's Dreams* (1968; 2nd ed., 1980), which includes some of Freud's jokes in its analysis.

Salcia Landmann, *Der jüdische Witz. Soziologie, Sammlung, Glossar* (1960; 5th ed., rev. and enlarged, 1962), has scored an almost legendary success with her abridged paperback edition, *Jüdische Witze, ausgewählt und eingeleitet von Salcia Landmann* (1963): my copy, dated 1976, is the eighteenth printing, showing almost 450,000 copies sold. In view of the way she garbles often excellent stories, this is unfortunate, as was noted in the devastating, irrefutable review by the Austrian novelist, journalist, and humorist Friedrich Torberg, " 'Wai geschrien!' oder Salcia Landmann ermordet den jüdischen Witz. Anmerkungen zu einem beunruhigenden Bestseller," *Der Monat,* no. 157 (October 1961), 48–65. Torberg's own wonderful collections of anecdotes (few of them jokes, mainly true stories), *Die Tante Jolesch, oder der Untergang des Abendlandes in Anekdoten* (1975), and its sequel, *Die Erben der Tante Jolesch* (1978), memorably conjure up a laughing Vienna that was long a-dying and given its final blow in March 1938 by Hitler and his assiduous Austrian adorers.

For Freud as a humorous man, I refer to the reminiscences by Hanns Sachs, *Freud: Master and Friend;* Martin Freud, *Freud: Man and Father;* Joan Riviere, "An Intimate Impression," *Lancet* II (September 30, 1939), 765–67; Franz Alexander, "Recollections of Berggasse 19," *Psychoanalytic Quarterly* IX (1940), 195–204; Roy R. Grinker, "Reminiscences of a Personal Contact with Freud," *American Journal of Orthopsychiatry* X (1940), 850–54; and Fritz Wittels, *Sigmund Freud: His Personality, His Teaching, and His School* (1924; tr. Eden and Cedar Paul, 1924), among others. In any event, on the subject of Freud and jokes, Freud and humor, the final word has most certainly not been said.

It should be obvious why I have no bibliographical comments for Six and Seven.

8: The Dog That Did Not Bark in the Night

In the bibliographical essay to *Freud,* 752–53, I have given details on why I am fairly confidently (though not dogmatically) persuaded that Jung's report of an affair between Freud and his sister-in-law Minna Bernays is untenable. To this I want now to add a persuasive paper that I overlooked before, by Alan C. Elms, "Freud and Minna," *Psychology Today* XVI (1982), 40–46.

. . . .
Acknowledgments

In writing and revising these essays over the years, I have incurred many debts which deserve acknowledgment. I am deeply grateful to my old friend Gladys Topkis for first suggesting this collection of essays on Freud and for seeing the manuscript through the press with her characteristic skill and generosity. (I want also to thank Margaret Kovach and Larry Kenney of the Yale University Press.) Elise Snyder encouraged me to pursue my lighter vein long before its products became controversial. Happily for me, John Merriman invited me to exercise my imagination. George Mahl, who worked so selflessly with me on my *Freud: A Life for Our Time,* was instrumental in my inquiry into the names Freud gave his children. Ronald S. Wilkinson, Manuscript Historian at the Manuscript Division of the Library of Congress, was at once scrupulous and forthcoming with information about unpublished Freud materials. Bill McGuire has long been disinterested and constructive, especially in matters concerning Jung. C. A. Meier cleared up an important question about the interview Jung granted John M. Billinsky in 1957. Stuart Feder gave me a welcome opportunity to discuss Freud's family romance (or, rather, its absence) before the New York Psychoanalytic Society. Ivo Banac called my attention to, and translated, a piece about my *Harper's* magazine article in a Yugoslav newspaper and further put me in his debt by writing a letter to the editor. Dr. Albrecht Hirschmüller kindly sent me xeroxes of an article in the *Neue Freie Presse* savaging an attempt to attribute Shakespeare's works to Bacon. Peter Demetz discussed with me the delay in the appearance of German biographies of Goethe. Mrs. Heinz Kohut kindly permitted me to publish an extract from a noteworthy letter she wrote me about Vienna in June 1938. Richard Wells, director of the Freud Museum in London, considerately supplied me with valuable material relevant to my paper "Freud and the Man from Stratford," as did Keith Davies. Rebecca Haltzel saved me a good deal of work with her timely assistance in the Yale libraries. Jackie Katwan introduced me to Friedrich Torberg. Gaby Katwan, Hank Gibbons, Iza Erlich, Thomas Greene, and Cyrus Hamlin talked Freud and Shakespeare with me, much to my profit. Alan Elms sent me an important paper on Freud and his sister-in-law. Sam Ritvo was right all along.

A number of other friends and colleagues read individual chapters or made suggestions that improved them. Quentin Skinner (who wrote me an exemplary letter), Harry Frankfurt, and Ernst Prelinger thoughtfully went over "Freud and Freedom." Anatole Broyard, whose stylistic suggestions I found helpful, skillfully edited my article on Freud's correspondence with Minna Bernays, while Lynne Lehrman Weiner helpfully questioned a passage in that same paper. Though these "assistants" by no means agree with everything I have said, all of them have made this exercise in nostalgia and revision a pleasure.

As for so many years, my wife, Ruth, was again exceedingly forthcoming, sustaining me through all this enterprise and taking time out from her own work to go over the whole manuscript with her usual care, much to its benefit.

Provenance

I want to thank the editors and publishers for granting me permission to reprint the six pieces that have appeared in print before.

"Freud and the Man from Stratford" has not been published before, but I was fortunate in trying out a variety of earlier versions before several generous (though, I am glad to say, not uncritical) audiences: at the Whitney Humanities Center at Yale in November 1988; at the Institute for Psychoanalysis in Chicago, on the occasion of delivering the Michael Littner Memorial Lecture and receiving the Irving B. Harris Media Award in January 1989; and at Columbia University, as a Paul Lazarsfeld Lecturer in March 1989.

"Six Names in Search of an Interpretation" started life as a paper for Dr. George Mahl, in his course "Freud, First Phase," at the Western New England Institute for Psychoanalysis in the fall of 1977. It reappeared, virtually unrecognizable, as a contribution to a festschrift for Fritz Bamberger under the enlarged title "Six Names in Search of an Interpretation: A Contribution to the Debate over Sigmund Freud's Jewishness," in *Hebrew Union College Annual* LIII (1982), 295–307. The version printed in this volume has restored the old, shorter title and has been extensively revised and somewhat enlarged.

"Freud and Freedom" was, in its original version, a chapter in Alan Ryan, ed., *The Idea of Freedom: Essays in Honour of Isaiah Berlin* (1979), 41–59, under the expanded title "Freud and Freedom: On a Fox in Hedgehog's Clothing." For the present version I have removed the subtitle and several references to Isaiah Berlin which seemed more appropriate for a festschrift. Still, in abiding admiration, I have retained some of these references even as I have, in thoroughly revising and substantially enlarging the essay, attempted to widen its appeal.

197

. . . .

"Reading Freud Through Freud's Reading" was first offered as a paper at Clark University, Worcester, Massachusetts, as part of a symposium celebrating the seventy-fifth anniversary of Freud's visit to Clark and as an offer of thanks for the honorary degree the university bestowed on me. That original version was printed in a brochure, William A. Koelsch and Seymour Wapner, eds., *Freud in Our Time: A Seventy-fifth Anniversary Symposium* (1988), 22–38. Revising the paper for this volume, I have taken the opportunity to go into the kind of detail about Freud's choices of "good books" that did not fit into a single lecture—the present version is twice as long as the original.

"Serious Jests" has not been published before, though I delivered a preliminary version in London for the British Institute for Psychoanalysis in October 1989, at a meeting commemorating the fiftieth anniversary of Freud's death, and, in Vienna, in November.

"Mind Reading: The Forgotten Freud" first appeared under the same title in the department "Revisions" in *Harper's* (September 1981), 83–86. Except for the addition of an epigraph, it is here reprinted without change.

"A Gentile Science?" first appeared in John M. Merriman, ed., *For Want of a Horse: Choice and Chance in History* (1985), 63–67. I have left the paper unchanged but added a cross-reference.

"The Dog That Did Not Bark in the Night" was published under the title "Sigmund and Minna? The Biographer as Voyeur," in the *New York Times Book Review* (January 29, 1989), 1, 43–45. I have revised the paper and somewhat expanded it for publication in this volume.

Index